Turkey and EU Integration

What has been achieved regarding Turkey's efforts at integration into the EU and what obstacles remain to it achieving full membership? Like other developing countries, Turkey displays visible signs of advancement with rapid increases in living standards, greater mobility and the rapid spread of technology. Much of its legislation and political, economic and administrative systems are also now aligned to the EU and this process has undoubtedly contributed to democratization and modernization. At the same time problems in politics and society persist; the Gezi protests, limitations of freedom of expression, frequent occupational accidents in the mining and construction sectors, honour killings and political upheaval which has manifested itself most starkly with the recent coup attempt all call attention to the challenges facing a country in the process of change.

Charting the political, legal and economic relations between Turkey and the European Union since 1959, this book explores the relationship through phases such as association, customs union and candidacy. Each chapter covers a particular period in the relations and/or a theme which has both current and overall relevance to the conduct of the relations. In this way, the authors examine the impact of the EU in effecting change, what has been achieved and the obstacles that remain.

Çigdem Nas is an associate professor in international relations and lecturer at the Department of Political Science and International Relations at the Yildiz Technical University in Istanbul. She also contributes to a non-governmental research organization called the Economic Development Foundation (IKV) specialized in EU studies. Her research interests comprise Turkey–EU relations, foreign policy, democratization, minorities, identity in international relations, migration and EU foreign policy. She has written articles on Turkey–EU relations and Turkish foreign policy.

Yonca Özer is an associate professor in international relations and lecturer at the European Union Institute of the Marmara University in Istanbul. Her research interests comprise Turkey–EU relations, democratization, europeanization, EU's external relations and international political economy. She has participated in many international conferences in international relations and is the author of papers and articles on Turkey–EU relations and EU's external relations.

Both authors edited a book titled "Turkey and the EU: Processes of Europeanization" which was published by Ashgate Publishers in 2012.

Turkey and EU Integration

Achievements and Obstacles

Çigdem Nas and Yonca Özer

Routledge
Taylor & Francis Group
LONDON AND NEW YORK

First published 2017
by Routledge
2 Park Square, Milton Park, Abingdon, Oxon OX14 4RN

by Routledge
605 Third Avenue, New York, NY 10017

First issued in paperback 2021

Routledge is an imprint of the Taylor & Francis Group, an informa business

Publisher's Note
The publisher has gone to great lengths to ensure the quality of this reprint but points out that some imperfections in the original copies may be apparent.

British Library Cataloguing-in-Publication Data
A catalogue record for this book is available from the British Library

Library of Congress Cataloging-in-Publication Data
A catalog record for this book has been requested

ISBN 13: 978-1-03-209686-5 (pbk)
ISBN 13: 978-1-4724-7355-4 (hbk)

Typeset in Times New Roman
by Apex CoVantage, LLC

Contents

List of abbreviations

AKP	Justice and Development Party
ANAP	Motherland Party
APD	Accession Partnership Document
ASEAN	Association of Southeast Asian Nations
CAP	Common Agricultural Policy
CCP	Common Commercial Policy
CCT	Common Commercial Tariff
CEEC	Central and Eastern European Country
CGE	Computable General Equilibrium
CHP	Republican People's Party
DEP	Democracy Party
DSP	Democratic Left Party
EC	European Community
ECHR	European Convention on Human Rights
ECJ	European Court of Justice
ECSC	European Coal and Steel Community
EEC	European Economic Community
EFTA	European Free Trade Association
EP	European Parliament
EU	European Union
FDI	Foreign Direct Investment
FETO	Fethullah Terrorist Organization
FTA	Free Trade Agreement
GSP	Generalised System of Preferences
GTAP	Global Trade Analysis Project
HDP	People's Democracy Party
HSYK	Supreme Council of Judges and Prosecutors
ICT	Independent Commission on Turkey
IMF	International Monetary Fund
ISIS	Islamic State of Iraq and the Levant
İKV	Economic Development Foundation
KCK	Union of Kurdistan Communities
MERCOSUR	Southern Common Market

MHP	Nationalist Action Party
MİT	National Intelligence Organisation
NATO	North Atlantic Treaty Organization
NGO	Non-Governmental Organization
OSCE	Organisation for Security and Cooperation in Europe
PKK	Kurdistan Workers' Party
PYD	Democratic Union Party
SAA	Stabilisation and Association Agreement
TBMM	Turkish Grand National Assembly
TDP	Communal Democratic Party
TOBB	Union of Chambers and Commodity Exchanges of Turkey
TRNC	Turkish Republic of Northern Cyprus
TTIP	Transatlantic Trade and Investment Partnership
TÜRKAK	Turkish Accreditation Agency
TÜSİAD	Turkish Industrialists and Businessmen Association
UK	United Kingdom
UN	United Nations
UNHCR	United Nations High Commissioner for Refugees
US	United States
USA	United States of America
WTO	World Trade Organization

Introduction

This book aims to provide a comprehensive picture of Turkey and European Union (EU) relations dating back to Turkey's application for an association to the European Economic Community (EEC) in 1959. Each of the chapters dwells on a particular period in the relations and/or a theme which has both current and overall influence on the conduct of the relations. In this way, progress of relations since the first application for association until today is analysed with a view to understanding the underlying factors shaping the process of Turkey's gradual integration to the EU.

Turkey together with Greece was one of the first countries in Europe that showed an early interest to be closely associated with the EEC following its foundation with the Treaty of Rome. Its application was greeted favourably by the fledgling Community as may be portrayed by the following words uttered by the president of the EEC Commission, Prof Walter Hallstein, in the signing ceremony of the Ankara Agreement on 12 September 1963 (Hallstein 1963: 1):

> Turkey is part of Europe. . . . We are, then, at the outset of an era of close cooperation between Turkey and the Community. . . . And one day the final step is to be taken: Turkey is to be a full member of the Community. This wish, and the fact that it is shared by us and our Turkish friends alike, is the strongest expression of our community of interest.

From the start, relations had an evolutionary character aiming to carry Turkey gradually closer to the Community and culminating in its accession as also mentioned in Article 28 of the Ankara Agreement. The agreement was modelled upon the treaty establishing the EEC and included provisions for the realization of the four basic freedoms of movement between the parties. The relations would evolve through three stages, the final stage to be based on a customs union. The Turkey–EU customs union was realized with the 1/95 Decision of the Association Council and started to function as of 31 December 1995.

The next important step came with Turkey's candidacy status to the EU announced at the Helsinki European Council of December 1999. Following a period of rapid reform in Turkey with the aim of fulfilling the Copenhagen criteria, Turkey's accession negotiations started on 3 October 2005. Negotiations have still not been completed, with eight chapters being suspended by a 2006 Council Decision and six more chapters blocked by the unilateral veto of Greek Cypriots in 2009. The last chapters opened to negotiations were 'Economic and Monetary Policies' in December 2015 and 'Financial and Budgetary Provisions' in June 2016. Currently a total of 16 chapters have been opened while only 1 was provisionally closed in the process. The Council's decision not to open eight chapters related to the customs union and not to close any chapter was a sanction imposed on Turkey as a result of Turkey's not opening its ports and airports to vehicles originating from Southern Cyprus. In the absence of a solution on the island leading to reunification, the negotiation process could not be accelerated with a view to its prompt completion. In the absence of a functioning negotiation between Turkey and the EU, such issues as the revision of the customs union, visa liberalization and cooperation in areas such as migration had to be managed in separate and parallel processes.

Although Turkey–EU relations have still not led to Turkey's membership in the EU, they have contributed to Turkey's alignment to EU norms, standards and *acquis* and increasing integration to the European market. Today's Turkey is much different from the country it was when it started off its relations with the EEC, exporting primarily agricultural goods and facing challenges of catching up with developing countries. The EU process played an important role in Turkey's development towards a middle-income economy, a member of the G20 group of states and a country with regional clout. At the same time, Turkey is still facing grave problems, such as social and political polarization, instability in the parliamentary regime, regression in rule of law, media freedoms, democratization, fast and unplanned urbanization, environmental degradation and the need to step up technological innovation. In this regard, the EU anchor plays an important role both as a model and as an external stimulus for reform and change in the country. However, the stalemate in the accession negotiations and the loss of credibility in the membership target have hampered the EU's influence over Turkey's transformation as may be witnessed in the slowdown of reforms in the last couple of years.

Unable to trigger the accession process, the EU and Turkey instigated alternative routes to manage common problems and to continue Turkey's convergence towards the EU. The Positive Agenda that started in May 2012 aimed to create a platform whereby issues of common concern, such as political reforms and fundamental rights, visa, mobility and migration, trade, energy, counterterrorism or dialogue on foreign policy, could be discussed among the parties. However, this initiative could not spark off a new dynamism in the relations. Momentum could be triggered in two areas due to pressing challenges in both spheres: the upgrading and modernization of the customs union and the issue area of migration management and mobility.

Turkey and the EU agreed to start a process of modernization of the customs union in May 2014. The Turkey–EU customs union dating back to 1995 included only trade in industrial goods and needed to be revised in line with changes in world trade and the EU's trade policy. As a customs union partner, Turkey also was committed to aligning its own trade policy to that of the EU's common commercial policy and common commercial tariff. With the failure of the multilateral trading system to provide further liberalization of world trade, significant actors such as the EU turned towards bilateral and regional trading arrangements. Turkey was faced with the challenge of new trade agreements signed between the EU and third countries, which created trade diversion effects and gradually eroded the advantages that Turkey enjoyed in the customs union. Moreover, the new generation of trade agreements included new areas, such as trade in services and liberalization of public procurement, thereby making the customs union outdated. Though both parties adopted a common approach towards the revision of the customs union, negotiations for that goal are expected to start in mid-2017.

The other area that is managed through a separate process is migration management and mobility. Turkey's demand for visa-free travel to the EU based on the Association and Article 41(1) of the Additional Protocol was supported by the Soysal Judgment of the European Court of Justice (ECJ) in 2009, which stipulated that demanding a visa from Turkish truck drivers travelling to Germany with the aim of providing a service is against EU law. However, the ECJ's judgment in the Demirkan case in 2013 dealt a blow to Turks' hopes of winning the legal battle over visas since the court ruled that provision of services does not cover recipients of services and Turkish citizens travelling to Germany for purposes of tourism, education and so forth are not exempt from the visa requirement. The visa-free travel issue was tied to the EU's expectations from Turkey regarding cooperation in the fight against irregular migration to the EU. A visa liberalization roadmap was adopted together with the signing of the Turkey–EU Readmission Agreement on 16 December 2013. Thus the implementation of readmission became one of the conditions for visa-free travel for Turkish citizens together with the 72 criteria embodied in the roadmap. Turkey had to take back all its citizens, stateless persons and third-country nationals who entered or stayed in the EU illegally, on the condition that they passed through Turkish territory on their way to the EU.

The refugee crisis erupting in 2015 with the outflow of Syrians fleeing from the worsening situation in the Syrian War brought a new urgency to the Readmission Agreement. The main routes used by the refugees and migrants on their way to the EU – that is the Western Balkans and eastern Mediterranean routes – passed through Turkey and the number of persons who made a passage through these routes reached 710,000 in the first nine months of 2015. Faced with the continuing influx of refugees, the EU turned towards Turkey in an attempt to solicit Turkey's cooperation in stemming this human movement.

A deal was struck between the parties in the summit meeting of 29 November 2015. Turkey would start to implement the Readmission Agreement in June 2016, cooperate with the EU in controlling migration, fight against migrant smuggling in the Aegean and work towards the integration of Syrians living in Turkey. To facilitate the deal, the EU promised to provide funds of €3 billion to be used for the needs of the Syrian refugees in Turkey, accelerate the accession process by opening chapters, start high-level dialogues in energy, foreign and security policy, and economy, grant visa-free travel to Turkish citizens by October 2016 dependent upon the fulfilment of the conditions by Turkey, and hold two summit meetings with Turkey annually. The EU–Turkey joint action plan involved a possibility of bringing the parties closer but also a risk of deteriorating the relations further by increasing the level of mistrust if the plan could not be properly put into action or did not produce the expected results.

The EU–Turkey joint action plan to fend off the refugee crisis was reignited in March with new demands coming from Turkey for more funds and visa-free travel in June 2016, while the EU was pushed into a corner since it depended on Turkey's cooperation to deal with the crisis. The summit of 8 March brought about a refugee agreement whereby Turkey agreed to readmit migrants travelling to Aegean islands from Turkey and the EU agreed to resettle a Syrian refugee from Turkey in return for each Syrian returned to Turkey. The deal also included a package of €3 billion to be allocated under the refugee facility until 2018, the target of visa-free travel for Turks to be realized until June 2016 and the opening of new chapters in accession negotiations. The deal was successful in eliminating the migrant smuggling activities in the eastern Mediterranean route as evidenced by a sharp drop in the number of persons using that route in April.

The momentum resulting from the refugee deal was not immediately reflected on the accession process despite Turkey's expectations. The promise of visa-free travel to the EU brought new life in the relations as Turkey passed a number of key reforms throughout April in order to fulfil the criteria embodied in the visa liberalization roadmap. The Commission in its evaluation report dated 4 May recommended the lifting of the visa requirement for Turkish citizens to the European Parliament and the Council, despite the remaining five criteria Turkey had still not completed. Controversy about the issue centred on Turkey's antiterror legislation that was found to be too extensive – that is on the point of infringing fundamental human rights. President Erdoğan and other leading figures of the Turkish government protested at the EU's intransigence regarding the lifting of the Schengen visa obligation and accused EU leaders of not fulfilling their promises. The issue remained unresolved and the target of June 2016 could not be kept, though technical negotiations among officials continued on the visa liberalization process. Despite the deteriorating relations, one more chapter was opened to negotiations at the end of June under the Dutch presidency of the Council – that is the chapter on financial and budgetary provisions.

The 15 July coup attempt in Turkey perpetrated by a faction in the Turkish armed forces started a period of tension and uncertainty in the relations. Its failure can be interpreted as a relief for the EU since it would lead to even worse results had the attempt gone through. However, the state of emergency declared following the coup attempt, the extensive purges that took place against functionaries alleged to have been associated with the Gulen organization, and allegations of torture and mistreatment of those arrested led to serious criticisms on the part of EU officials and several European politicians. Especially President Erdoğan and other prominent figures in Turkish government, such as minister for EU affairs Ömer Çelik, criticized the EU for not supporting Turkey in its difficult period. President Erdoğan noted that not even one EU leader visited Turkey in the aftermath of the coup attempt as a sign of solidarity with a candidate country.

Austrian prime minister Christian Kern on the other hand demanded an end to Turkey's EU negotiations due to an insufficiency in Turkey's democratic standards (Chadwick 2016).

The EU's need to maintain the refugee deal and prevent further refugee flows along the eastern Mediterranean route and the concomitant dependence of Turkey on the European market for its trade and economy could be seen as the vital guarantee of preventing a total breakup of the relations. Looking back over the long history of Turkey–EU relations spanning nearly 60 years, it would not be wrong to argue that the relations will endure this crisis and will set on a new course after some turbulence. At the time of writing of this book, relations between the two sides soured, especially following the arrests of several journalists, columnists and the editor-in-chief of *Cumhuriyet* newspaper, a landmark establishment dating back to the first years of the foundation of the Republic, and the arrests of members of the People's Democracy Party (HDP), including the co-chairs, on 4 November 2016. President of the European Parliament (EP) Martin Schulz reacted to the detentions and arrests and said that 'Turkish authorities . . . are turning their backs on the values, principles, norms and rules underpinning Turkey–EU relations' (European Parliament 2016) while the EP called for the suspension of negotiations. According to the negotiation framework guiding Turkey's accession negotiations, the Commission either on its own initiative or upon the request of one-third of member states may bring a suspension of negotiations to the agenda, while it would be up to the Council to make the final decision based on qualified majority voting (European Commission 2005b). This would take 55 per cent of the member states equalling at least 65 per cent of the EU's population to be able to make a decision to suspend the talks. While a complete suspension of negotiations is a possibility, even if the required number of votes does not materialize, it would not be wrong to put forth that negotiations will be in a state of coma. Considering that the situation regarding rights and freedoms might worsen in the days to come, and depending on the result of the April 16 referendum, this situation might impact not only the negotiations but also other areas of cooperation, such as the refugee deal, visa liberalization, high-level dialogue mechanisms and even the customs union modernization process, which is expected to commence in 2017. At the end of the day, the mutual need of both sides would still bring them together in enhancing cooperation in the aforementioned fields. However, unless Turkey makes a U-turn with regard to its present direction of moving away from democracy towards authoritarianism, any relations Turkey and the EU would shape in the future would have been based on sheer interests without any expectation of adoption of European norms and values.

What is critical at this stage is the future of the accession process. Will Turkey ever be able to become a member of the EU? After the British referendum of 23 June leading to a process of withdrawal from the EU, in which direction will EU integration proceed? Will Turkey be able to accede to a multi-speed, multi-tiered EU? What kind of a relationship will evolve between Turkey and the EU if accession negotiations are cut off and the goal of membership is forsaken? These are all critical questions about the future of Turkey–EU relations. The book will attempt to lay out a general perspective of Turkey and EU relations by focusing on some of the key areas, aiming to help the reader to develop his/her answer to the aforementioned questions.

Synopsis of chapters

The book contains seven chapters involving the historical progress of Turkey–EU relations and several thematic areas that stand out in the process of Turkey's alignment towards the EU.

The first chapter examines Turkey–EU relations in the period between Turkey's associate membership application to the EEC in 1959 and the realization of the customs union between Turkey and the EU in the 1990s. In other words, the first two stages of the Association, which was envisaged to be completed in three stages, are covered by this chapter. Why Turkey and the EEC established the Association relationship, the characteristics of the Association Agreement and what it involves and aims at are all examined with reference to the concurrent Greek case in order to provide a full assessment of the origins of the relations. The first stage of the Association (1960s) represents 'the honeymoon' of the relations since it did not suffer any major problems or challenges. However, the second stage (1970s and 1980s) might be regarded as the 'uneasy' period of the Association. Serious problems in the relations were experienced relating particularly to economic concerns in the 1970s and political issues in the 1980s. This situation led to the malfunctioning of the Association until the early 1990s. For this reason, Turkey felt the urge to bypass the indirect and problematic association path towards its membership objective and resorted to a shortcut attempt in 1987 for reaching this objective. However, the Commission in its Avis as a response to the Turkey's full membership application in 1987 noted that it was too early to contemplate Turkey's membership in the EC and recommended, instead, reviving the existing Association relationship with a view to the establishment of a customs union.

The second chapter analyses the customs union between Turkey and the EU. The Association Agreement already envisages the establishment of a customs union between the parties as the basis of the Association with a view to integrating the Turkish economy into the Community. Article 28 of the Agreement also stipulates the possibility of Turkey's membership in the EEC depending on 'full acceptance' of membership 'obligations'. Therefore, the establishment of a customs union has always been regarded by the Turkish side as the main device for eventually achieving full EU membership. It has constituted a gradual integration with the EU in the long term. However, the customs union remained unrealized until the 1990s due to economic and political problems and a new initiative by the parties for its achievement was needed. Indeed, the decision on the long-planned customs union in March 1995 by the Association Council characterized the next major watershed in the evolution of Turkey's relations with the EU since the Association Agreement in 1963. The customs union has always been a moot point in the relations, particularly in the context of its implications for the Turkish economy and the asymmetric nature of the bond it has created between the parties.

The second chapter analyses these issues by focusing on its implementation process, starting with the customs union decision of 1995 and on the concerns arising out of its *sui generis* features. Whether, in the absence of full membership, the customs union constitutes a true form of integration between Turkey and the EU is questioned. The chapter also examines whether the customs union needs to be revised with a view to resolving the attendant problems.

The third chapter depicts the progress of relations following the Helsinki European Council of 1999, declaring Turkey as a candidate to join the EU. The Helsinki Summit was a watershed in the relations since it upgraded Turkey's status to that of a candidate country starting a pre-accession process with the aim of joining the EU. The obligation to fulfil the political aspects of the Copenhagen criteria with a view to the opening of accession negotiations triggered an unprecedented reform process in Turkey. Until 2004, two major constitutional amendments and eight harmonization packages were adopted by the Turkish Grand National Assembly (TBMM), including the abolishment of capital punishment, adoption of new penal and civil codes, widening the scope of fundamental rights and freedoms, and expansion of cultural rights. The result was a favourable recommendation on the part of the European Commission to start accession negotiations with Turkey, which was approved by the Council, leading to the opening of negotiations on 3 October 2005. What was once a dream turned into reality, only to lead to disappointment once again with the suspension of eight chapters and the decision not to close any chapter by the Council of the EU, aiming to punish Turkey for failing to open its ports to Greek Cypriot ships and planes. Although a total of 14 chapters have been opened to negotiations to this day, negotiations may be said to be in a state of stalemate. Reforms in Turkey have slowed down and serious issues emerged in the political area, such as problems in the independence of the judiciary, media freedom and rule of law. The chapter discusses in detail the developments following Turkey's candidacy to the EU and aims to explore the multiple factors that led to a divergence between the parties in recent years.

The fourth chapter analyses Turkey's performance regarding realization of democratic reforms under the influence of the EU's conditionality by mainly categorizing the democratization process as the pre-candidacy period and the post-candidacy period that is also examined in three succeeding stages until recently. While the EU's conditionality had quite limited effectiveness for Turkey's democratic transformation during the pre-candidacy period, Turkey undertook radical democratic changes particularly after achieving candidacy status in the Helsinki European Council in December 1999. With its recognition as a candidate state, the EU introduced a strict conditionality mechanism and linked the improvement of Turkey's institutional ties with the EU to compliance with the Copenhagen political criteria. In other words, the declaration of its candidacy status, which offered a credible and conditional membership perspective, constituted an important incentive for Turkey to transform its political and legal system with a view to the fulfilment of the Copenhagen criteria. Repeal of the death penalty, adoption of new penal code and civil code, revision of the status of the National Security Council, adoption of several international human rights conventions and recognition of the right to broadcast in and learn ethnic languages were among the reforms passed during this era. However, from the opening of the negotiations Turkey dramatically lost its momentum in this respect and except for some minor changes its performance therefore severely decreased. As stated in the Negotiating Framework Document and progress reports, the irreversibility of the political reform process and the full, effective and comprehensive implementation of reforms are essential for the success of the accession process. However, since the 2011 general elections in Turkey, Turkish democracy has been getting worse and going through a quite critical process which can generally be marked as regression. This chapter explains this differentiation in Turkey's performance regarding realization of democratic reforms with the varied application and, therefore, effectiveness of conditionality by the EU, along with the changing domestic conditions and the interaction between these two factors.

The fifth chapter concerns an issue dating back to at least the 1960s that continues to have an impact on Turkey–EU relations: the Cyprus conundrum. It is largely argued that the unsettled dispute of Cyprus, which has seriously affected the accession negotiations with Turkey, constitutes a major impediment to Turkish accession. Apparently, Greek Cypriot EU membership in 2004 imported the Cyprus problem into the EU and altered the position of the EU in this matter in favour of the Greek Cypriots. Cyprus's EU membership has posed important concerns for Turkey since it led to an awkward situation whereby Turkey is aiming at entering a bloc of countries, one of which it does not formally recognize. The first stumbling block for Turkey materialized when the Council decided to penalize Turkey for not opening its seaports and airports to ships and aircrafts originating from Southern Cyprus by blocking eight chapters associated with the customs union and deciding not to provisionally close any of the negotiation chapters. The Cypriot government also used its veto power as a member state to block the opening of six other chapters in Turkey's negotiation process.

The chapter examines how the Cyprus dispute has become an issue between Turkey and the EU, how influential the Greek factor has been in Europeanizing the issue and how the issue has affected EU–Turkey relations since a connection between the Cyprus problem and the relations was first established until the current impasse. The chapter also questions if the issue constitutes a permanent obstacle undermining Turkey's EU vocation since there is little prospect for settlement or if it is an issue that can easily be settled by the parties on the condition that sufficient political will for resolution exists on all sides.

The sixth chapter eyes Turkey–EU relations from the perspective of the EU's assessments regarding its integration capacity to accept Turkey as a future member state. The prospect of Turkey's membership in the EU presents various challenges in terms of integration capacity. Turkey, being a populous country, second only to Germany if admitted to the Union, a country with regional imbalances and a massive agricultural sector, candidate to become a major recipient of EU structural funds, having cultural and religious differences, and residing in a turbulent region of the world likely to bring with it a heavy burden upon the foreign, security and defence policies of the EU, will not be just another member state but one likely to make a considerable impact upon the working and institutional balances in the Union. Remarks by several prominent figures in EU member states, such as French presidents Giscard d'Estaing and Nicholas Sarkozy, reveal the opposition to Turkey's EU accession mostly upon grounds of cultural difference and destructive impact on European integration if admitted to the Union. The chapter explores the integration capacity concept with special reference to the case of Turkey's probable integration to the EU.

The last chapter concerns a topical issue influencing Turkey–EU relations, visas and migration. Turkey's quest for visa-free travel to the Schengen Area has entered a new phase with the signing of the Turkey–EU Readmission Agreement on 16 December 2013 and the concomitant approval of the 'Roadmap towards a Visa-Free Regime with Turkey'. The roadmap contained a total of 72 criteria that Turkey had to fulfil in order for its citizens to qualify for visa-free access to the Schengen countries. In an effort to align with the EU's requirements in this field, the Directorate-General for Migration Management started to operate within the Ministry of Internal Affairs and a Law on Foreigners and International Protection was adopted, which had the effect of modernizing Turkey's migration policies. The Syria refugee crisis of 2015 brought about a new deal between Turkey and the EU whereby Turkey demanded to bring the date for visa-free travel forward, first to October 2016 and lately to June 2016, when the Readmission Agreement is also due to be put into implementation. The chapter examines the trajectory of the Schengen visa for Turkish citizens within the context of the EU's increasing concern about irregular migration and the role Turkey plays in this regard. It may be contended that migration and mobility issues will continue to occupy a central position in Turkey–EU relations for the foreseeable future.

Straddling six decades, Turkey and EU relations have gone through ebbs and flows, with periods of convergence followed by divergence. Turkey is one of few countries other than the miniscule states of Andorra and San Marino which have established a customs union prior to acceding to the Union. It is a candidate country negotiating for accession for 11 years without a clear perspective of its completion in sight. It is a negotiating country with which the refugee deal was adopted on a bilateral platform rather than as part of accession negotiations under Chapter 24. It is an official candidate country, which is not expected to become a member until 3000, as out forth by the British prime minister. It is a country which has experienced a coup attempt, a serious attack on its constitutional order, yet not visited by any EU official or leader as a sign of solidarity. It is a country for which calls are being made for the culmination of accession negotiations by the prime minister of a member state, Austria, yet a country that the EU needs badly in order to deal with its refugee and irregular migration problem. Such depictions clearly testify to the peculiar and sui generis nature of Turkey–EU relations, which can be seen as a dilemma between 'with or without you' as the famous U2 song goes.

Assuming that the EU is a community of values, one of the most important priorities of an accession process for a candidate country is not only to adopt the EU *acquis* but to also internalize these values. In the case of Turkey internalization of EU values has been quite limited so far, owing not only to Turkey's internal problems regarding the establishment of a stable democratic order but also to inconsistencies and double standards in the EU's approach to Turkey, which diminished the EU's credibility and deterioration of EU values even within the member states, as exemplified by violations of democratic and rule of law standards in Poland and Hungary. Reciprocal criticisms and accusations have not been rare between the two sides, which attest to a lack of mutual trust and understanding.

At the end of the day, Turkey and EU relations are very much interlinked with the idea of Europe and its borders. The success or failure of Turkey's EU accession would clarify the issue of where Europe's borders lay and what unites Europe. At the moment, it seems that Turkey is being located outside of these borders as a partner country rather than a member state. Developments in Turkey are not in the direction of more Europe – that is greater freedom and democracy – while the EU, with impending ultra-right-wing populism, ineffective foreign policy and growing rift among its member states, is also being far from welcoming to Turkey. However, the jury is still out on the issue as Turkey's accession negotiations are still ongoing and both sides still have a chance to advance the relations. The relationship between Turkey and the EU is of an interdependent nature due to the extent of trade and economic relations as well as Turkey's importance with regard to European security. Regardless of whether membership is on the cards, it is in the interests of both parties that Turkey–EU relations should be settled on a firm basis, making way for extensive cooperation and coordination of policies in diverse areas, such as trade, migration, foreign policy, energy and security.

The recent referendum held in Britain on 23 June resulted in a decision to withdraw from EU membership. This unprecedented development is to be followed up by the EU and the British government in accordance with Article 50 of the Lisbon Treaty. The Brexit vote has once again exposed the democratic deficit in European integration and the need for a substantial reform of EU institutions making way for greater participation by and representation of EU citizens. Underneath it all are much deeper problems about the EU linked to the decline in its output – that is benefits accruing to governments and people, pitfalls in dealing with major crises, such as the euro crisis and the refugee crisis, problems in achieving solidarity among member states, the crisis of European democracy where mainstream parties can no longer appease the grievances of the population, and growing challenges of globalization and global competition. In the next years, the EU is expected to undergo yet more changes as Britain's fate in or out of the EU unravels, leading to several possible outcomes. Britain will negotiate the conditions of its withdrawal from membership with the EU. There is the possibility that other member states may follow Britain's example or Britain may renege on the decision to leave the EU. Ensuing developments will most probably impact on the nature, method and pace of European integration, leading to a major revision of the Founding Treaties, which may allow for the institutionalization of a multi-tier, multi-speed EU. Turkey's EU perspective may also be influenced by such an outcome, leading to the negotiation of a particular kind of membership where Turkey participates in selected policies and not others. It is beyond the confines of this book to speculate on upcoming developments regarding European integration and impact on Turkey. Suffice it to say at this point that critical developments in the EU following the Brexit vote are also likely to influence Turkey's EU perspective and the shape of its relations with the EU.

1 Association relationship with full membership perspective

The ongoing significance of the Ankara Agreement

Relations with Turkey can be described as one of the most arduous and complex aspects of external relations of European integration. There has been a gradual integration process between Turkey and the EU, which started with the Association Agreement and is planned to culminate in Turkey's full membership. This process has lasted much longer than planned, taking four decades for Turkey to be declared as a candidate for EU membership, and with accession negotiations being finally launched in 2005. It is really unknown how long this process will last. This chapter looks back over several decades in order to examine how these relations have evolved over time and turned out to be problematic.

Turkey occupies a special place in the history of external relations of the EU. It is the one country which has sought closer relations since the initial years of integration, and one of two countries that Europe first established formal relations with. Relations with Turkey formally started with the Turkish application to the then EEC on 31 July 1959 for an association relationship with the ultimate objective of full membership. This application, made in terms of Article 238 of the EEC Treaty that regulated association relations of the EEC with the third countries, paved the way for the Association Agreement that has since constituted the basis of relations. The motivations of the parties for establishing the association relationship, the characteristics and objectives of the agreement, and what it involves and how it was implemented until Turkey's membership application in 1987 are all examined with references to the concurrent Greek case in order to provide a full assessment of the origins of these relations.

The chapter analyses relations in the period from this application until the completion of the customs union between Turkey and the EU in 1995. In other words, it covers the first two stages of the association, which was envisaged to be completed in three stages and is now in the final stage. The first stage of the association (1960s) represents the honeymoon of relations since it did not suffer any problems or challenges, while the second stage (1970s and 1980s) might be regarded as the uneasy period. Serious problems in relations were experienced particularly regarding economic concerns in the 1970s and political issues in the 1980s. This situation led to the malfunctioning of the association until the early 1990s. For this reason, Turkey had to bypass the indirect and problematic association path towards its membership objective and resort to a shortcut in 1987.

It therefore applied to the then European Community (EC) for full membership on the legal basis of Article 237 of the EEC Treaty that regulated full membership of the European countries in the Community. However, the Commission in its Avis recommended reviving the existing association relationship and the establishment of the customs union instead of proceeding on the second path, which was opened via Turkey's full membership application.

Establishment of the Turkey–EC association

Turkey is highly integrated into the EU today, although it is not a member. Instead, the association relationship between them constitutes the basis of this integration. Formal relations with the newly established European integration initiative – that is the EEC – were established through the Ankara Agreement, which was signed on 12 September 1963 and entered into force on 1 December 1964 after ratification by Turkey and the member states in accordance with the procedure laid down in Article 238 of the EEC Treaty.[1] It was the Turkish application in 1959 to the EEC and the negotiations following this application that led to the conclusion of the Ankara Agreement. Turkey made its application just 16 days after Greece's application on 15 July. Both Turkey and Greece based their applications on Article 238 of the EEC Treaty, which regulates association relations of the Community with non-members (Saraçoğlu 1991: 49). That is, they applied to the EEC to establish an association relationship with the objective of gradually becoming a full member.

Political, security and economic factors played an important role in Turkey's application. Since the foundation of the Republic in 1923, westernization has always been the main objective of Turkish foreign policy, with the construction of a Western and modern model determined as the fundamental concern. Turkish policymakers have always been preoccupied with the aim of catching up with Western civilization in economic, legal and political terms. Since Western civilization was represented mainly by Europe, taking Europe as a model to reach this aim became the primary principle of the Turkish Republic, so Turkey became involved in all the European political, economic and military organizations formed after World War II. It joined the Organisation for European Economic Co-operation (OEEC)[2] in 1948 and the Council of Europe in 1949 as a founding member, and also became a member of the North Atlantic Treaty Organization (NATO) in 1952.

In the conjuncture of the post–World War II era European states realized that they had to form a deeper cooperation model between themselves with a view to preventing new wars in the continent. Therefore, they established the EEC. Turkey considered EEC membership as a reasonable outcome of its westernization and modernization policies, and an Association Agreement with the EEC providing an important degree of institutional, economic and political integration was regarded as a crucial stepping stone to becoming an integral part of Europe. Although the newly elected Turkish government emphasized, a few months after conclusion of the EEC Treaty in 1957, its political will to take part in European integration (Arıkan 2003: 53), it could not act immediately since it had been experiencing economic and political instability. However, Turkey's inactivity in this respect did not last too long and shortly after the Greece's application to the EEC for establishing an association relationship, Turkey applied to the EEC for the same aim.

Actually, inactivity would have been an unexpected response to this integration initiative because Turkey's republican state policy had always been economically and politically in close relationship with Europe. Indeed, in the succeeding years until recently, the Turkish political and economic elite considered EU membership as the ultimate aim that would make westernization and modernization processes, which have been proclaimed as official state ideologies, irreversible for Turkey (Öniş 2003: 17). However, it was obvious that Greece's application for association relationship speeded up Turkey's decision on what kind of relationship was to be established with the EEC (Tsakaloyannis 1980: 43). Turkey's quick response to the Greek application should therefore be assessed in the context of its concern that Greece would use the political and economic advantages arising from an association relationship with the EEC to the disadvantage of Turkey. Politically, Turkey had long-standing hostile relations with Greece and was preoccupied with the concern that Greece would gain more concessions with respect to its bilateral disputes with Turkey. That is why Turkey's foreign policy towards Greece depended on the principle of being represented in every international platform where Greece was represented (Birand 1978: 52). Additionally, Turkey wanted to obtain the same trade concessions as Greece through the customs union that would be established within the framework of the Association Agreement. Otherwise, Turkey would lose its competitiveness against Greek products in European markets since Turkey exported similar products to Greece to the EEC. Evidently, Turkish foreign policy depended both on ensuring Turkey's European vocation and on monitoring what Greece did or did not do in the international arena. That is, Greece's application and Turkey's established westernization policy were undoubtedly both important factors behind Turkey's application to the EEC.

Security concerns also played an important role in Turkey's decision to apply for establishing an association relationship with the EEC. After World War II, concerns arising from Soviet claims regarding the Turkish straits and the northeastern part of Turkish territory, as well as fear of the Communist threat from the Soviet Union, motivated Turkey to get involved in the Western alliance. Turkey considered integration with the EEC as one of the major components of being a part of the Western alliance, although the EEC did not include a common security policy at that time and, therefore, did not have sufficient capacity by itself to allay the security concerns of its members. Nevertheless, it would be able to anchor Turkey more firmly to the Western alliance by providing economic and political integration (Arıkan 2003: 54).

The application for an association relationship with the EEC was also in part prompted by economic considerations, including the benefits of preferential market access and the need for economic aid to implement its economic development programme and to reduce economic disparities between it and the EEC countries.

Another economic motive behind the application was the expectation of foreign direct investment both from the EEC members and from other developed countries encouraged by the prospect of increasing economic stability and development through close relations with the EEC. Moreover, as Heinz Kramer (cited in Arıkan 2003: 54) stated, the prospect of free movement of workers through the agreement was regarded as a means not only of reducing Turkey's huge unemployment level but also of obtaining foreign currency in the form of guest worker remittances. Through association relationship Turkey aimed at getting rid of its economic problems and also financing the cost of providing security as a NATO member on the south-eastern flank of the Western alliance.

The EEC accepted Turkey's application quite swiftly and negotiations started in September 1959. The EEC's economic interest in accepting the application and establishing an association relationship was evidently less important than its security and political interests. In view of the huge developmental gap between the EEC and Turkey, Turkey was not regarded as important for the EEC's external economic relations in either trade or foreign investment terms. Rather security concerns regarding the Communist threat arising from the environment of the post–World War II era were considered to play the main role on the EEC's side in its association policy with both Turkey and Greece. After World War II, maintaining security constituted a fundamental concern for Western European states as well as ensuring economic development as they did not feel secure while they had borders with the Communist bloc. Turkey and Greece therefore had a strong strategic and geopolitical importance on the south-eastern flank of the Western alliance as buffer states against Soviet expansion towards Southern Europe. EEC members desired to bind those countries closer to the West since they were regarded as necessary allies in countering the strategic threat from the Soviet Union. They were perceived as very important elements of the 'containment policy' of the Western alliance. As Arıkan (2003: 54) states, deepening relations with Turkey was regarded as necessary for European security and for the strategic objective of strengthening NATO's south-eastern flank by ensuring the economic and social, and therefore political, stability of Turkey.

Additionally, the Turkish and Greek applications provided important support for a newly established integration initiative which had not yet had much influence in the international arena. The EEC considered the establishment of association relations with those European countries as a good way of expanding its influence. The EEC's first generation of association policy should thus be assessed in the context of the EEC's willingness to win friends in its formative years, given the fact that the direction the new European integration initiative would take in the future was uncertain for many (Redmond 1994: 8). These applications to the EEC meant its recognition and therefore led the EEC to gain prestige in political terms. The European states were also extremely pleased that Turkey and Greece made their choice in line with the EEC and not with the European Free Trade Association (EFTA), which was the main rival in those years. According to Tunç Aybak (cited in Arıkan 2003: 55), association agreements with Greece and Turkey, which might eventually lead to membership, were seen as examples of encouraging and preparing European countries that were not yet willing to join or capable of joining the EEC.

Association negotiations with Turkey lasted four years and concluded two years after the conclusion of the negotiations with Greece, although they started earlier.[3] This long negotiation process arose from some setbacks experienced during negotiations. Firstly, because of the 27 May 1960 military coup, negotiations stopped until 24 July 1962 (Müftüler-Baç 2001: 27). The military intervention generated doubts among EEC members regarding whether Turkey was a suitable country for establishing such a close relationship like an association. For example, French president de Gaulle pressed for suspending relations with Turkey due to the execution of death penalties following the coup. Another factor that protracted the negotiation process was disagreement on the form of the relations. Turkey, on the one side, demanded to establish the association relationship on the basis of a customs union with an automatic transition after a short preparation period and with ultimately full membership at a specific date. On the other side, the EEC offered only a cooperation agreement including agricultural trade preferences and financial aid instead of an association agreement. However, Turkish negotiators, highlighting Turkey's geostrategic importance for the EEC, insisted on their demands in order to reach an association agreement identical to the Athens Agreement, which was signed with Greece in 1961 (Arıkan 2003: 56).

As Sena Ceylanoğlu (cited in Mayer 2008: 9) has argued, the Commission was not willing to offer Turkey a far-reaching agreement like the Athens Agreement due to concerns about the backwardness of the Turkish economy and overstretching the EEC's capacities. The Commissioners (except for External Relations Commissioner Jean Rey, who actively supported the agreement) thought Turkey would not be economically prepared to meet its commitments arising from customs union. However, the Council of Ministers, which was aware of the importance to the EEC of treating Greece and Turkey equally, and of keeping a delicate balance in relations with these countries due to their positions in south-eastern Europe against the Soviet Union, decided to conclude an association agreement with Turkey in parallel to the Athens Agreement in response to the insistence of Turkey on the establishment of an identical association relationship to that of Greece. Finally, the Association Agreement involving the establishment of a customs union in stages was signed with Turkey in September 1963, and the prospect of full membership was also included.

The objectives, characteristics and instruments of the Association Agreement

The Ankara Agreement, establishing an association between the EEC and Turkey, was only the second such agreement including a full membership objective, after the Athens Agreement. The legal basis of the Ankara and the Athens Agreements was Article 238 of the EEC Treaty, which regulates the association relationships of the EEC with non-member countries (Saraçoğlu 1991: 49). An association agreement is a sui generis international treaty in terms of its nature, signifying less than admission to the EU but more than a mere trade agreement, according to EU law (Lasok 1991: 27). That is, it goes far beyond the mere regulation of trade, involving close economic cooperation and wide-ranging financial assistance from the EU for the country concerned.

The first-generation association policy of the EU towards European countries mainly included three different types of association agreements. The first ones were made with EFTA countries. Economic factors, rather than political ones, constituted the main motivation for this kind of agreement. These agreements envisaged the establishment of the European Economic Area (EEA), to be based on four freedoms in order to create a common market between the European integration and the EFTA countries without having a common trade policy against third countries. Secondly, association agreements with Cyprus and Malta (entered into force in 1973 and 1971 respectively) were designed to establish a customs union between the parties in two stages within a ten-year period, but without any reference to eventual membership. The last kind of association agreement was designed as preparation for accession to the European integration, such as those with Greece and Turkey. Both of them envisaged the establishment of a customs union as a tool for obtaining eventual membership. In these cases, the association formula of Article 238 was used as a form of pre-accession. That is, they were association agreements for the integration of those two countries into the EEC, so they were more comprehensive than those with Cyprus and Malta.

The Ankara Agreement, first of all, provided the parties with an association which was economic in nature. The economic objectives that characterized the agreement were stated in Article 2:

> The aim of this agreement is to promote the continuous and balanced strengthening of trade and economic relations between the Parties, while taking full account of the need to ensure an accelerated development of the Turkish economy and to improve the level of employment and living conditions of the Turkish people.
>
> (Official Journal of the EC 1977a)

However, the agreement also provided the parties with an association relationship with the prospect of full membership. In other words, it covered not only economic (development) objectives and related trade matters but also the political objective of ultimately becoming a full member. Indeed, the Ankara Agreement, in the fourth paragraph of its preamble, makes a reference to the ultimate objective of the association: ‘the support given by the EC to the efforts of the Turkish people to improve their standards of living will facilitate the accession of Turkey to the Community at a later date’. Additionally, Article 28 of the Agreement clearly regulates the prospect of full membership. It commits the contracting parties to examining the possibility of Turkey’s accession to the Community. Its wording does not certainly state that Turkey will become a member of the EC. Rather, it states the intention of the parties that is expressed tentatively, creating only an expectation (Lasok 1991: 36). It regulates that whenever Turkey reaches, through the operation of the Agreement, a level at which it can fully assume the obligations arising from the EEC Treaty, the possibility of Turkey's accession will be examined. That is, this provision rules that performing economic, social and legal commitments resulting from full membership and reaching a certain level of economic development are preconditions of Turkey's accession (Can and Özen 2005: 22). But it can also easily be understood that, even if Turkey can reach a level at which it can fully assume the obligations arising out of being a member of the Community, it may still not become a member at the end of the examination of the possibility of its accession. This is because the conditions stated by the agreement were for the examination of the possibility of accession, not for the final accession. Therefore, according to Article 28, full membership is not automatic. There is no automatic transition from the status of an associated state to membership of the Community on the completion of the programme laid down by the Association Agreement. Instead, any change in status will result from a political decision depending on the examination. In other words, Article 28 offers no guarantee of admission even if Turkey becomes capable of accepting the obligations arising not only from the Ankara Agreement but also from the EEC Treaty. Therefore, the EEC is obliged only to examine the possibility of Turkey's accession (Lasok 1991: 36–7).

Nevertheless, since it was a precise intention of the contracting parties to use the Association Agreement as a stepping stone to accession, Article 28 provides a clear full membership perspective as the ultimate aim of the association (Lasok 1991: 36). Subsequent association agreements have not included a provision similar to Article 28 with its clearly stated prospect of full membership, although the Stabilisation and Association Agreements (SAAs) with the countries of the Western Balkans refer in their preambles to the 'potential candidate' status of the Western Balkan partners (Cremona 2009: 250–1).[4] The Ankara Agreement did not envisage only an association for the purposes of Turkish economic development, but appeared to serve as a pre-accession agreement to prepare Turkey for full membership. That is why it was regarded as a '*Beitrittsassoziation*' agreement (Can and Özen 2005: 22). It aims at free movement of goods, services, workers and capital between the parties by predicating on the relevant provisions of the treaty establishing the EEC. Although progressively establishing a customs union between the parties is the main aspect of the association as provided by Article 10 of the Ankara Agreement, it was not only the elements of free movement of goods between the parties and the adoption by Turkey of the Common Customs Tariff (CCT) of the EC in its trade with third countries (along with an approximation to the other EC's rules on external trade) which were aimed at during the association relationship. As an association agreement leading to full membership, it also included provisions related to free movement of workers (Article 12), services (Article 14) and capital (Articles 18, 19 and 20) and harmonization of some economic policies, like agriculture (Article 11), transportation (Article 15), competition and taxation (Article 16) and external trade (Article 21) between Turkey and the EU as envisaged by the EEC Treaty between member states. This meant that while the association was mainly based on a customs union between Turkey and the EC, it also envisaged closer and deeper economic relations in accordance with the ultimate aim of the association. Its objective was far more ambitious than establishing a customs union because it envisaged developing other areas of economic integration in addition to the customs union to serve as a preparatory stage to membership of the Community (Lasok 1991: 27; Can and Özen 2005: 22–5). That is, the agreement's ultimate objective was not a customs union. Rather, a customs union was aimed at with the full understanding that it would lead to full membership (further integration). That is why the agreement envisaged a customs union as an instrument which would ultimately facilitate the way towards Turkey's accession to the EC (Can and Özen 2005: 21).

Regarding the main characteristics of the Ankara Agreement, as Ahmet Gökdere (cited in Can and Özen 2005: 24) and Burak Erdenir (2012: 478) stated, it is firstly a 'framework agreement', like the Athens Agreement. Framework agreements or treaties have a 'programmatic character providing a broad framework for further integration' (Cremona 2009: 252). They establish an institutional structure and authorize the institutions to realize their programmes and, therefore, to reach their objectives. The Ankara Agreement as a framework agreement describes the framework of a programme to establish a customs union in three successive stages and to integrate the Turkish economy gradually into the EC. It stipulates general rules and principles of the association rather than clear commitments of the parties, and implementation of its provisions are largely left to the discretion of the parties due to its programmatic nature (Can and Özen 2005: 24–5). Subsequent developments in the association relationship could take place through both the Additional Protocol,[5] which was signed on 23 November 1970 and annexed to the Ankara Agreement, and decisions of the Association Council. While providing a general framework for the association, it gave details regarding the contents of just the first stage (Saraçoğlu 1991: 49) through the Provisional Protocol and the Financial Protocol[6] that were attached to it.

Similarly, Lasok (1991: 37–9) emphasizes, from the international law perspective, the 'non-self-executing' nature of the Ankara Agreement as an association agreement providing only a framework for future action or set of rules which become operative upon the implementation by the parties. Even if containing similar textual provisions to the EEC Treaty, which came into operation automatically as a self-executing treaty, such agreements do not necessarily create directly enforceable individual rights unless implemented since their rules are indirectly applicable,[7] being in the nature of programmes or framework provisions. As Lasok (1991: 41–2) highlighted, in the *Demirel* case[8] the European Court of Justice (ECJ) ruled that the provisions of an association agreement were directly applicable if they imposed a clear and precise obligation on the parties. However, it characterized the Ankara Agreement as specifying the objectives of the association and laying down the guidelines for their attainment without providing any specific rules to that end. The relevant article in this case, Article 36 of the Additional Protocol of 1970 depending on the principles set out in Article 12 of the Ankara Agreement, conferred exclusively on the Association Council the power to lay down specific rules for securing the free movement of workers.

The ECJ concluded that the provisions which merely imposed upon the contracting parties a general duty to cooperate for achieving the objectives of the Ankara Agreement could not directly confer rights on individuals.

As a framework and non-self-executing agreement, it provided for an institutional structure with a view to realizing its programme. In other words, it established and then gave authority to relevant institutions in order to fill in the framework defined by it. The main institution of the association is the Association Council.[9] It was established to oversee the functioning of the agreement and to ensure the implementation of its provisions and the progressive development of the association. The Association Council was given authority to take decisions[10] for attaining the objectives of the agreement and to settle disputes[11] arising in relation to the application or interpretation of its provisions. The importance of the Association Council arises from the fact that it provides for the progressive development of relations and the implementation of the Ankara Agreement by laying down specific rules to that end and making the provisions of the agreement a clear and precise obligation for both parties. As Erdenir (2012: 479) pointed out, the ECJ ruled in the *Sevince* case[12] that the Association Council decisions taken to implement the provisions of the Ankara Agreement included sufficiently clear and precise commitments that did not necessitate any further act, thereby being an integral part of the EC law order and directly conferring rights on individuals. Therefore, the ECJ highlighted the crucial role of the Association Council decisions in making provisions of the Ankara Agreement and the Additional Protocol (related to the issue of free movement of workers in this case) operative.

A second characteristic of the Ankara Agreement was that, like the Athens Agreement, it did not have a provision to terminate its existence at a specific time. That is, its existence can only come to an end when the objectives of the agreements are fully achieved. Thus, the Athens Agreement came to an end when Greece became a full member of the EC, so whenever the ultimate objective of the Ankara Agreement that is Turkey's full membership is reached, the agreement will have completed its function and its existence will come to an end. Thirdly, the Ankara Agreement is substantially similar to the Athens Agreement. Their structural characteristics, contents, objectives and even the wording of some of their provisions are identical. There is just one difference between them: in the case of the Ankara Agreement, the association was envisaged as being completed in succeeding three stages, while in the case of the Athens Agreement the association was designed to be completed in just one stage (Saraçoğlu 1991: 49). Another important feature of the Ankara Agreement was that it is asymmetrical concerning the reciprocal commitments of the contracting parties. Asymmetry meant in this case more rapid liberalization on the Community side than on the Turkish side. For example, in the first stage, only the Community assumed obligations, and in the second stage it performed its obligations arising from the Additional Protocol of 1970 to establish the customs union earlier than Turkey.

The Ankara Agreement envisages a progressive and gradual integration process through the establishment of a customs union between the parties, and this process is designed to be completed in three stages: preparatory, transitional and final. The transition from the preparatory stage to the transitional stage, according to Article 4 of the agreement, would not be automatic, but provided for by the parties through a protocol by negotiating on conditions of the transitional period. Indeed, the Additional Protocol which regulated the conditions, detailed rules and timetables of the transitional period was concluded in 1970. However, how the parties would transit to the final stage was not regulated by the agreement. It was left to the discretion of the parties. The Association Council took on 6 March 1996 a decision on implementing the final phase of the customs union which commenced the final stage of the association on 1 January 1996.[13] The Ankara Agreement left the length of the final stage undetermined. Transition from the status of associated country to membership will take place in this stage with the successful conclusion of accession negotiations.

The scope of the preparatory stage was regulated by Article 3 of the Ankara Agreement. In accordance with this article, Turkey did not undertake any commitments concerning the improvement of its relations with the EC. Consistent with the asymmetric character of the agreement the Community alone undertook commitments to prepare the Turkish economy to meet its commitments in the transitional and final stages. The preparatory stage was designed to strengthen the Turkish economy through financial aid of 175 million ECU in loans under the first Financial Protocol, and through preferential tariff reductions for some agricultural products (hazelnut, tobacco, dried fig and raisin) provided by the Community. From 1967 on, the scope of the agricultural goods which were subject to tariff reductions was extended to include grapes, citrus, wine and some seafood (Çayhan 1997: 52). The preparatory stage was envisaged to last a minimum of five years, and a maximum of ten.

According to Article 4 of the Ankara Agreement, the aim of the transitional stage was to establish progressively a customs union between Turkey and the Community on the basis of mutual and balanced obligations and to align the economic policies of Turkey with those of the Community. The EC and Turkey would progressively abolish all trade barriers on exports and imports (customs duties on imports and exports and all charges having equivalent effects, quantitative restrictions and all other measures having equivalent effects) in order to ensure free movement of goods. Additionally, Turkey would gradually adopt the CCT of the EC against third countries in order to establish the customs union with the EC. The Additional Protocol, which was signed on 23 November 1970 and entered into force on 1 January 1973, provided for conditions, detailed rules and timetables relating to the implementation of the transitional stage and therefore the completion of the customs union. The Protocol, which was prepared in accordance with Article 4 of the Ankara Agreement, may be regarded as an implementation agreement since it to some extent filled in the framework regarding the transitional period provided for by the agreement, and led to the implementation of its provisions regarding establishment of a customs union.

In accordance with the asymmetric character of the Ankara Agreement, the Additional Protocol envisaged an asymmetric trade liberalization. The Community was required to remove all customs tariffs on imports from Turkey in industrial goods and charges having equivalent effects on the entry into force of the Additional Protocol, except for sensitive products, like agricultural and energy goods, steel and textiles,[14] while Turkey was obliged gradually to remove, with some exceptions, the same barriers on imports from the EC over a period of 12 years from the entry into force of the Protocol.[15] Since the ratification of the Additional Protocol by both the parliaments of member states and the Turkish Parliament would take a long time, a Provisional Protocol was signed on 1 September 1971, in order to be able to implement the commercial provisions of the Additional Protocol (Saraçoğlu 1991: 51). The Community started to abolish customs duties on imports from Turkey and charges having equivalent effects immediately after the Provisional Protocol entered into force, without waiting for the entry into force of the Additional Protocol. That is, the EC started to perform its obligations regarding customs tariffs and charges before it was obliged to. With the Provisional Protocol, the preparatory stage ended and the transitional stage started de facto while the transitional stage started *de jure*, through the entry into force of the Additional Protocol on 1 January 1973.

With respect to quantitative restrictions on imports from the EC and measures having equivalent effects, Turkey was required to abolish them not later than 22 years after the entry into force of the Additional Protocol. The EC was also obligated to abolish all measures having equivalent effects to quantitative restrictions on imports from Turkey within 22 years after the entry into force of this Protocol, while it was obliged to abolish quantitative restrictions on the entry into force of the Protocol. Turkey was also required to align its customs tariffs against third countries with the CCT of the EC mainly over a period of 12 years following the entry into force of the Protocol, while for some sensitive products listed in Annex 3 to the Additional Protocol Turkey was permitted to align its tariffs with the CCT over a period of 22 years. With some exceptions, the Ankara Agreement in Article 4(2) envisaged the transitional stage to last not more than 12 years. However, the exceptions were envisaged not to impede the final establishment of the customs union within a reasonable period. It should be noted that the customs union was intended to be completed in its entirety at the end of the twenty-second year of the Additional Protocol, while it would basically be completed at the end of the twelfth year.

The issue of extension of free movement to agricultural goods was regulated by Articles 31–35 of the Additional Protocol, and Turkey was obliged to adjust its agricultural policy over a period of 22 years from 1973, with a view to adopting the measures of the Common Agricultural Policy (CAP) of the Community. In other words, the Additional Protocol made it necessary for Turkey to adjust its agricultural policy to the CAP to gain free access of its agricultural goods to the EC markets.

In accordance with the Ankara Agreement, the Additional Protocol involved provisions regulating the objectives of free movement of workers, services and capital as well as free movement of goods, since it envisaged an economic integration between Turkey and the Community beyond just a customs union. Indeed, Article 36 of the Protocol provided a time schedule for the gradual realization of the free movement of workers as between the end of the twelfth and twenty-second years after the entry into force of the Ankara Agreement. Therefore, free movement of workers should have been progressively achieved between the end of 1976 and 1986. Additionally, Article 36 made it necessary for the Association Council to decide on the detailed rules and procedures necessary for achieving the free movement of workers by the stated deadlines. Just like the provisions for the free movement of goods leading to a customs union, the substantive provisions for free movement of workers were defined in the Ankara Agreement while the timetable was given in the Additional Protocol. Likewise, the related article of the Protocol, Article 36, depended on the principles set out in Article 12 of the Ankara Agreement, which envisaged that the contracting parties should be guided by Articles 48, 49 and 50 of the EEC Treaty for the purpose of progressively achieving the free movement of workers between them. However, there was something missing from the framework: Article 51 of the EEC Treaty. It provides that previous working periods are taken into account in calculating the amount of social security benefit. The lack of Article 51 meant that there could be free movement for just new workers, or for those workers who were willing to sacrifice their acquired rights arising from previous working periods. In this case, one can argue that the envisaged free movement of workers between the EC and Turkey was deficient.

Similarly, Article 41(1) of the Additional Protocol regulated the issues of free movement of services and right of establishment, stating that 'the contracting parties shall refrain from introducing between themselves any new restrictions on the freedom of establishment and the freedom to provide services.' Just like the free movement of workers, Article 41, in its second paragraph, made it necessary for the Association Council to take decisions regarding the timetable and detailed rules for the progressive abolition by the contracting parties between themselves of restrictions on freedom of establishment and on free movement of services. Regarding the free movement of capital, Article 51 required Turkey to try to facilitate its regime regarding foreign capital coming from the EC that could contribute to the development of the Turkish economy. Moreover, the contracting parties were obliged to try to refrain from introducing between themselves any new restrictions on the free movement of capital and making the existing arrangements more restrictive in Article 52.

The final stage was intended to start on the completion of the transitional stage, depending on the progressive and gradual establishment of the customs union. The customs union decision taken by the Association Council on 6 March 1995 determined the conditions relating to the completion of the customs union. The final stage, then, started on 1 January 1996 on the completion of the customs union between the parties. Currently, the association is in its final stage, involving a functioning customs union and closer coordination of economic policies between the parties. As the Ankara Agreement envisaged the possibility of the accession of Turkey in Article 28, the conditions for full membership would be negotiated in the final stage of the association.

Problems experienced in the implementation process of the Association Agreement and non-fulfilment by the parties of their contractual commitments

The preparatory stage was the honeymoon period of relations between Turkey and the EC since, during this stage, the association did not experience important problems compared to the next stage. In this stage, security concerns were of primary importance, so Turkey's geostrategic importance played the main role in the development of relations. Moreover, Turkey had no obligations arising from the Ankara Agreement with the EC side alone providing a reasonable amount of financial aid, and implementing tariff reductions on those Turkish agricultural exports that did not pose a burden that the EC could not cope with. The Turkish economy benefitted from financial aid of approximately $200 million and from the increasing trade with the Community members resulting from these tariff reductions. This situation induced the Turkish side to launch the next stage with high expectations that the transitional stage would provide greater access to EC goods and labour markets and to more financial aid from the EC. Turkey also expected, following the military coup in Greece in 1967, to obtain better concessions from the Community which would restore the economic imbalance between the Ankara and Athens Agreements, since it considered the Athens Agreement to be a more favourable agreement with the aim of establishing customs union in just one stage (without a preparatory stage) (Arıkan 2003: 59). With closer relations in the framework of the transitional stage, Turkey also hoped to gain the support of the EC member states for its Cyprus policy to counterbalance the US policy towards the dispute (Bourguignon 1990: 53). Additionally, membership applications by the UK, Denmark and Norway, and the emergence of the EC's Mediterranean Policy, also made Turkey's request to start the transitional stage more urgent because it would be easier for Turkey to gain concessions from the Community before this first enlargement. Turkey also wanted to obtain financial aid and trade preferences before the Mediterranean countries obtained them in the framework of trade and cooperation agreements. Therefore, the Turkish government applied to the EC to start the transitional stage two years earlier than had been planned (Arıkan 2003: 60).

Although the EC was reluctant to negotiate the transitional stage with Turkey at that time due to the unpreparedness of the Turkish economy for meeting commitments in relation to the establishment of the customs union, it agreed to start negotiations because of security concerns arising from regional instabilities, like the Arab-Israeli dispute and the military takeover in Greece. The EC thought that the stability of Turkey had to be supported through further economic aid and the preferential access of Turkish goods into its markets. Therefore, the transitional stage was launched on 1 January 1973, with the entry into force of the Additional Protocol, signed on 23 November 1970 at the end of the negotiations started in 1968.

In contrast to the preparatory stage, serious problems, particularly relating to economic issues in the 1970s and political issues in the 1980s, were experienced in the transitional period in relations between the EC and Turkey. Actually, the Turkish economy was not ready to start the transitional stage, which imposed reciprocal obligations on the parties for liberalizing trade between them, because at that time the Turkish economy was being considerably protected by import substitution policies and there was a high degree of state intervention in the economy. Under the influence of political considerations, Turkey underestimated the unpreparedness of its economy for adapting to an important degree of trade liberalization, even though it would be gradual in nature. Therefore, its willingness to start meeting its commitments regarding the customs union can be seen as less than rational. Indeed, Turkey experienced serious problems in complying with its contractual commitments arising from the transitional stage of the association, due to its economic inadequacies.

First of all, following the entry into force of the Additional Protocol, and the activation of Turkey's commitments, a critical debate on the customs union in general, and on the timetable of the customs union in particular, started in Turkey. Turkish producers, who had operated in a quite protective economic environment, claimed that the transitional period into the customs union was too short, which would hinder the industrialization of the Turkish economy. Even the foundations, like the Istanbul Chamber of Industry and the Economic Development Foundation, which always support closer relations with the European integration, adopted a suspicious stance towards the customs union in this period. With respect to the bureaucracy, such an approach was also dominant in the State Planning Organisation, which argued that the customs union would interfere with Turkey's industrialization and import-substitutive development strategy. Influential circles in Turkish society stood against the customs union out of the same concerns, stating that they were not against the EC but they were against the customs union timetable determined by the Additional Protocol. This situation was aggravated by the negative approach of one of the two major political parties in Turkey and by the inability of the other major party to cope with this situation, although it was in favour of developing the relations with the EC. Additionally, the other minor but influential political parties in terms of maintaining coalitions were strongly against the EC. This picture reflects the fact that consensus with respect to developing relations with the EC had been lost and views against the customs union gained influence.

Another problem for Turkey in its relations with the EC, which damaged its implementation of the transitional stage, related to developments in the EC's external and internal policies. Due to the Global Mediterranean Policy of the EC, adopted in 1975,[16] trade concessions that Turkey obtained in the framework of the Ankara Agreement and the Additional Protocol became insufficient to provide preferential treatment or privileges to Turkey vis-à-vis the Mediterranean countries. The policy gave similar trade concessions, particularly to those countries which produced substantially similar products to Turkey, and whose exports therefore competed with Turkey's exports to the EC markets.

The Community also gave similar trade concessions for textiles and agricultural goods to less developed countries within the framework of the Generalised

System of Preferences, which also harmed Turkey's preferential access to such EC markets. Turkey also had concerns about the EC's first enlargement that included the UK, Ireland and Denmark, and its forthcoming Mediterranean enlargement to involve Greece, Spain and Portugal (Bourguignon 1990: 55). Turkey's preferential access to EC agricultural markets was also undermined by the UK's accession because it extended the EU's preferential treatment to those countries where the UK had colonial ties. The UK's membership also impacted Turkey's textile exports to the EC since the UK imposed trade barriers on Turkish cotton yarns. Turkey regarded all these developments as undermining already-agreed privileges resulting from its associate member status. Because the Association Agreement with Turkey went beyond a mere trade and cooperation agreement and included the ultimate objective of membership, Turkey claimed that the EC should have provided it with further privileges in order to offset the negative impacts of changes occurring through the EC's external and internal policies (Arıkan 2003: 62).

All these concerns aggravated the increasing reluctance in Turkey regarding the customs union that mainly resulted from the existing incapacity of the Turkish economy to meet its obligations regarding the customs union. Mehmet Uğur has argued that the import substitution policy, which prevailed during 1970s, was also responsible for the reluctance, since its protectionist nature contradicted liberal economic policy regarding the free movement of goods (Uğur 1999: 5–6). For this reason, Turkey failed to integrate its economy with the EC through the customs union. Indeed, Turkey applied to the EC to delay the implementation of its obligations regarding customs duties shortly after the gradual implementation process formally started in 1973, since its third Five-Year Development Plan for the period 1973–1977 was incompatible with its commitments arising from the Additional Protocol (Uğur 1999: 67).

Turkey's performance concerning its commitments in the transitional stage was quite weak. Only two reductions of tariff rates for imports from the EC, of 10 per cent each, were realized for barriers subject to elimination in 12 years, and of 5 per cent each for the barriers subject to elimination in 22 years in 1973 and 1976. The adjustment to the CCT was not even started, and the process of reducing quantitative restrictions, by 40 per cent of total imports, on imports from the EC also came to an end in 1976 after hardly having been launched. Furthermore, Turkey demanded greater EC concessions in agricultural trade without making substantial efforts to adapt its agricultural policy to the conditions of the CAP (Kramer 1996: 207). Finally, in 1978, when the EC did not accept Turkish demands and Turkey faced important economic and political difficulties, the coalition government in Turkey proposed to revise the relations regarding the customs union, to suspend its commitments unilaterally for a period of five years, and to require further financial assistance and new concessions regarding agricultural and sensitive industrial goods (Birand 1990: 384–8). Although the new government, which came to power at the end of 1979, withdrew the decision regarding suspension, obligations arising from the customs union could not be met until the early 1990s because of economic and political disturbances in Turkey.

It was not only Turkey that was responsible for the fact that implementation of the Ankara Agreement and the Additional Protocol was never really launched properly until the early 1990s. Although the Community abolished all customs duties and quantitative restrictions by 1973 for Turkish manufactures, trade in textiles and clothing constituted an important exception to the elimination of trade barriers on Turkish exports. Trade in this sector was regulated firstly under the EC textile policy in the framework of the international multi-fibre arrangement and then by so-called voluntary export restraint agreements concluded between Turkish textile exporters and the EC. As discussed in Chapter 2 in this volume, the EC had continued to protect its domestic producers from Turkish textiles through quotas in the framework of voluntary export restraints until 1996 when the customs union between Turkey and the EC started to operate. Additionally, although the Community abolished all customs duties for agricultural imports from Turkey in 1987, trade in agriculture remained restricted by the CAP's very effective non-tariff barriers on the grounds that Turkey's commitment to align its agricultural policy with the CAP remained unfulfilled (Kramer 1996: 205–6).

Another issue of Turkish concern was the non-fulfilment of obligations concerning the free movement of workers. At the beginning of 1973, the German government imposed a ban on the recruitment of migrant workers from non-EC countries, and the other member states soon followed it. This ban was later supplemented by the introduction of visa requirements for Turkish citizens visiting Germany and other member states. Since then, immigration into the EC has been made possible for Turkish citizens only when family members join an already legally settled worker. The German government exerted great efforts to prevent the relevant provisions of the Association Agreement from being effectively implemented by vetoing the related agenda of the Association Council in the Council of Ministers,[17] and other member states supported German efforts by remaining silent. The Association Council could not take decisions necessary to lay down specific rules for securing by stages the freedom of movement of workers as required by the Additional Protocol.[18] Consequently, one of the important pillars of the association could not be implemented. At the beginning, it was basically economic and social concerns that motivated the German government to adopt its restrictive attitude towards the free movement of Turkish workers. In more recent years, however, this issue has increasingly became intermingled with European domestic political issues, such as policies towards asylum-seekers and the resurgence of xenophobia in Germany and elsewhere. In November 1986, the EC proposed clear regulation of the issue of free movement of labour, whereby immigration of new workers would be virtually suspended for the duration of the association relationship. The Turkish government rejected this proposal and since then the issue has been pending (Kramer 1996: 206).

An additional reason for Turkish criticism regarding non-performance by the Community side was the fact that the fourth Financial Protocol, agreed on in 1981 in the framework of the Association Agreement, never entered into force due to the EC's inability to prevent the Greek veto. This protocol, which envisaged loans to Turkey in the amount of 600 million ECU, would have provided financial assistance to mitigate the negative impacts of the customs union on Turkish industry. However, it could not be implemented because the association relationship was suspended following the military coup in 1980 until a democratic regime was reapplied. Since then, its implementation has been continuously blocked by Greece in EC institutions. The EC had provided financial assistance of up to $705 million through the previous three Financial Protocols of the association relationship.

Relations in the 1980s and Turkey's full membership application to the EC

The 1980 military coup aggravated existing problems between Turkey and the Community in relation to the implementation of the transitional stage of the association. Throughout the 1980s, democracy and human rights issues gained importance in relations, as compared to the 1970s, when economic concerns and considerations had been dominant. While Turkey was experiencing difficult times regarding its democracy and human rights situation, the EC determined that these issues were essential conditions for obtaining membership status when it assessed the membership applications made by Greece, Spain and Portugal. The EC did not react immediately to the military coup in Turkey and pursued a 'wait and see' policy for a while. However, after the National Security Council's decision concerning the banning of all existing political parties, the EC's attitude towards Turkey hardened. In January 1982, through a decision by the European Parliament, the Ankara Agreement was suspended until democracy and human rights could be secured in Turkey. Accordingly, the association institutions could no longer convene.

Even the 1983 general elections failed to change relations, and this attitude continued until the 1984 local elections. The Community evaluated the participation of the previously prohibited parties in these elections as a clear step towards democracy, so the first messages of normalization in relations started to come from it. The Community also considered that keeping relations with Turkey functioning was important for the political, economic and security interests of the EC. Since the Turkish government desired to normalize relations as well, the Community attempted to revive the Association Agreement without ignoring its sensitivity regarding democracy. Therefore, after a long hiatus, the Association Council reconvened in 1986, and both the issue of the entry into force of the fourth Financial Protocol and how relations were to be normalized were negotiated. Although both parties had common interests in working for a strengthened relationship, their ways to reach this and their objectives differed.

Turkey applied for full membership in the EC on 14 April 1987 on the basis of Article 237 of the EEC Treaty that regulated full membership of the European countries to the Community. Turkey thought that the association path, which had started with the association application in 1959 in terms of Article 238, and was mainly based on the customs union, had not been able to operate as intended. The consequences of the Association Agreement were unsatisfactory for Turkey as its ultimate aim was full membership and Turkey was still very far from achieving this aim, although 23 years had passed. On the contrary, relations were worse than at the beginning of the association, and by the mid-1980s, the customs union seemed to have become a failure. The EC and Turkey experienced considerable economic and political difficulties in completing the customs union, which was the means to full membership. Free movement of workers seemed impossible, and financial aid was repeatedly blocked by Greek vetoes in EC institutions. That is the association relationship had seemingly reached an impasse, so the Turkish authorities came to the conclusion that the association became an inappropriate framework for becoming a member, and that applying directly for membership on the basis of Article 237 was the best way for Turkey regarding its political, economic and security interests. In other words, the first path (association path) would be bypassed and a new path towards full membership would be opened. This led relations to proceed under two parallel tracks, with different starting points and legal bases, but the same ultimate aim.[19]

However, one may assert that the timing was wrong for this application. It did not seem possible for the EC to react positively since relations, which had been seriously damaged, were only beginning to normalize, and the EC was still anxious about Turkey's political and economic suitability as a candidate for membership. Additionally, the EC was turning its concentration totally onto its internal affairs to deal with problems arising from the incomplete internal market and the slowing down of its decision-making process. It tried to reform itself to overcome this long period of internal stagnation or 'Eurosclerosis' through the Single Market Programme defined by the Single European Act, signed in 1986. Additionally, the EC had just begun the process of digesting the southern enlargement (Greece, Spain and Portugal).

The EC, engaged in such a critical reform process and concentrating on its internal affairs, could not be expected to assess Turkey's application positively, particularly as it was a large and economically less developed country. Indeed, the Commission's Avis, which was resent to the Council in 1989, did not include a clear and certain positive or negative answer (European Commission 1989). While it stated that Turkey was eligible to be a member, it added that Turkey was not ready to meet the commitments arising from full membership due to its inadequate economic and political situation, particularly considering the political and economic objectives of the EC declared in the framework of the Single European Act. The Commission also made reference in its opinion to disputes with a member state (Greece) and to the Cyprus issue as obstacles to Turkey's membership. Additionally, the Commission stated that the EC itself was not ready to negotiate accepting new members until 1993 because of its concentration on the completion of its internal market. Instead, the Commission proposed firstly to revive and then to develop relations based on the existing Association Agreement. It emphasized the EC's vital interest in deepening relations with Turkey in the framework of the association, and in supporting the country to complete its political and modernization process as soon as possible (European Commission 1989). This meant that the Commission proposed to leave aside the second path towards membership opened by Turkey through its full membership application and to reactivate the first path. The Council adopted the Commission's opinion unanimously. In other words, the

EC did not decide on Turkish membership. It just delayed the issue, since it had reservations about Turkey's membership bid. This answer reflected the EC's continued, and critical, indecisiveness regarding Turkey's full membership.

In accordance with the Commission's proposal made in its opinion on the Turkish membership application regarding reviving relations in the existing association framework, the Council requested the Commission to prepare and present a comprehensive package of measures. Commissioner Abel Matutes, responsible for relations with Mediterranean countries, prepared a cooperation package called the Matutes Package and presented it to the Council in June 1990. This package consisted of four interrelated aspects in order to bring Turkey as close to the EC as possible: the completion of the customs union by the end of 1995; the revival and extension of financial cooperation through the entry into force of the fourth Financial Protocol, which had been frozen since 1981; industrial and technical cooperation; and the development of political and cultural relations (European Commission 1990). This package, which asked Turkey to reactivate and develop the association relationship through the completion of the customs union, reflected the way chosen by the EC side to strengthen the relationship.

To begin with, Turkey was unwilling to complete the customs union since the issue of full membership had not been resolved by the EC. However, in the radically changing international environment that had shifted from a bipolar Cold War era to an uncertain and instable multipolar post–Cold War era, the customs union began to seem once more to be the most appropriate way for Turkey to maintain relations with the Community. When it was understood in Turkey that it would not be able to become a member in the short run through the shortcut of a full membership application, the EC's proposal to revive the frozen and non-functioning Association Agreement became more attractive. Consequently, completion of the customs union became a priority for Turkey in its relations with the EC.

Although the Matutes Package could not be implemented due to the Greek veto, its aim of completing the customs union between the parties by the end of 1995 constituted the basis of relations thereafter. The Commission prepared a Working Programme in January 1992 that envisaged similar instruments to the Matutes Package. It also prepared guidelines under which Turkey had to take the measures necessary to complete the customs union. In the Association Council meeting of November 1993, the parties agreed to establish a customs union between themselves by the end of 1995 with a one-year delay compared to the timetable envisaged by the Additional Protocol. After that, Turkey took important steps towards the establishment of the customs union by introducing necessary measures. Finally, the Association Council took a decision on 6 March 1995 to conclude a customs union between the EC and Turkey by 1 January 1996. All these developments, which began with the Matutes Package regarding the completion of the customs union, were simply confirmation of the Ankara Agreement and the Additional Protocol. Nothing was new in terms of relations between Turkey and the Community.

Notes

1 For the Agreement see Official Journal of the EC (1977a).
2 OEEC was reformed into the Organisation for Economic Co-operation and Development (OECD) in 1961.
3 Association negotiations with Turkey started in September 1959, while association negotiations with Greece started in March 1960.
4 As a much older form of agreement that the EU concluded, the Ankara Agreement does not include any provision for political dialogue or justice and home affairs cooperation (Cremona 2009: 252).
5 For the Additional Protocol see Official Journal of the EC (1977b).
6 These protocols regulated the details regarding the commercial and financial privileges unilaterally provided by the Community in the preparatory stage of the association.
7 A distinction is made between 'direct applicability' and 'direct effect' in EU law. Directly applicable rules of EU law do not require domestic implementing legislation in member states by taking effect as soon as they are published by the European Commission. They must be fully and uniformly applied in all member states from the date of their entry into force. Direct effect refers to the principle that rule of EU law may, if appropriately framed, confer rights on individuals which the courts of member states are bound to recognize and enforce. Initially, these terms were used interchangeably in the case law of the Court of Justice of the EU. But in time the distinction between the two has become clearer due to the expansion of principle of direct effect to include directives. Direct effect can be considered as a consequence of direct applicability since directly inapplicable rules, in principle, are also directly ineffective as they cannot be used in court until they have been enacted by national legislation with the exception of direct effect of directives. Despite being directly inapplicable, directives have been granted direct effect in some exceptional situations, for the sake of fostering private enforcement of the EU law, through individual parties' actions. For more information about direct effect see Craig and Burca (2015: 184–204).
8 For more information regarding the *Demirel* case see InfoCuria (1987).
9 The others include the Association Committee, Joint Parliamentary Commission, Customs Cooperation Committee, Customs Union Joint Committee and Joint Consultative Committee.
10 The Association Council takes decisions unanimously. Both the EU side as a whole and the Turkish side have one vote each. The EU reaches this common position, or voice, in the Council of Ministers by unanimity voting before the meetings of the Association Council. Since the decisions taken by the Association Council are binding on the parties, each of the parties must take the measures necessary to implement the decisions.
11 Any disputes relating to the application or interpretation of the Agreement which concern the Community, a member state or Turkey may be submitted to the Association Council by the contracting parties. In the case of a dispute submitted to itself it may either resolve the dispute by a decision or decide to submit the dispute to the Court of Justice of the EC or to any other existing international court or tribunal.
12 For more information regarding the *Sevince* case see InfoCuria (1990).
13 For the decision see Official Journal of the EC (1996).
14 The Community was obliged to abolish progressively customs duties and charges having equivalent effects on imports from Turkey in these products over a 12-year period from the entry into force of the Protocol.
15 For the products which were considered to gain competitiveness against the European goods in the long term, Turkey was required to remove these barriers over a period of 22 years. The list of these sensitive products was annexed to the Additional Protocol.

Additionally, the contracting parties were obliged to abolish customs duties on exports and charges having equivalent effects between themselves at the latest four years after the entry into force of the Additional Protocol.

16 The Global Mediterranean Policy was based on bilateral trade and cooperation agreements with the Maghreb (Algeria, Morocco and Tunisia) and the Mashreq countries (Egypt, Jordan, Lebanon and Syria) and Israel. These agreements provided these countries with preferential market access to EC markets particularly in some agricultural goods and financial assistance. This policy was adopted for developing relations between the EC and the Mediterranean countries in relation to the EC's security concerns, such as its dependence on oil, increasing migration from these countries and conflict between the Arab states and Israel.

17 The agenda of the Association Council needs to be decided unanimously in the Council of Ministers.

18 The only decisions adopted by the Council was Decision 2/76 followed by Decision 1/80, which prohibited the imposition of any new restrictions on the access to employment (Lasok 1991: 42).

19 One may argue that, with the opening of accession negotiations on 3 October 2005, the existing two parallel ways towards full membership functionally met, although relations are institutionally still under these two parallel paths. While accession negotiations that are, one way or another, proceeding cover all the areas of integration, the Ankara Agreement and its instruments like the Association Council are still in force since the ultimate aim of the Association has not been reached yet. Some may also argue that Turkey–EU relations are still not only institutionally but also functionally under these two parallel paths due to the suspension of the eight negotiation chapters related to the customs union. Similarly, Tezcan (2013: 45) argues that Turkey–EU relations are today simultaneously proceeding in the framework of both association relationship and accession/enlargement process. When Turkey's accession/enlargement process is successfully completed, existing relations proceeding in the framework of two platforms will automatically come to an end and relations will be founded on a sole legal basis since Turkey will gain the status of EU member state. Considering another approach to the current state of relations, the pre-accession dimension of the Ankara Agreement entails that although it is a contractual basis of the relations between Turkey and the EU, it functions along with other instruments of the accession process, like Accession Partnership, and its institutional framework provides the structure through which the Association Partnership is monitored (Cremona 2009: 252).

2 The customs union as the basis of EU association

An appropriate device for accession?

Turkey's full membership application of 1987, which was made after 23 years of unsuccessful association, was not assessed positively, mainly due to both parties' unpreparedness for launching the process towards membership. In response to this application, the EU offered to continue with more progressive integration as intended by the Ankara Agreement of 1963[1] and the Additional Protocol of 1970.[2] Turkey had no choice but to accept this offer and complete the customs union as the main instrument for progressively integrating with the EU in the absence of a more direct and short route towards membership. It therefore endorsed this offer at the thirty-third meeting of the Association Council on November 1992. While there seems to have been some enthusiasm for this development, the EU actually offered nothing new, resembling instead a rediscovery of what had already been included in the Ankara Agreement. While the association between the parties stood still, the EU developed its own brand of customs union.

It should be noted that Turkey regarded the customs union as a stepping stone towards membership rather than an end itself, as becomes also clear from the statement of the then Turkish foreign minister, Murat Karayalçın, during the thirty-fifth meeting of the Association Council of 19 December 1994 (EU–Turkey Association's Annual Report 1994: 28). Accordingly, referring to the Ankara Agreement, Turkey emphasized that the customs union was the final phase of the association before the country's accession to the EU. Indeed, the Ankara Agreement itself envisaged the establishment of a customs union between the parties as a means for reaching the ultimate objective of full membership. Thus, in concluding the customs union, Turkey had been driven not only by economic considerations but also by the political expectation that the customs union would facilitate its integration with the EU as a full member. Even the economic considerations were motivated by the view of preparing the Turkish economy for EU membership, using the customs union as a pre-accession instrument. The EU itself was based on a customs union, and according to Article 28 of the Ankara Agreement, Turkey's accession would be considered once it reached a level at which it could fully assume the obligations arising out of membership. Thus, at every opportunity during the establishment of the customs union, Turkey drew the EU's attention to the clear and direct correlation between the customs union and Turkey's membership, as conceived by the Ankara Agreement. Turkey therefore expected that EU membership would be achieved in a quite short period of time, ranging from four to eight years, after the customs union was established (Kabaalioğlu 2012: 14).

The EU, however, did not take the same approach towards the customs union, refusing to accept Turkey's view that the customs union would serve as a stepping stone to EU membership. Instead, the EU tended to regard the customs union as establishing closer economic cooperation rather than being a pre-accession instrument. Thus, the EU saw the customs union decision taken by the Association Council on 6 March 1995[3] as a trade agreement to revitalize the stalled Association Agreement, and accordingly it was voted through in the European Parliament under the assent procedure.[4] It is worth noting that while the EU was negotiating the completion of the customs union with Turkey, it had already started its next wave of enlargement to include the former Communist countries of Central and Eastern Europe. That was mainly why Turkey made great efforts during these negotiations to establish a direct connection between the issue of Turkey's membership and the customs union. However, in the post–Cold War era, the EU preferred to reform its relations with Turkey within the framework of the Association rather than the framework of its enlargement perspective adopted after the conclusion of the internal market and the dissolution of Central and Eastern Europe's Communist regimes. Indeed, the EU did not even consider Turkey as a prospective member when it took a decisive step towards the eastward enlargement at the Copenhagen European Council of 1993 by agreeing that 'the associated countries in Central and Eastern Europe that so desire shall become members of the EU' (European Council 1993: 13) and when the Essen European Council of 1994 decided to launch a pre-accession strategy for preparing these countries for membership. In the conclusions of these European Council summits, and in the other official documents of the EU, Turkey's membership issue or, more specifically, the issue of Turkey's preparation for membership was not mentioned. This was because the EU, instead of committing itself to accept Turkey as a member, intended for both economic and security reasons to improve its relations with Turkey institutionally, economically and politically, and to anchor it to the EU as a stable country with a large market through the customs union.[5]

Obviously, therefore, Turkey and the EU had different motivations and expectations in focusing on the completion of the customs union. Turkish policymakers were mainly stimulated by the country's long-standing bid for EU membership, and therefore regarded the customs union as the final step before EU membership. In contrast, the EU was not keen to treat the customs union as a pre-accession strategy to prepare Turkey for membership, being motivated instead by economic and security factors. That is mainly why the Association Council decision on the customs union did not include sufficient and efficient instruments to prepare Turkey for EU membership.

Main characteristics and scope of the customs union

The customs union decision of the Association Council on 6 March 1995 terminated the transitional period, whose conditions, detailed rules and timetables had been determined by the Additional Protocol of 1970. In other words, the Association Council decided that the final stage of Association, based on a customs union, was to commence as of 1 January 1996 in accordance with the Association Agreement and the Additional Protocol. This decision laid down the rules for implementing the final phase of the customs union. In this respect it firstly envisaged various measures and a timetable regarding the remaining aspects for the establishment of the customs union. These aspects included removal of existing trade barriers on imports and exports between the EU and Turkey and Turkey's adoption of the EU's CCT. It also specified other aspects concerning the proper functioning of the customs union once it had been established. The customs union, which mainly focuses on the free movement of goods between the parties and the implementation of a common customs tariff vis-à-vis third countries, has also necessitated the adaptation of relevant Turkish legislation to the common trade and competition policies of the EU in accordance with developments in these policies.

Because the decision required critical trade policy changes on the Turkish side rather than the EU's, it was believed that the customs union represented a form of unilateral trade liberalization by Turkey. First, Turkey had to eliminate all remaining customs duties and other charges, quantitative restrictions and measures of equivalent effects on industrial imports from the EU by 1 January 1996. Various other trade barriers that were not listed in the decision but that formed part of Turkey's national practices were also all removed. The EU had already removed most customs duties and quantitative restrictions on industrial goods imported from Turkey in the first two stages, so, through this decision, Turkey gave a delayed response. Most export-oriented industries in Turkey, except the textiles and clothing sectors, had already benefitted from an open EU market so the main effect of the customs union for Turkish exporters was that EU markets were also opened to Turkish products in these sectors since the EU, in accordance with the decision, had to abolish the voluntary export restraints that had previously limited the export of Turkish textiles to its market. That is why these sectors strongly supported the customs union in order to expand their market shares in the EU.

There was one exception to the obligations regarding the ensuring of the free movement of goods with the EU by 1 January 1996: the removal of standards and technical barriers to trade. As regulated in Article 8(1) of Decision No 1/95 of the EC-Turkey Association Council, Turkey undertook to incorporate into its internal legal order the EU's instruments relating to the removal of technical barriers to trade within five years from the date of entry into force of the decision. Harmonization in standards and technical barriers is an important pillar of achieving free movement of goods between the parties. Accordingly, the decision obliged Turkey to harmonize its related legislation with that of the EU. Since this difficult task required more time, the Association Council decided to give an extra five years to Turkey to complete harmonization. In accordance with Article 8(2) of Decision No of 1/95, the Association Council agreed in 1997 where Turkey had to align its legislation with the EU.[6] Accordingly, the Turkish Accreditation Agency (TÜRKAK) was established in 1999 in order to develop infrastructural arrangements in the fields of calibration, accreditation, testing and certification.

However, although work on harmonizing national legislation to remove technical barriers to trade with the EU continued, progress was slow and the process was still uncompleted by the end of 2000.

The customs union covers products other than agricultural products and those within the scope of the European Coal and Steel Community (ECSC). However, since Turkey signed a free trade agreement (FTA) for ECSC products with the EU in July 1996, which has allowed these products to circulate freely since 1999, all industrial products, including processed agricultural goods,[7] benefit from free movement. In addition, the customs union applies not only to industrial and processed agricultural goods originating from EU member states or Turkey but also to those coming from third countries and in free circulation in the Union or in Turkey once import formalities have been complied with and any customs duties and charges have been levied in the state of entry.

Regarding agricultural products, the situation is different. The parties did not find it appropriate to begin free movement of agricultural products in view of the differences in their agricultural policies, realizing that to implement a customs union for agricultural products without first aligning the parties' pricing policies would cause distortion in agricultural trade. Therefore, since Turkey had not adapted its agricultural policies to the EU's Common Agricultural Policy (CAP) during the transitional period in spite of its commitment arising from the Additional Protocol,[8] trade in agricultural products was not included in the customs union. Indeed, Article 24 of Decision 2/97 acknowledged 'the parties' common objective to move towards the free movement of agricultural products' but noted that 'an additional period is required' to establish the conditions necessary to achieve this free movement. That is, Turkey has to align its agricultural policy with the CAP in order to have free access to European agricultural markets. Meanwhile, processed agricultural products are not completely industrial products but contain an important 'agricultural component'. According to Article 18 of the decision, customs duties and charges having equivalent effects may be imposed by the parties on 'agricultural components' of those products while leaving their 'industrial components' free of any customs duties, levies or charges.[9]

Article 13 of the Customs Union Decision also requires Turkey to align itself with the CCT in relation to non-EU countries. Furthermore, according to Article 14, Turkey should not apply any import tariffs lower than the CCT for any product. Accordingly, Turkey aligned its customs tariffs with the EU's CCT in relation to these countries by 1 January 1996, which meant that the average nominal protection rates applied to non-EU countries decreased considerably, from 22.1 per cent in 1994 to 1.3 per cent at least and 6.9 per cent at the most in 2001 (Togan 2012: 2). Consequently, the customs union has given both EU members and non-EU countries substantially increased access to Turkey's markets in all industrial products except coal and steel. However, Turkey was allowed to retain customs duties higher than the CCT until 1 January 2001 in respect of non-EU countries for various products[10] that the Association Council agreed as sensitive in terms of competition.[11] As Yılmaz (2011: 237) reports, the then Turkish government had met significant opposition from some sectors, particularly the automotive industry, to foreign competition while working to complete the customs union. After leading representatives of this sector successfully lobbied for keeping a certain level of protection, this sector was included in the list of sensitive industries for which Turkey could impose customs tariffs higher than the CCT until 2001 on relevant products from third countries.[12] With the alignment of Turkey's customs duties on sensitive products with the CCT of the EU in 2001, Turkey's openness to imports of third countries increased further.

Although the original intention of the association was that the customs union would be achieved mainly by eliminating all trade barriers between the parties and Turkey's adoption of a CCT towards third countries, by the time the customs union decision was taken, the commitments involved in establishing a properly functioning customs union had become much more complicated since the EU's legislation had in this respect evolved considerably. This also necessitated the harmonization of Turkey's trade policy with all the other much more complicated Community trade measures against third countries and the Community's trade agreements with them. Because the common commercial policy (CCP) has evolved considerably and its scope has become more comprehensive, Turkey's commitments regarding harmonizing its commercial policy with the CCP have multiplied compared to the 1960s and 1970s. Accordingly, Turkey adopted the Community Customs Code and all Community legislation regarding trade policy instruments against third countries by 1 January 1996. Community legislation covers all trade policy instruments and measures applied to third countries, such as anti-dumping and anti-subsidy measures, common rules for imports and exports, and rules for textile imports.

Articles 16 and 54 of the customs union decision further obliged Turkey to harmonize its commercial policies concerning third countries with the Community's trade arrangements involving preferential trade arrangements and the Generalised System of Preferences (GSP)[13] of the EU. However, it became apparent that negotiating and concluding preferential trade arrangements would naturally take some time, so Article 16 of the decision provided that 'Turkey shall align itself progressively with the preferential customs regime of the Community' within five years from the date of its entry into force. Since then, Turkey has negotiated and concluded such arrangements on a mutually advantageous basis with European Free Trade association (EFTA) countries, some Central and Eastern European countries (CEECs),[14] some Mediterranean counties (including the Palestinian Authority), Macedonia, Croatia, Bosnia-Herzegovina, Albania and Georgia, in accordance with the commitments arising from the decision. Turkey has also harmonized its GSP regime with the EU's. Its performance was significant in this respect as it has largely aligned its preferential customs regime with the EU's. As Akman notes, these arrangements, which constituted the first wave of such agreements bilaterally concluded by Turkey, increased access for Turkish exports to these markets (Akman 2013). However, as the EU's bilateral trade relations have further developed in the form of free trade agreements with major trading partners, particularly after 2006 following the introduction of a new trade policy in the aftermath of the failure of the 2003 Cancun Ministerial Meeting of the World Trade Organization (WTO), Turkey has needed to revise its commercial policies and negotiate new bilateral free trade agreements (with the countries concerned) representing the second wave. In spite of its successes in harmonizing its commercial policies with the EU's regarding the first wave of preferential trade arrangements, Turkey has faced significant problems in dealing with the second wave, as discussed later in this chapter.

The decision, which mainly regulated free movement of goods between the parties and the implementation of a common customs tariff vis-à-vis third countries in order to create the customs union, also envisaged that Turkish legislation would adapt to the EU's trade and competition policies as these policies developed. Thus, Turkey also had to align its legislation with EU legislation related to the proper functioning of the customs union, like competition rules, protection of intellectual and industrial property rights, and protection of consumer rights. Turkey adopted the EU's competition policy in 1994 and established its Competition Authority in 1997. Regarding intellectual and industrial property rights, Turkey has adopted the EU's copyright and patent laws, while also harmonizing its rules with the WTO's for pharmaceutical processes and products patents by January 1999. Accordingly, it set up the Patent Institute (Akman 2013: 140). In order to have a properly functioning CU, it is also necessary to equalize the competition rules or production conditions of the parties because implementing a customs union without first aligning these would cause trade distortions at the expense of the party with the stricter competition rules and implementations – the EU, in this case. Since the EU would take countervailing measures in such a situation, no one would be able to regard the customs union as functioning properly. Therefore, Turkey had to align its legislation regarding these areas with the EU's so that the competition conditions were equal and a properly functioning customs union relation could be maintained.

In conclusion, the scope of the Turkey–EU customs union not only has included both the elimination of trade barriers and the adoption of a CCT as a conventional and limited definition of the term 'customs union' suggests, but also has required 'harmonisation of the structure, standards and legislative framework of the Turkish economy' with those of the European single market (Arıkan 2003: 83). The customs union has thereby provided a programme for Turkey to integrate its economy into the EU's single market within a reasonable time period.

Effects of the customs union on the Turkish economy

Obviously, the customs union has been a major tool for integrating the Turkish economy with European and global markets, which increased trade volume from $67 billion to $389 billion between 1996 and 2012. The Turkish economy, owing to the customs union, has become the most integrated non-member country with the EU in the European periphery. More specifically, the customs union has allowed deeper trade and investment linkages between the EU and Turkey, with bilateral trade reaching $147 billion in 2012, making Turkey the EU's sixth largest trading partner and the EU Turkey's biggest. Regarding investment relations, the EU is the largest foreign investor in Turkey, accounting for three-quarters of total foreign direct investment (FDI) inflows in manufacturing and services sectors[15] while Turkish companies have become loosely integrated into European production networks for automobiles and clothing (World Bank 2014: 1). Therefore, both Turkey and the EU have considerably benefitted from the customs union since 1996, particularly after 2004.

Two decades on, rather than considering short-term static effects, it is more reasonable to assess the customs union's dynamic effects on the Turkish economy,[16] which one can argue have been mainly positive. First of all, the customs union created an important degree of incentive for the Turkish manufacturing industry to transform itself and increase its competitiveness by undertaking new investments and improving production technology. Additionally, harmonization of the domestic competition rules, customs regulations, quality and technical standards with those of the EU improved the regulatory base in which Turkish producers operate. Consequently, the quality and, therefore, capacity of the Turkish manufacturing industry as a whole to cope with both global and European competitive pressures and market forces have improved since 1996. Regarding export-oriented sectors, the customs union has consolidated the privileged situation of Turkish industry in EU markets against third-country rivals, providing Turkish industry with the opportunity to access a stable market with a high level of per capita income. Moreover, since the customs union provided an important degree of liberalization for EU and third-country goods in Turkey's domestic markets, the Turkish manufacturing industry has also faced an increased competition from imports. Thus, the customs union constitutes an important motivational force domestically so that both export-oriented and import-competing industries within Turkey have needed to transform themselves and adapt to new economic conditions in order to survive in the more competitive environment arising from the bilateral elimination of barriers to trade between the parties and the decrease in Turkey's protection rates against third-country products to the level of the EU's CCT. Indeed, adaptation to the new economic environment forced by the increased competition contributed significantly to the fivefold increase in Turkish exports, from $31 billion in 2001 to $152 billion in 2012 (Yılmaz 2015: 5).

Although this import liberalization process had already started in 1984, some industries, like automobiles, durable home appliances, electrical machinery and basic metals, had continued to be protected through high tariffs before the customs union was established. Thus, the customs union further opened up Turkish industry to global competition. While this increased competition arising from imports could have resulted in factory shutdowns and job losses in these sectors and harmed the manufacturing industry's growth prospects, the actual experience of the sector in response to the customs union was not as initially feared. Instead, increased competition from imports motivated import-competing sectors to introduce important changes in their behaviour, which increased productivity growth and improved competitiveness in the aforementioned sectors, while other import-competing sectors have grown even more than export-oriented and non-traded goods sectors (Yılmaz 2011: 240).

Concerning overall trends in manufacturing, the increased competition from imports following the customs union has led to Turkish industry becoming more productive much faster than it would have otherwise. This increase in competitiveness and productivity has also caused a favourable change in Turkey's foreign trade structure in that domestic demand for Turkish import-competing products has increased while Turkey has started to export more technology-intensive products than before the customs union. There has also been a shift from the exports in unskilled, labour-intensive and low-technology sectors, like textiles and clothing, to relatively skilled, labour-intensive and medium-technology sectors, like road vehicles, durable home appliances, electrical machinery and basic metals. That is, more competitive products with higher added value have started to be produced in technology-intensive sectors. The share of low-technology sectors in Turkey's total exports decreased from 57 per cent in 1996 to 32 per cent in 2009, while the share of medium-technology sectors increased from 40 per cent in 1996 to 66 per cent in 2009 (Akman 2012: 220). The customs union's contribution to increasing the quality and sophistication of Turkey's exports is particularly well exemplified by the automotive industry. When the advisability of the customs union was still being debated, many were concerned that the industry would be uncompetitive against EU automotive imports, with the sector expected to be one of the industries worst affected by the customs union. However, this turned out not to be the case. Rather, after a short period of adaptation, the industry's share in Turkey's export increased considerably, reaching 13.5 per cent in 2009 from 4.8 per cent in 1996 (Akman 2012: 221).

Problems arising from the asymmetric nature of the customs union

The main asymmetry regarding the customs union arises from the fact that while Turkey needs to align its trade policy with the EU's CCP, it cannot be involved in the EU's decision-making mechanism in this respect because it is not an EU member state. Thus, despite having no opportunity to influence EU decisions that may directly affect it, Turkey has entirely aligned its trade policies against non-member countries with the EU's CCP by adopting all the CCTs, instruments, agreements and protocols and a substantial part of the related *acquis*, while also continuously updating its legislation and policies in accordance with any developments in the CCP framework as required by Articles 13, 14, 16 and 54 of Association Council Decision 1/95. In March 1995, the Turkish government signed the customs union decision under the expectation that full membership would be obtained in a short period of time. This was why Turkey's exclusion from the EU's decision-making procedure regarding the CCP was not considered by the then Turkish government as a significant problem. However, two decades on, EU membership is still not on the short-term agenda, and seems not to be even on the medium-term agenda. This makes the operation of the customs union quite problematic for Turkey since the EU sets the CCP in line with its own priorities. It negotiates and concludes bilateral trade agreements with third countries without allowing Turkey any effective involvement in determining the EU's common negotiation position[17] and without taking Turkey's commercial interests into account. In other words, Turkey's trade relations with non-members are decided by EU member states in Brussels without any involvement by Turkey, which potentially leads to unfair trade competition.

The EU has even failed to implement the consultation procedure provided in Articles 54–60 of Decision 1/95. According to Article 55, when a new legislation bill is drafted by the European Commission in an area of direct relevance to the operation of the customs union,[18] the Commission should informally consult Turkey by sending copies of the draft bill. Additionally, the parties may also consult each other within the Customs Union Joint Committee at either's request before the final decision is taken by the EU Council. More importantly, during this consultation process, the parties are expected to cooperate in good faith in order to facilitate the decision most appropriate for the eventual proper functioning of the customs union. However, this consultation mechanism remains far from satisfying Turkey's need to be involved in the EU's FTA negotiations with third countries.

This issue has been particularly important for Turkey since 2006, when the EU developed its new trade policy, called 'Global Europe', after the Doha Development Round was suspended, which weakened prospects for further multilateral liberalization, at least in the short to medium term. In the 1990s, when the customs union was first concluded, the EU did not have as many FTAs as it currently has.[19] However, the Commission issued its Communication 'Global Europe' in response to the stalemate in multilateral negotiations to ensure greater openness and fair rules in other markets. Inspired by the Lisbon competitiveness agenda, and to increase access to more competitive markets, like South Korea, India, MERCOSUR and ASEAN, the Commission gave more importance to engaging in new FTAs, which are much deeper and more comprehensive than covering just trade in goods.[20] This led to the EU abandoning its long-standing moratorium, since 1999, on launching new bilateral trade negotiations. Some scholars (Rollo 2006; Elsig 2007; Elsig 2009) argue that the October 2006 Communication represented a radical change in trade policy from one with a tendency towards multilateral liberalization to one with a bilateral/regional tendency to increase economic growth and employment. According to a World Bank report (2014: 28), the impacts of these recent FTAs are expected to be much more important for Turkey and the future of the customs union than when the customs union was first concluded since there are more and deeper agreements between the EU and third countries. Accordingly, problems arising from the asymmetric nature of the customs union are likely to get worse as the number of FTAs that the EU concludes with non-EU countries increases.

The problem of EU FTA partners refusing to conclude FTAs with Turkey

Because the EU has been negotiating and concluding such agreements without complying with the aforementioned articles of the customs union decision, which implicitly requires it to agree a common position with Turkey before starting negotiations with third countries, Turkey has been forced to conclude similar agreements of its own with the countries concerned.[21]

Concluding its own FTAs with these countries has provided Turkey with commercial benefits that might not have happened if the customs union had not been established. However, third countries are not obliged to conclude such agreements with Turkey, and if there is no convincing commercial motivation from them then they do not do so. Indeed, some of those countries that either have or are negotiating FTAs with the EU are reluctant to reach similar agreements with Turkey.[22] Since these countries can already gain preferential access to Turkish markets indirectly via the EU, which causes trade deflection due to the customs union, they are unwilling to open their markets to Turkey's industrial exports in return, particularly if their domestic industries are less competitive their Turkish counterparts. In this case, it cannot retaliate against third countries by raising its own tariffs to their exports by claiming that they failed to provide similar trade privileges to Turkish industrial exports through any equivalent FTA because Turkey agreed to align its customs regime and duties to the EU's under the customs union (Akman 2010: 26).

However, trade deflection risks the imposition of origin controls for imports coming from the EU, particularly on sensitive goods, to determine whether they really originate from the third countries with which the EU has concluded an FTA. Accordingly, Turkey has introduced protection measures based on rules of origin for imports of cars from Mexico to reduce trade deflection. However, the use of such measures, especially if they were to proliferate, undermines one of the key benefits of the customs union, to remove the need for costly origin requirements (World Bank 2014: 25). In the absence of significant progress regarding the FTA issue, and relying on the terms of Article 58/2 of Decision No 1/95 of the Association Council,[23] Turkey had to impose protection measures on imports of various EU FTA partners transhipped via the EU in order to counter the resulting trade deflection.[24]

The effects of trade deflection at the expense of Turkey while its exports still face protection can be seen from simulations in version 8 of the Global Trade Analysis Project (GTAP) database regarding the ten EU FTA partners that currently do not have an FTA for industrial goods with Turkey: if they concluded such an agreement so that Turkey could export duty-free to these markets, the highest income gains for Turkey would be obtained from concluding FTAs with Mexico (US$111 million), South Africa (US$115 million) and Colombia (US$41 million). Regarding Algeria, which is another important market for Turkish exports but is not included in version 8 of the GTAP database, a partial equilibrium analysis carried out by Turkey's Ministry of Economy showed that, if an FTA between the two countries had entered into force at the same time as the FTA between the EU and Algeria, Turkey's exports could have been approximately US$450 million higher in 2010, reaching US$1.9 billion (World Bank 2014: 25, 26).

The problem of losing market share with EU FTA partners to European firms

The fact that Turkish firms have not received automatic reciprocal access to those third-country markets with which the EU has negotiated FTAs leaves them at a competitive disadvantage to EU exporters. Since the EU does not allow Turkey 'to negotiate jointly', or ask for its partners to continue 'parallel negotiations' with Turkey, Turkey needs to conclude its own FTAs with these countries, usually a certain time after the EU's own agreement. This situation leads to a disadvantageous position on the part of Turkish exporters vis-à-vis EU exporters, who can obtain a preferential status by penetrating into third-country markets earlier than their Turkish rivals.

This problem is particularly important in recent FTAs concluded with commercially more prominent countries. The time lag for Turkey to conclude its own FTAs after the EU's can increase the costs of late access for Turkish exporters. Although Turkey's growing experience of negotiating FTAs has reduced the average time required to conclude such agreements, it still results in lost market access opportunities (Akman 2010: 28). The main markets where Turkey has lost market share to European firms to date have been in Algeria, Mexico and South Africa. Turkey has also suffered preference erosion in EU markets as the latter has signed FTAs with countries that actively compete with Turkey, such as Chile and Morocco (World Bank 2014: 25).

Difficulties in negotiating FTAs with third countries on similar terms to the EU's FTAs

The fact that Turkey can neither negotiate with third countries jointly with the EU nor conduct parallel negotiations forces it to conclude FTAs with these countries later on their own terms, which has made it quite difficult for Turkey to obtain trade privileges as beneficial as the EU's. Instead, Turkey is usually compelled by its FTAs with third countries to eliminate its own trade barriers as soon as the agreement enters into force, while allowing the partner country to remove its trade barriers progressively. Thus, the liberalization is asymmetrical. Additionally, even if the third country agrees to conclude an FTA with Turkey, it may demand sectoral exceptions during the negotiations or safeguard mechanisms for its domestic industries that are uncompetitive against Turkish rivals.

TTIP as a significant example of an FTA with the EU excluding Turkey

The Transatlantic Trade and Investment Partnership (TTIP), which the EU and the US are currently negotiating in order to create a comprehensive FTA including all aspects of trade (both goods and services), tariff and non-tariff barriers (especially regulations) and FDI is particularly noteworthy in this respect. A GTAP CGE simulation of the US signing an FTA with the EU while excluding Turkey, which is included in the World Bank Report of 2014, suggests that Turkey's trade and welfare would be adversely affected. According to the simulation, the welfare loss would be US$130 million, of which US$120 million derives from deterioration in Turkey's terms of trade due to increased competition in US and EU markets, even assuming no trade deflection via the EU. The welfare loss increases to US$160 million if trade deflection via the EU occurs and US imports enter Turkey duty-free[25] (World Bank 2014: 27). Turkish exports will face more competition from the US goods in the EU markets compared to the one from the EU goods in the US markets when the TTIP comes into effect since non-tariff barriers imposed by the EU on imports from the US are more restrictive than those imposed by the US on the EU goods. Therefore, the size of the trade diversion effect is likely to be much bigger for Turkey in the EU markets. Moreover, the effect of trade deflection will be less than the impact of the competition from the US goods in the EU markets since the total amount of US exports to the EU is almost five times that of US exports to Turkey (Yılmaz 2015: 3–4).

However, if Turkey was able to conclude an FTA with the US together with the EU then its welfare gain would be US$130 million as a result of the TTIP.[26] Therefore, Turkey has a strong incentive to conclude an FTA with the US as simultaneously as possible as the EU does. This is particularly important if the TTIP becomes a comprehensive agreement going beyond just free movement of goods since potential losses would exceed US$160 million in the absence of such an agreement between Turkey and the EU (World Bank 2014: 27). On the other hand, if Turkey can be associated with the TTIP through having an agreement with the US that includes services, agriculture, investment protection and the liberalization of public procurement laws, then this could also facilitate deepening of the customs union since the Turkish government will need to address problems in these sectors with more effective domestic policies. In this respect, the TTIP could constitute a watershed for the future of the customs union.

Concluding an FTA between Turkey and the US will also be beneficial for both the US and the EU while making a lot of sense for the Turkish side. According to the study by Güneş et al. (2013) the income gains of the EU and the US could be $30–$50 billion more than those without an FTA between Turkey and the US. Therefore, both the EU and the US as well as Turkey are expected to work for the best outcome for all sides. It seems more possible for Turkey to negotiate an FTA with the US bilaterally instead of being included in the TTIP negotiation process directly. Since these countries are strategic partners and business circles in both countries state their will for stronger links between the parties, an FTA between them seems also politically feasible. However, there are significant difficulties to conclude an FTA with the US. In addition to the fact that the estimated income gains (just about 0.2–0.3 per cent of the GDP)[27] do not seem motivating for the US side to negotiate an FTA with Turkey, the Turkish side may not be ready to accept some of the US demands regarding including agriculture, services, public procurement and investment. Additionally, on the political front the US Congress's rising concerns over the Turkish government's recent authoritarian tendencies and diverging foreign policy perspectives in the Middle East and Ukraine make ratification of the US government's decision of negotiating an FTA with Turkey difficult (Yılmaz 2015: 4–5, 7). Under these circumstances whether the EU, as Turkey's customs union partner, will take the initiative in ensuring an FTA between Turkey and the US is concluded is vital.

Solutions to the problems of 'asymmetric' relations in the customs union

Because the problems discussed here mainly arise from the fact that Turkey cannot participate in forming the EU's common commercial policy with third countries, the most important solution would be to implement some kind of joint negotiation process. For example, an effective procedure could be implemented to allow Turkey observer status in the relevant Council meetings discussing trade negotiations, or in Committee 133, where the EU's common negotiation position is determined, particularly when decisions are made in areas directly related to the customs union with Turkey. This would enable future FTAs to be negotiated and concluded to include truly common arrangements and measures to ensure the integrity of the common commercial policy and prevent any possibility of trade deflection.

If this cannot be achieved due to the EU's institutional constraints the second-best solution might be to introduce parallel negotiations whereby Turkey would negotiate its own FTAs that mirror the EU's negotiations. However, both processes would have to be conducted and concluded simultaneously, although the final agreements could differ in some respects. Nevertheless, to eliminate important differences, a common position would still need to be reached in general terms through increased consultation and greater information sharing with Turkey on potential FTAs.

Finally, the European Commission has proposed incorporating a clause into the EU's agreements with third countries asking these countries to conclude a similar agreement with Turkey. Indeed, this 'Turkey Clause' was first used in FTA negotiations with Algeria in 2005. However, it is not legally binding on the country concerned so it cannot force third countries to conclude a separate agreement with Turkey, as in the case of Algeria, where an FTA with Turkey has still not been agreed. As the World Bank Report of 2014 acknowledges, since the EU's negotiating mandate does not include a Turkey Clause, it may sometimes be ignored in negotiations, as with South Africa, which refused to include it in its FTA negotiations. In the case of South Korea, although the clause was weakened to a declaration, it still helped Turkey to conclude an agreement with this country almost simultaneously with the EU's FTA. Mexico and Algeria are other partner countries that the EU has not yet been able to persuade to make similar agreements with Turkey (World Bank 2014: 29).

The Turkish government proposed strengthening the Turkey Clause to the European Commission (Wold Bank 2014: 30) to ensure that the parallel negotiating track is binding for future EU FTAs. According to the Turkish government's proposal, third countries and Turkey could conclude an FTA between the two parties on a mutually advantageous basis to enter into force simultaneously with the entry into force of the agreement between the EU and FTA partner. If the agreement between the EU and third country enters into force before the agreement between the latter and Turkey, the latter could be required to negotiate and conclude an FTA with Turkey within a set time period in the context of a revised Turkey Clause.[28] Meanwhile, Turkish industrial exports would be accepted by the third country as having originated in the EU until the entry into force of the FTA between that third country and Turkey.

The problem of transport quotas

Another concern of the Turkish side regarding the customs union is the restrictive impact of the insufficient and slow allocation of quotas for the road transport of goods that constitute an important barrier to the free movement of goods between Turkey and the member states. While 41 per cent of Turkey's export volume is carried by road transport according to 2012 figures, total number of road transport quotas allocated by EU countries has fallen behind Turkey's export capacity growth (UN Economic and Social Council 2013: 1).[29] Insufficient quotas, which simply limit the number of vehicles carrying export goods to member states, constitute measures having equivalent effect with quantitative restrictions since they obviously restrict the volume of goods exported from Turkey. This then restricts Turkey's foreign trade revenue like any other country subject to quantitative restrictions. The limited number of transit permit quotas also forces road vehicles carrying export goods to use indirect (longer) routes, which increases transportation costs. This situation constitutes charges having equivalent effects with tariffs. The Turkish authorities argue that these types of barriers, coupled with visa requirements for Turkish truck drivers, contradict the terms of the customs union decision. Indeed, all tariffs and charges having equivalent effects as well as quantitative restrictions and measures having equivalent effects are expressly prohibited by Articles 5 and 6 of Association Council Decision 1/95 on the customs union.

The European Commission, however, approaches the issue of transport quotas from a different point of view, considering it to be a matter of free movement of services instead of free movement of goods. Therefore, it claims that the issue has nothing to do with the customs union because it does not include free movement of services according to Decision 1/95 of the EC-Turkey Association Council. Turkey, however, argues that road vehicles carry export goods so any limitation imposed on such vehicles by issuing transit permit documents actually restricts their export because these measures have equivalent effects with quantitative restrictions while extra transportation costs constitute charges having equivalent effects with tariffs, as discussed earlier.[30] Kabaalioğlu (2012: 21) and Karakeçeli (2011: 11) argue that transportation of goods constitutes a fundamental aspect of road transport while the service aspect is subsidiary. That is, issues concerning the qualifications of drivers or standards of transport vehicles relate to the free movement of services, while issues which directly affect the transportation of goods, like transport quotas, relate to the free movement of goods.

In addition, the European Commission's argument has been found inadequate by several decisions of the European Court of Justice (ECJ). In the *Geddo* case,[31] the ECJ ruled that all measures that restrict fully or partially the import, export or the transit of the goods are equivalent to quantitative restrictions (cited in Kabaalioğlu 2012: 21). In the *SIOT* case,[32] which is directly related to the issue of transportation, the ECJ decided that if the transit of goods is restricted or if there is a threat of restriction in any form (e.g. a transit tax or difficulty preventing the transit of goods between member states), free movement of goods cannot be exercised fully (quoted in Kabaalioğlu 2012: 21, 22).

Strikingly, the EU does not even take a consistent perspective in its relations with Turkey regarding the issue of the transportation of goods. While the EU approaches restrictions on road transport of goods from the perspective of the free movement of services instead of the free movement of goods, as discussed earlier, it considers the issue of Turkey's refusal to open its harbours to Greek Cypriot vessels as a restriction on the free movement of goods, and has blocked eight chapters of the accession negotiations, including the free movement of goods chapter. That is, the EU's argument regarding transport quotas contradicts its approach regarding Turkey's ban on Greek Cypriot vessels.[33]

The problem of visa requirements

The visa requirements that the EU imposes on Turkish citizens, including businessmen, industrialists, service providers and market analysts, constitute an important difficulty for a fair customs union. Turkish economic actors currently need to obtain an entry visa to undertake normal economic activities in EU countries, such as participating in fairs and tendering, negotiating and concluding business agreements, while their EU counterparts can travel without visas to Turkey or, at worst, obtain a visa at the point of entry. This situation disadvantages Turkish economic actors and also contradicts the logic of the customs union because while goods are allowed to move freely between the parties, the Turkish citizens trying to market, sell or transport these goods are disqualified, restricted or, at best, hindered by visa procedures. In order to get visas, Turkish citizens, despite being included in the functioning of the customs union, suffer an onerous and lengthy procedure requiring redundant official documents and unreasonably high visa fees, which is quite harmful in business terms.

In line with the trend to remove visa restrictions after World War II, Turkey signed bilateral visa liberalization agreements with many of the Western European countries during the 1950s, before becoming a signatory party to the European Agreement on Regulations governing the Movement of Persons between Member States of the Council of Europe in 1961, which had been opened for signature by the Council of Europe member states in 1957. In the aftermath of World War II, those European countries that lacked labour also started to conclude labour recruitment agreements with certain countries (preferably with Southern

European countries) to secure their economic development. Turkey also signed such agreements with Germany (in 1961), the Benelux countries (in 1964), France (in 1965) and Sweden (in 1967). Given these labour recruitment agreements, the eventual free movement of workers between Turkey and the EC countries, as envisaged by the Ankara Agreement and the Additional Protocol, was seen as a realistic objective (Erdenir 2012: 476).

Article 36 of the Additional Protocol envisaged a timetable for the gradual realization of the free movement of workers between Turkey and the EEC member states between the end of the twelfth and the twenty-second year after the entry into force of the Association Agreement, clearly setting a specific date for the full introduction of the free movement of workers in Article 12 of the Ankara Agreement, which referred to the relevant articles of the treaty establishing the EEC.[34] The final date for the full introduction of the free movement of workers was 1986, while the free movement of goods was to be realized at the latest in 1995 in accordance with Articles 2–35 of the Additional Protocol. In other words, the free movement of workers would have been achieved before the achievement of the free movement of goods. However, despite being an important pillar of the Association Agreement, the free movement of workers could not be realized, although the customs union, concerning the free movement of goods, has been in operation since 1996.

Moreover, instead of removing all restrictions on the free access of Turkish workers to EEC labour markets, Germany took the lead in ending the recruitment of migrant workers by issuing a ban in 1973, and the other member states soon followed in order to bring the constant inflow of low-skilled labour under control (Kramer 1996: 206). Worse, Germany repealed its visa liberalization agreement of 1953 with Turkey and introduced a new restriction of entry visa requirements for Turkish people on 5 October 1980 on the grounds that the significant increase in requests from Turkey for political asylum following the 1980 coup d'état would threaten public order.[35] Following Germany, the other Western European countries started to introduce visa requirements for Turkish citizens on similar grounds. Initially, due to mainly socio-economic reasons, Germany took a restrictive stance regarding the free movement of persons because it viewed the influx of low-skilled labour as an economic burden during a period of economic hardship.[36] Since then, political considerations, such as policies towards asylum-seekers and the revival of xenophobia, have also started to play an important role in Germany's stance towards Turkish citizens. Another significant factor behind a strong public backlash against Islamic elements in European society has been religious and cultural differences, particularly after 11 September 2001 (Kramer 1996: 206).

The visa requirements imposed by EU countries on Turkish citizens not only are unfair in terms of customs union relations but also contradict the Turkey–EU association law[37] as ruled by the ECJ in 2009 in the *Soysal* case (InfoCuria 2009). As in previous cases,[38] the ECJ clearly concluded that Article 41(1) of the Additional Protocol, which included a standstill clause on the free movement of services and the right of establishment, is a directly applicable provision, and therefore has direct effect on Turkish citizens (InfoCuria 2009). In other words, Turkish citizens can seek justice in member state courts by depending on this provision, which states that 'the Contracting Parties shall refrain from introducing between themselves any new restrictions on the right of establishment and the freedom to provide services.' Indeed in the *Soysal* case, the Turkish truck drivers applied to the German court by depending on this article, claiming that Germany's visa requirements breached their rights to provide an international transport of goods service since an entry visa had not been required by the German authorities from Turkish citizens on 1 January 1973, the date of entry into force of the Additional Protocol. The German court, through 'preliminary ruling' procedure of the EU law, asked the ECJ whether a visa requirement implemented in 1980 could be regarded as a new restriction concerning Article 41(1) of the Additional Protocol. The ECJ concluded that any visa requirement introduced by Germany after the entry into force of the Additional Protocol was indeed a new restriction on the freedom of Turkish service providers and the right of establishment of Turkish citizens, and was therefore contrary to Article 41(1).[39]

Thus, the *Soysal* decision clearly demonstrated that introducing new visa requirements or increasing the existing burden of getting a visa for Turkish nationals who want to provide services or establish a business in EU members states is contrary to law if these restrictions were imposed after the entry into force of the Additional Protocol in 1973 by the existing member states or after the membership date of current member states that were not members at the time of entry into force of this protocol. Particularly since this decision, it has become necessary to ensure that the related rights of Turkish nationals are respected throughout the EU in terms of the lawfulness of member states' border policies. As the guardian of the treaties, the European Commission is expected to monitor the situation in member states and take necessary initiatives in accordance with what the *Soysal* ruling requires (Karakeçili 2011: 9). However, the Commission has merely asked member states whether their legislation is compatible with the ECJ's decision, arguing that it lacks the power to force members states to comply since this issue falls under national jurisdiction (Kabaalioğlu 2012: 20). As a result, except for a few countries, including Germany and Denmark, that have complied with the decision in a limited sense, most member states, which also did not impose a visa requirement on Turkish nationals either at the time of the entry into force of the Additional Protocol or at the time of their own entry into the EU, have done nothing to comply fully with the ECJ's ruling (Karakeçili 2011: 10). Nevertheless, the process that started with signing an agreement on visa liberalization dialogue, together with the Readmission Agreement of 16 December 2013 between Turkey and the EU, and more recently the refugee deal on 18 March 2016 including visa liberalization might be all regarded as positive developments in this respect.[40]

Notes

1 See Official Journal of the EC (1977a).
2 See Official Journal of the EC (1977b).

3 For Decision No 1/95 of the EC-Turkey Association Council on implementing the final phase of the Customs Union see Official Journal of the EC (1996).
4 Some argued that the assent procedure of the European Parliament should not have been used since this was not a new international agreement but simply an implementation measure for an Association Agreement already in force (see Kabaalioğlu 1998: 117).
5 Harun Arıkan (2003) called this approach of the EU 'containment policy for Turkey'.
6 For the Association Council decision of 1997 see Official Journal of the EC (1997).
7 Processed agricultural goods have an industrial component which is subject to free access in the case of the Turkey–EU customs union.
8 See Article 33 (Official Journal of the EC 1977b).
9 According to Article 19 of the Customs Union Decision, agricultural components can be measured by 'adding together the quantities of basic agricultural products considered to have been used for the manufacture of the goods in question multiplied by the basic amount corresponding to each of these basic agricultural products'.
10 Examples include motor gasoline, petroleum ether, gas oils, diesel, fuel oil, trunks, suitcases, bags, sacks, footwear, porcelain, midibuses, minibuses, motor cars and lorries.
11 For the Association Council decision regarding sensitive products in competitive terms (Decision No 2/95 of the EC-Turkey Association Council on temporary exceptions to Turkey's application of the Common Customs Tariff in respect of third countries) see DPT (2001: 261–64).
12 Additionally, the Customs Union Decision envisaged that Turkey could restrict imports of used motor vehicles from the EU for a period of ten years, which was extended in August 2008 until Turkey's full EU membership (Yılmaz 2011: 237 and Note 1).
13 This is an autonomous regime providing preferential treatment unilaterally.
14 These countries became EU members in 2004 and 2007.
15 European banks invested billions of euros after the EU's decision regarding the opening of accession negotiations with Turkey on 17 December 2004, and they control some of the biggest private banks in Turkey. Istanbul is used as regional headquarters by many European companies. Subsidiaries or joint ventures of European companies in Turkey export to the Middle East, Africa and Central Asia as well as to Europe (Yılmaz 2015: 5).
16 These are improvements in competitiveness, economies of scale, stimulation of investment and better utilization of resources.
17 For example, the lack of any effective procedures for Turkey's involvement in EU trade negotiations for discussion and consultation includes Committee 133, where the EU's common negotiation position is determined.
18 According to Article 54/2, areas of direct relevance to the operation of the customs union are commercial policy and agreements with third countries comprising a commercial dimension for industrial products, legislation on the abolition of technical barriers to trade in industrial products, competition and intellectual property law and customs legislation.
19 It had Europe Agreements with former candidate countries in Central and Eastern Europe, the European Economic Area with the EFTA countries except Switzerland, and association agreements with some Mediterranean countries.
20 These include trade liberalization in areas relevant to foreign direct investment, services, non-tariff barriers, trade-related intellectual property rights, competition rules and government procurement, as well as other regulatory issues, like environmental and labour standards.
21 'Currently, the EU has FTAs with 48 countries while Turkey has concluded FTAs with just 19, two of which the EU does not have FTAs with (Syria and Georgia). Turkey has 17 FTAs in force, namely with EFTA, Macedonia, Bosnia-Herzegovina, Albania, Israel, Palestine, Morocco, Tunisia, Egypt, Syria (suspended), Georgia, Serbia, Montenegro, Chile, Jordan, South Korea and Mauritius. Agreements with Lebanon and Kosovo will be in effect after the completion of internal ratification procedures. Meanwhile, there are 14 countries/country blocs that Turkey has started FTA negotiations;

namely Peru, Ukraine, Colombia, Ecuador, Malaysia, Moldova, Dem. Rep of Congo, Ghana, Cameroon, Seychelles, Gulf Cooperation Council, Libya, MERCOSUR and Faroe Islands. Moreover, Turkey has launched initiatives to start negotiations with 12 countries/country blocs, which are the USA, Canada, Japan, Thailand, India, Indonesia, Vietnam, Central American Countries, other ACP Countries, Algeria, Mexico and South Africa' (World Bank 2014: 25).

22 The EU FTA partners that have abstained from concluding an FTA with Turkey are Mexico, South Africa, Colombia, Algeria, Peru, Panama, Costa Rica, Dominican Republic, Guatemala, El Salvador, Honduras, Jamaica, Trinidad and Tobago, Nicaragua, Papua New Guinea, Haiti, St. Lucia, Bahamas, Antigua and Barbuda, Guyana, Suriname, Barbados, Belize, Seychelles, St. Vincent and the Grenadines, St. Kitts and Nevis, Dominica and Grenada (World Bank 2014: 25, footnote 17).

23 'If discrepancies between Community and Turkish legislation or differences in their implementation in an area of direct relevance to the functioning of the Customs Union cause or threaten to cause impairment of the free movement of goods or deflections of trade and the affected Party considers that immediate action is required, it may itself take the necessary protection measures and notify the Customs Union Joint Committee thereof; the latter may decide whether to amend or abolish these measures. Priority should be given to measures which least disturb the functioning of the Customs Union.'

24 'Turkey has also decided to apply additional customs duties for some textiles products originating from some countries outside the EU and EU FTA partners. The additional duties vary for countries benefiting from the GSP scheme, LDCs and others. In order to apply these differentiated duties, origin controls are being conducted based on customs declarations' (World Bank 2014: 25).

25 According to another study by Felbermayr and Larch (2013: 55), the long-run welfare effects of the TTIP on Turkey are estimated to reach 2.5 per cent of GDP.

26 According to another study by Güneş et al. (2013) if Turkey signed an FTA with the US, Turkish GDP would increase by $31 billion together with close to a 7 per cent increase in Turkish exports.

27 This is the income gain that is estimated in percentage terms by the study by Güneş et al. (2013). The amount that is estimated in real terms by this study was referred to earlier.

28 This was not included in the Turkish proposal, but was included in the World Bank Report (2014: 29).

29 Indeed, the permit quotas allocated to Turkey lag well behind the percentage growth in exports to certain EU countries. For example, while Turkish exports carried by road transport in 2011 increased by 9.4 per cent on the previous year, the total number of road transport quotas allocated to Turkey increased by only 3.9 per cent (UN Economic and Social Council 2013: 1).

30 A permit is required for every border crossing and movement within a foreign country.

31 For more information for the *Geddo* case see InfoCuria (1973).

32 For more information for the *SIOT* case see InfoCuria (1983).

33 Turkey does not open its seaports and airports to ships and aircrafts under the Cypriot flag on the grounds that it does not politically or legally recognize the Republic of Cyprus, although Turkish harbours are open to Greek Cypriot goods carried by vessels under any other flag. Therefore, Turkey's target is not to restrict (the Greek Cypriot) goods.

34 Articles 48, 49 and 50.

35 According to Erdenir (2012: 477), Germany imposed this new restriction on the free movement of persons by depending on Article 7 of the 1957 Agreement between Member States of the Council of Europe, which states that 'Each Contracting Party reserves the option, on grounds relating to ordre public, security or public health, to delay the entry into force of this Agreement or order the temporary suspension thereof in respect of all or some of the other Parties' (Council of Europe 1957).

36 Oil crisis and stagflation (economic stagnation and high inflation together) affected EC economies negatively and resulted in high unemployment.

37 The Turkey–EU association law depends on the association agreement together with its protocols and decisions of the Association Council.

38 The Queen v. Secretary of State for the Home Department, ex parte Abdülnasır Savaş, C-37/98, (2000) ECR I-2927; Eran Abatay and Others and Nadi Şahin v. Bundesalstalt für Albeit, C-317/01, (2003) ECR I-1230; Tüm and Darı v. Secretary of State for the Home Department, C-16/05, (2007). Before these cases specifically related to Article 41(1) of the Ankara Agreement, the issue of direct effect of the provisions of the Ankara Agreement and the Additional Protocol in general was decreed by the ECJ in 1987 in the *Demirel* case. In this case the ECJ decided that Turkish citizens can seek justice in member state courts by depending on the provisions of the Ankara Agreement and the Additional Protocol which are sufficiently clear, certain and unconditional and do not necessitate a further measure or act in order to be implemented (InfoCuria 1987). Similarly, the ECJ decided in the *Sevince* case that the provisions of the Association Council decisions which are sufficiently clear, certain and unconditional and do not necessitate a further measure or act in order to be implemented have direct effect for Turkish citizens (InfoCuria 1990).

39 The ECJ stated that 'the visa requirement made it more difficult for Turkish nationals to exercise their economic freedoms granted by the Ankara Agreement, especially because of the additional and recurrent administrative and financial burdens involved in obtaining it' (InfoCuria 2009: para. 51–7).

40 For details regarding the visa liberalization dialogue together with the readmission agreement and more recent developments in the relations around the refugee deal liberalization on 18 March 2016, see the last chapter in this volume.

3 Turkey as a candidate to join the EU

The turning point in Turkey–EU relations and its aftermath

The Helsinki decision of the European Council declaring Turkey as a candidate country 'destined to join the EU on the basis of the same criteria as applied to the other candidate States' was a watershed in Turkey–EU relations (European Council 1999). Relations that were until then shaped within the framework of the association relationship acquired a new dimension that had the aim of Turkey's integration to the EU as a member state. Two years earlier, the exclusion of Turkey from candidacy in the Luxembourg European Council had sparked adversity in the relations and the then prime minister Mesut Yılmaz accused the EU of applying double standards to Turkey (Hürriyet Daily News 1997; Hale 2002: 240). In Helsinki, the EU aimed to undo the damage inflicted on Turkey–EU ties and provide a new perspective to the country by including it among the candidate countries of the EU in addition to the 12 countries mentioned in Luxembourg. The goal of EU accession had never been so clearly set for Turkey.

In the period that followed the Helsinki decision, this new status vis-à-vis the EU unlocked the reform potential of the country by bringing together mainstream political parties, triggering civil society in favour of reforms and stimulating the general public to support the process leading to EU membership. From academia to non-governmental organizations, Turkey–EU relations became a renewed area of interest which was displayed by the opening of new departments and programmes on EU studies, the proliferation of EU-funded projects and civil society initiatives calling for reform to fulfil the Copenhagen criteria. The government in power at the time composed of centre, centre-left and centre-right parties united to pursue the EU candidacy agenda and drew up controversial reforms, such as the lifting of capital punishment and repeal of the military member of state security courts. The coalition government decomposed following the 2001 economic crisis and left its place to a majority government under a newly founded party in the November 2002 elections, the Justice and Development Party (AKP). One of the most intriguing puzzles of the EU reform process afterwards was the upholding of the EU membership goal by a party coming from an anti-European ideological stance. AKP was able to join forces in the parliament with the main opposition party, the Republican People's Party (CHP), acquired the support of liberal forces and intelligentsia in the country and was able to avail itself of the EU reform process in dealing with dominant forces which it saw as obstacles in front of its sustained power, the civil and military bureaucracy.

Background to the Helsinki conclusions and Turkey's EU candidacy

The European Council meeting in Helsinki declared Turkey as 'a candidate State destined to join the Union on the basis of the same criteria as applied to the other candidate States' (European Council 1999). It commended positive developments in Turkey and its will to engage in reforms with a view to fulfilling the Copenhagen criteria. The Council also stipulated that a 'pre-accession strategy' would be put into action to prepare Turkey for the accession process, including political dialogue, participation in Community programmes and agencies, and financial assistance in addition to an accession partnership and 'appropriate monitoring mechanisms' (European Council 1999: para. 12). With regard to political dialogue, the European Council made reference not only to the aim of improving the country's human rights provisions but also to two other paragraphs in the conclusions, 4 and 9(a).

The Turkish government of the time led by Bülent Ecevit was uneasy and reluctant to accept the offer, owing to these other conditions in the presidency conclusions that had a particular relevance for Turkey. One of these provisions was Paragraph 9(b), which stipulated the EU's approach to the Cyprus issue. Cyprus had already made its application to join the EU in 1990 and was included among the candidate countries in the Agenda 2000 document. Accession negotiations had started in 1998 and the EU noted that it supported a comprehensive settlement of the Cyprus problem, but resolution of the issue was no longer a precondition for Cypriot membership of the EU (European Council 1999):

> 9 (a) The European Council welcomes the launch of the talks aiming at a comprehensive settlement of the Cyprus problem on 3 December in New York and expresses its strong support for the UN Secretary-General's efforts to bring the process to a successful conclusion.
>
> (b) The European Council underlines that a political settlement will facilitate the accession of Cyprus to the European Union. If no settlement has been reached by the completion of accession negotiations, the Council's decision on accession will be made without the above being a precondition. In this the Council will take account of all relevant factors.

The other clause had to do with bilateral conflict and stipulated that the candidate countries should resolve their border disputes until they actually accede to the Union (European Council 1999):

> The European Council stresses the principle of peaceful settlement of disputes in accordance with the United Nations Charter and urges candidate States to make every effort to resolve any outstanding border disputes and

> other related issues. Failing this they should within a reasonable time bring the dispute to the International Court of Justice. The European Council will review the situation relating to any outstanding disputes, in particular concerning the repercussions on the accession process and in order to promote their settlement through the International Court of Justice, at the latest by the end of 2004.

Since Central and Eastern European states that were EU candidates had already signed various agreements with the aim of resolution of disputes within the framework of the Stability Pact pioneered by the EU and OSCE (Möttölä 1997: 25), this clause was particularly pertinent to the disagreement between Turkey and Greece over the extent of territorial waters on the Aegean and related bilateral problems. Although Cyprus was also a candidate country with an unresolved political conflict, the burden of responsibility was mostly associated with Turkey and the Turkish Cypriots according to the EU. The Turkish government was apprehensive about accepting candidacy to the EU since it suspected that this would bring further commitments upon Turkey in addition to the fulfilment of the Copenhagen criteria. Turkey would have to shift its position in Cyprus and make an intensive effort to resolve disputes with Greece and facilitate the reunification of Cyprus. Since Greece was already a member state of the EU and frequently used its veto to block relations with Turkey, and Greek Cypriots had already started negotiations with the EU, it would be expected that the EU would be also a party to these disputes. The EU was using its leverage over Turkey to instigate change in this direction and while doing this was imposing pressure on Turkey incommensurate with pressure placed on the other relevant parties. Practically, Greek Cypriots were left to their own devices regarding whether to support the reunification of the island since this was no longer a precondition for Cypriot accession to the EU.

The EU side took some steps to ease the apprehension felt by the Turkish government. Javier Solana, the high representative for common foreign and security policy, and Gunther Verheugen, member of the European Commission responsible for enlargement, flew to Ankara in order to convince Ecevit to accept the candidacy offer. They were also carrying a letter written by the Finnish prime minister, Paavo Lipponen, who was at the time leading the term presidency of the Council. The Lipponen letter of 10 December 1999 was instrumental in allaying the concerns of the Turkish government regarding Cyprus's accession prospects: 'Regarding Cyprus, a political settlement remains the aim of the EU. Concerning the accession of Cyprus, all relevant factors will be taken into account when the Council takes the decision.' Ecevit also wrote two letters to Lipponen, dated 10 and 24 December, stating Turkey's approach to the situation: 'I welcome the remarks in your letter that shed light on some misunderstandings. Your letter is an inseparable part of the European Council conclusions.'

Ecevit's press release was attached to the letter dated 24 December and stated,

> It is a great success on the part of Turkey that our candidacy was recognized on equal terms at Helsinki. However, there are also some hints which cannot

> be accepted by Turkey. It is not acceptable for us that the Aegean problems should be submitted to the Court of Justice at The Hague in 2004 the latest. It was a positive development that Turkey was declared as a candidate to the EU. The door to EU membership was opened unconditionally for Turkey.
>
> (Hürriyet 2000)

Ecevit later made a statement concerning the unacceptability of a linkage between Turkey's EU candidacy and Cyprus and referred to Lipponen's letter as proof that the EU understood Turkey's position on this issue right after the Helsinki European Council (Ministry of Foreign Affairs 2000). Commenting on Greek prime minister Simitis's words that Lipponen wrote the letter not in his capacity as the president of the Council but in his capacity as the prime minister of Finland, Ecevit said, 'I take Lipponen's letter seriously; I do not take Simitis' words seriously' (Türkiye 1999).

Convinced by the diplomatic efforts of the EU and affirmed by the letter of Finnish prime minister Lipponen, Ecevit together with minister for foreign affairs Ismail Cem and minister of state for the EU Mehmet Ali Irtemcelik went to Helsinki and took part in the family photo taken at the end of the summit. Thus Turkey officially accepted the status of EU candidacy. This status was important in triggering changes in the country in the direction of meeting the membership criteria. It was a development that would bolster Turkey's international image, contribute to Turkey's value as a model country for the newly independent states of Central Asia and countries in the Middle East aspiring for modernity and democracy, enhance Turkey's role as a regional hub and destination for international financiers, and most importantly trigger an internal reform process in the direction of democratization as well as changes in conventional foreign policy stances of the country (Öniş 2003; Saatçioğlu 2013: 8–10; Yeşilada 2013).

Several developments formed the background of the EU's decision declaring Turkey as a candidate country. Although the change between the European Council's approach to Turkey at the Luxembourg Summit of 1997 and Helsinki Summit of 1999 could be evaluated as a U-turn, the EU's insistence on the Cyprus issue and settlement of border disputes remained the same. What was different was the EU's strategy towards Turkey. While at Luxembourg the EU proposed a 'European strategy for Turkey' which would be tailor-made for the country,[1] at Helsinki Turkey was included in the enlargement process that already comprised 12 countries. Several factors could be enlisted that would explain this shift. First, Turkey's reaction to the Luxembourg conclusions was quite harsh. The Turkish government of the time adopted a counter-strategy to the EU declaring that political dialogue with the EU would be suspended; Turkey would accelerate integration with the TRNC as the EU would continue Cypriot accession negotiations. The prime minister at the time, Mesut Yılmaz, criticized the EU and particularly the German chancellor, Helmut Kohl, of applying double standards to Turkey (Milliyet 1998; Ergin 1998). Thus the EU felt the need to recalibrate its policy towards Turkey based on the insufficiency of the European strategy offered at Luxembourg in terms of Turkey's membership ambitions (Arıkan 2006: 76).

Another related factor was the resolution of the coalition government led by Bülent Ecevit to accelerate reforms in the country, which was evidenced by a letter addressed to the German chancellor, Gerhard Schröder, before the Cologne European Council of 26 May 1999. In this letter Ecevit gave assurances concerning the government's resolve to carry out democratic reforms including the southeast of the country, in line with the Copenhagen criteria, and put forward that an open membership perspective would greatly accelerate the reform process, and that Turkey demanded a non-discriminatory approach towards Turkey (Hürriyet 1999). Gerhard Schröder, differently from Helmut Kohl or Angela Merkel, had a positive stance regarding Turkey's membership perspective and these assurances certainly had a positive effect on him (Deutsche Welle 2004; Inal 2005). In a letter he wrote to Ecevit as a reply to his letter, Schröder expressed his support for Turkey's request for a roadmap from the EU and wrote that he was pleased about the assurances given on the Kurdish issue and a more amicable approach to relations with Greece that may also have a positive impact on the resolution of the Cyprus conflict (Hürriyet 1999).

A third factor had to do with the changing approach of Greece to Turkey's EU ties and the lifting of its veto on Turkey's EU candidacy. Greece had already consented to the 1996 Turkey–EU customs union on the condition that membership talks with Cyprus would be opened. The start of a process of rapprochement between the two sides under ministers of foreign affairs Ismail Cem and George Papandreu came to the fore during the 1999 Kocaeli earthquake in Turkey. Earlier the fiasco of the PKK leader Öcalan being captured in Kenya with a Cypriot passport in the Greek embassy led to the resignation of the former minister of foreign affairs in Greece and Prime Minister Simitis's search for a restoration of Greece's international image. The change in Greece's approach to Turkey's EU relations was critical in the candidacy process and can be linked to a changing perception in Greek diplomacy, which preferred a Europeanizing Turkey over an overly militaristic or fundamentalist one (Grigoriadis 2003).

A fourth factor was related to consideration about the evolving common foreign and security policy and the EU's aim to initiate a European security and defence policy. As a member of NATO, Turkey could have an obstructive influence in this process since it could veto the use of NATO assets and capabilities by the EU. A need to come up with a solution to this issue may also have an impact on the EU's readiness to include Turkey in the enlargement process. The eruption of ethnic violence in Kosovo and the use of force against the Serbs by NATO in March 1999 demonstrated that south-eastern Europe was still not stabilized. Security threats that may emanate from conflicts in the Balkans were threatening European order. In such a setting, Turkey could be a valuable ally in bringing about stabilization of south-eastern Europe. An inclusive enlargement policy could be one of the best tools that the EU could employ in extending the zone of peace further east and south of the continent.

A fifth factor influencing the EU's approach to Turkey was related to the Kurdish question, the capture of the PKK leader Öcalan and the declaration of ceasefire by the PKK as a result. In a letter addressed to the German chancellor, Ecevit underlined that now the threat of terrorism was over, Turkey was in a condition to proceed with democratic and social reforms in the south-east of the country (Hürriyet 1999). The EU and especially the European Parliament in a number of resolutions about Turkey noted its concerns for the situation in the south-east of the country and advised that the problem should be resolved by political measures. The imprisonment of Öcalan provided the chance now to deal with the Kurdish issue from the perspective of democracy and human rights. The abolishment of capital punishment and the civilianization of the State Security Courts, where Öcalan was put on trial, could be seen as the first moves heralding reforms in Turkey in the line of the Copenhagen criteria.

A last factor could be related to US president Clinton's support of Turkey's EU bid and the telephone diplomacy he initiated during the Helsinki Summit. The US has been one of the staunch supporters of Turkey's entry into the EU. This could be attributed to the importance the US attached to Turkey as a strategic partner and ally in the Near East and its important role in the resolution of Europe's problems, such as instability in the Balkans, integrating Russia and bridging the West and the Islamic world (Clinton 1999: 2091). The American view sees Turkey as a part of Europe and is anxious about the consequences of the EU's exclusion of Turkey for its future, such as radicalization or destabilization in the country. Strobe Talbott, deputy secretary of state in the Clinton administration, was reported as saying the following in 1998 (Sayarı 2003: 171):

> Turkey's ties to Europe are irreversible and unbreakable; they are a fact of life, not a privilege that comes with membership in this or that institution . . . We do not believe that European unity and integration will be fully successful if a key European country is set uniquely alone and apart.

Reform process after Helsinki

The EU perspective provided an external incentive for reform in Turkey owing to the necessity of fulfilling the political aspects of the Copenhagen criteria. The first progress report prepared by the European Commission on Turkey was published in 1998 and concluded the following on Turkey's situation with regard to the political criteria stressing serious problems in human rights, treatment of minorities, the Kurdish question, the role of the army and disputes with Greece (European Commission 1998: 20):

> On the political side, the evaluation highlights certain anomalies in the functioning of the public authorities, persistent human rights violations and major shortcomings in the treatment of minorities. The lack of civilian control of the army gives cause for concern. This is reflected by the major role played by the army in political life through the National Security Council. A civil, non-military solution must be found to the situation in south-eastern Turkey, particularly since many of the violations of civil and political rights observed in the country are connected in one way or another with this issue.

> The Commission acknowledges the Turkish government's commitment to combat human rights violations in the country but this has not so far had any significant effect in practice. The process of democratic reform on which Turkey embarked in 1995 must continue.

Problems in Turkey with regard to weakness of democratic institutions, violations of human rights and the role of the army in political life impeded the opening of accession negotiations with Turkey. The government and the parliament were now under an obligation to instigate reforms with a view to the fulfilment of the EU criteria. The EU progress reports and accession partnership documents incorporated the criticisms of the EU with regard to the political system in Turkey and also included a roadmap for reforms. The first Accession Partnership Document was published in March 2001 and included short- and medium-term priorities which Turkey had to take into consideration with the aim of fulfilling the Copenhagen criteria. It included goals for reform in accordance with political and economic criteria and alignment to the EU *acquis* in the various policy areas of the EU (Official Journal of the EC 2001a). The Accession Partnership Document was reciprocated by the National Program for the Adoption of the *acquis* prepared by the Turkish government outlining the content, time frame and cost of reforms and legislative changes Turkey would undergo in line with the EU criteria. The first Accession Partnership Document was followed by updated documents in 2003, 2006 and 2008, and so were the National Programs prepared by Turkey in 2003 and 2008. Turkey also prepared a national programme for alignment with the EU *acquis* for the period 2007–2013 (Ministry for EU Affairs 2015).

The reforms that were started under the coalition government led by Ecevit were continued by the AKP government that came to power in 2002. The first step was taken by the Ecevit government with the amendment of the Constitution in 2001 and adoption of two harmonization packages. After the capture of PKK leader Abdullah Öcalan, his trial in accordance with European standards and repeal of the death penalty which was not implemented since 1987 but nevertheless remained in law acquired an urgency. The government worked out a formula whereby the military judge in the state security court that tried Öcalan was replaced by a civilian judge and the death penalty that was inflicted on Öcalan was put on hold according to a protocol among political leaders which stipulated that the court should wait for the final decision of the European Court of Human Rights on this issue and the final decision should be referred to the TBMM (TBMM 2002). The TBMM later passed the first harmonization package whereby the death penalty was repealed in August 2002. Later Turkey also adopted Protocol Number 6 of the ECHR and repealed the death penalty, including in times of war and for acts of terror.

The TBMM legislated major reforms in this period with the aim of fulfilling the Copenhagen criteria. The political parties represented in the parliament following the November 2002 elections, the AKP and CHP, worked in harmony and passed two constitutional amendments as well as eight harmonization packages between 2001 and 2004. Two hundred and eighteen legal provisions in 53 different laws were amended in this period. Consensus among the political parties and the speed of the legislative process showed that the existence of a clear membership perspective and credible conditionality implemented by the EU acted as a powerful stimulus for reform. The economic crisis of 2001, the political stalemate and crises of the 1990s and the challenge of the Kurdish insurgency were also instrumental in creating an environment of internal support for EU-induced reforms in Turkey.

The elections of November 2002 could be regarded as a political earthquake. The coalition partners were ousted from the parliament as a result of the elections and only two parties received the favour of the electorate. The AKP, founded in 2001, received the highest percentage of votes and the mandate to form a majority government. The party came from an Islamic tradition, called the National view, and was established by former members of the Welfare Party, closed by the Constitutional Court in 1998 owing to its anti-regime activities (Hürriyet Daily News 1998). The AKP drew upon the lessons of the process of 28 February, whereby the Welfare Party–True Path Party coalition was forced to resign by the National Security Council dominated by the military (Atacan 2006: 54). The party adopted a different stance compared to its predecessor. While the Welfare Party was quite sceptical towards the EU and the West in general, and advocated alternative groupings, such as the Developing 8-D-8 initiative, the newly established AKP had a much more liberal stance towards the EU and the global economy. The party programme stated the party's approach to EU membership: 'Turkey shall rapidly fulfil its promises in its relations with the European Union and the conditions, which the Union demands of other candidate nations as well. Thus, it shall prevent the occupation of the agenda with artificial problems' (AKP Party Programme 2015).

The leader of the AKP, Recep Tayyip Erdoğan, immediately upon taking office went to Brussels to convince the EU leaders about the start of accession negotiations with Turkey on the eve of the Copenhagen European Council of December 2002. The aim was to receive a date for the start of accession negotiations. The EU adopted a cautious stance on this issue and delayed the decision on opening accession negotiations with Turkey to 2004 contingent upon a positive assessment by the European Commission (European Council 2002): 'If the European Council in December 2004, on the basis of a report and a recommendation from the Commission, decides that Turkey fulfils the Copenhagen political criteria, the European Union will open accession negotiations with Turkey without delay.' This statement accelerated the reform process even more and instigated further amendments of the Constitution and harmonization packages to be enacted by the parliament until the Commission's critical assessment of Turkey's fulfilment of the political criteria for accession in 2004. Several critical pieces of legislation were passed that carried Turkey towards the fulfilment of the Copenhagen criteria. The 2001 and 2004 constitutional amendments aimed to strengthen freedom and democracy in Turkey by way of adopting reforms in a whole array of issues, including

> freedom of thought and expression, the prevention of torture, strengthening of democracy and civilian authority, the freedom and security of the individual,

> the right to privacy, the inviolability of the domicile, the freedom of communication, the freedom of residence and movement, the freedom of association and gender equality.
>
> (Secretariat General for EU Affairs 2007: 4)

The eight harmonization packages adopted by the TBMM until 2004 aimed to enact changes to relevant legislation, such as the penal code, antiterror law, press law, law on associations, law on political parties, and aimed to achieve coherence and consistency between the Constitution and relevant laws. Reforms also included the adoption of a new civil code in 2002 based on principles of gender equality, protection of the child and freedom of association. Among the changes introduced with the constitutional amendments and harmonization packages, the following points are particularly important in terms of democratization and liberalization of legislation:

- Abolishment of the death penalty under all circumstances including terrorism except in times of war and its replacement by aggravated life sentence;
- Equality between men and women;
- Repeal of national security exceptions for press freedom;
- Abolishing of state security courts;
- Provision for being a party to the International Criminal Court;
- Precedence of international agreements on fundamental rights and freedoms over domestic law;
- Reduction of pretrial detention periods, reduction of applicable sentences for crimes against state organs;
- Abolishment of fines for praising a criminal act, calling for disobedience or inciting hatred on the basis of class, race, religion, sect or territory;
- Improving rights of detainees and prisoners;
- Expanding scope of freedom of thought and expression;
- Expanding freedom of association, such as repeal of prohibition of associations that are established 'to protect, develop or expand languages or cultures other than the Turkish language or culture' and prohibition of international activities and activities in Turkey of foreign associations;
- Greater freedom for meetings and demonstrations;
- Provision for retrial in accordance with judgments of the European Court of Human Rights;
- Repeal of prison sentences for criminal offences in the media;
- Repeal of ban on broadcasting in the different languages and dialects traditionally used by Turkish citizens in their daily lives, such as Kurdish;
- Repeal of the restriction on the learning of languages and dialects traditionally used by Turkish citizens in their daily lives;
- Abolishing of the permission requirement for the prosecution of civil servants and public employees for allegations of torture and mistreatment;
- Protection of journalists against being forced to reveal their sources of information;

- Amendments to the Law on Political Parties making it more difficult for the Constitutional Court to close political parties;
- Amendment of the penal code by repealing the provision used for reduction of sentences in cases of 'honour killings';
- Improvement in the legal conditions of community foundations, including property rights;
- Amendment of the law on the National Security Council underlining its purely advisory role and allowing for a civilian to be elected as the secretary general.

The Commission's 2004 report on Turkey was of critical importance with regard to opening of accession negotiations. The Commission appreciated the comprehensive reforms the Turkish Parliament enacted until that date and concluded in its 2004 report that 'Turkey sufficiently fulfilled the Copenhagen political criteria.' A communication recommending opening of accession negations with Turkey was also attached to the 2004 report. This recommendation evaluated the success of the reform process in Turkey. The Commission in its recommendation noted that 'there has been substantial legislative and institutional convergences in Turkey towards European standards' in areas such as civil-military relations, human rights, freedoms, the judicial system, cultural rights and strengthening of civil society (European Commission 2004a). It also listed some laws that had not yet entered into force, such as the Law on Associations and the new penal code, and warned that there was a need for effective implementation of legislative changes. The Commission's conclusion of Turkey's sufficiently fulfilling the criteria was contingent upon entry into force of the mentioned legislation.

In a separate paper titled 'Issues Arising from Turkey's Membership Perspective' and also incorporated into the recommendation, the Commission also evaluated the potential effects and significance of Turkey's EU membership. The Commission described the process as 'challenging both for the EU and Turkey' and underlined the special nature of Turkey's accession (European Commission 2004b): 'Turkey's accession would be different from previous enlargements because of the combined impact of Turkey's population, size, geographical location, economic, security and military potential.' The Commission noted a number of issues that had to be taken into consideration. Among these points were Turkey's role as a model country for Muslim countries, the economic impact of Turkey's accession on the EU, which was evaluated as 'positive but relatively small', the increase in regional disparities in the EU as a result of Turkey's membership, the large number of Turks residing in the EU, the possible demographic contribution to ageing EU societies, the need for adjustment of Turkey's agriculture, Turkey's role as a transit country for energy supply, the extension of the EU's borders with Turkey's entry, the budgetary impact of Turkish membership, and the impact of Turkey's membership on the institutions of the EU.

The recommendation of the Commission included a number of caveats with regard to the reforms in Turkey. It noted that reforms should continue in Turkey and the progress should be watched closely by the EU 'in order to guarantee the sustainability and irreversibility of the political reform process' (European Commission 2004c). The Commission also mentioned the possibility of 'suspension of negotiations in the case of a serious and persistent breach of the principles of liberty, democracy, respect for human rights and fundamental rights and the rule of law' (European Commission 2004c). As if predicting what was going to happen after the opening of accession negotiations, the Commission also underlined that 'both the EU and Turkey will need a considerable amount of time to create the conditions that will ensure a smooth integration of Turkey into the EU.' The recommendation to start accession negotiations with Turkey also included precautions and safeguards with regard to the probable impact of Turkey's membership in the EU and reservations as to the effectiveness of the reforms in Turkey.

The Commission's 2004 report on Turkey and the recommendation for opening accession negotiations were presented to the European Council meeting on 16–17 December 2004. Turkey's membership had been a contentious issue for the EU at least since Turkey's first application for membership in 1987. The declaration of the European People's Party congress in 1997 that 'Turkey had no place in European civilization' was a watershed since it was a high-level rejection of Turkey's credentials for EU membership based on fundamental notions of Europe and Europeanness coming from official representatives of parties having a considerable role in European politics. As Turkey approached the EU further by taking such steps as realizing the customs union in 1996 and applying for membership, its probable accession to the Union became an even more controversial issue where major alignments among political families and member states took place in the EU. The evaluation of Turkey's suitability for EU membership was increasingly couched in cultural or civilizational terms, referred to as a culturalist approach (Küçükcan 2008: 204).

It was later reported in newspapers that one member state was particularly opposed to opening of accession negotiations with Turkey and showed resistance until the last minute. This country was Austria, represented at the meeting of foreign ministers by its minister of foreign affairs, Ursula Plassnik. Plassnik argued that negotiations with Turkey should be 'open-ended, and that the opening of negotiations will not inevitably lead to Turkey's EU membership'. She also called for 'derogations, long transition periods, specific arrangements and permanent safeguard clauses in the event of an opening of accession negotiations with Turkey' (Federal Ministry for Europe, Integration and Foreign Affairs 2004). Apparently, safeguards and long transition periods regarding free movement of persons, structural funds or agriculture were also supported by other member states of the EU that were also sceptical concerning the anticipated burden that Turkey's integration to the EU would result in (Arıkan 2006: 237).

The European Council after lengthy discussions approved the recommendation of the Commission with the aim of starting accession negotiations with Turkey. The official date for the start of negotiations was set as 3 October 2005. The Council also asked the Commission to prepare a framework for negotiations and identified some protective measures to take into consideration, such as long transition periods, derogations or permanent safeguards, and also underlined the open-ended nature of the accession process (European Council 2004: para. 23).

This identification of the nature of negotiations as 'open-ended' was noticed and scorned in Turkey. It was mostly interpreted as a sign of the insincerity of and double standards imposed by the EU on Turkey compared to other candidate countries. The leader of the main opposition party CHP, Deniz Baykal, said that the terms of the negotiation framework would always be controversial as far as Turkey was concerned, while minister of foreign affairs Abdullah Gül spoke of the last-minute efforts of the governments to include the statement that the final aim of the negotiations is accession in the conclusions and the negotiations framework (Ministry of EU Affairs 2005). A report was prepared by the CHP under the guidance of the vice-chairman of the party, Onur Öymen, concerning the 'traps' of the EU report on Turkey and warned against the 'open-ended nature' of the process. The report argued that 'It is not possible to give concessions regarding Turkey's major interests unless the aim of full membership is openly stated' (Hürriyet 2004). Thus the precautions included in the Commission recommendation, conclusions of the European Council and the negotiation framework aroused national sensitivities in Turkey and were largely interpreted as evasions and pretexts employed by the EU to avoid granting membership to Turkey as a result of the negotiations. The door was kept open to an alternative sort of relationship short of full membership, such as that propagated by the Austrian minister of foreign affairs: 'a tailored partnership' with Turkey owing to the limits of EU's absorption capacity (Küçükcan 2008: 206). The commissioner for enlargement of the time, Olli Rehn, explained this issue of the 'open-ended' nature of negotiations in a meeting he had with the leader of the opposition, Deniz Baykal. He said that 'the common aim of the negotiations is definitely accession.' He added that there are no alternatives to membership; however, the process of negotiations is open-ended since 'we do not yet know whether Turkey will achieve the expected target as a result' (Ministry of EU Affairs 2005).

The Negotiating Framework Document guiding the negotiations embodied provisions on how, according to which rules and with which intentions the process would advance. The document stipulated the end result of the process as accession. However, it also made provision for failure of this goal (Council of the EU 2005):

> The shared objective of the negotiations is accession. These negotiations are an open-ended process, the outcome of which cannot be guaranteed beforehand. While having full regard to all Copenhagen criteria, including the absorption capacity of the Union, if Turkey is not in a position to assume in full all the obligations of membership it must be ensured that Turkey is fully anchored in the European structures through the strongest possible bond.

According to the Negotiating Framework Document, the negotiations will proceed within the framework of an intergovernmental conference which will make decisions by unanimity. The Council will determine benchmarks for the closing and, if applicable, opening of each chapter to negotiations. The document makes room for the application of 'long transitional periods, derogations, specific arrangements or permanent safeguard clauses' for Turkey in the areas of free movement of persons, agricultural policy and structural funds. The framework also stipulates a procedure to be employed

> in the case of a serious and persistent breach in Turkey of the principles of liberty, democracy, respect for human rights and fundamental freedoms and the rule of law . . . In such a case, negotiations may be suspended upon the proposal of the Commission and approval of the Council by qualified majority.
>
> (European Commission 2005b)

Thus, the negotiations framework document may be deemed as an overly cautious document that tries to take precautions against any mishap that may occur during the process of Turkey's accession to the EU. Even if Turkey becomes a member state at the end of this process, transition periods and safeguards will continue to bar it from benefitting from some of the fundamental rights and policies of the Union at least for a considerable time.

While the negotiations started with an official ceremony on 3 October 2005, it could be said that from the start, the process carried within it the seeds of its own destruction (Kaygusuz 2010). The fact that Turkey started negotiations with a Union of now 25 states including one that it did not officially recognize was bound to cause problems. The first problem emerged within the context of the expansion of the customs union to the newly acceding member states of the Union. The protocol expanding the customs union to the newly acceding states was signed on 29 July 2005 between Turkey and the EU, accompanied by a declaration by Turkey that the signing of this protocol did not amount to a formal recognition of the Greek Cypriot administration. In the declaration, Turkey stated that it remains committed to a political solution of the Cyprus problem; however, the Republic of Cyprus referred to in the Protocol is not the state founded in 1960 and for this reason Turkey recognizes that the Greek Cypriot authorities exercise control south of the buffer zone and do not represent the Turkish Cypriots (Ministry of Foreign Affairs 2005).

Turkey's declaration was met with a counter-declaration adopted by the Council on 21 September 2005 (Council of the EU 2005). The EU reacted to Turkey's declaration in solidarity with the 'Republic of Cyprus' and stated that it is unilateral, not legally binding and not a part of the Protocol. The Council further noted that the EU expects Turkey to implement the Protocol fully and in a non-discriminatory manner and repeal all limitations on free movement of goods, including limitations regarding means of transport. Turkey had closed its ports and airports to vehicles originating from the south of Cyprus since 14 May 1987 upon the instruction of the Ministry of Foreign Affairs as a reciprocal measure against the Greek Cypriot administration's similar practise (Köse et al. 2014). It was also noted that implementation by Turkey will be closely monitored by the EU and an evaluation will be made in 2006. The Council furthermore hinted that the opening of the relevant chapters in the negotiations is dependent on Turkey's fulfilment of its commitments and reminded it that the 'Republic of Cyprus' is a member of the EU since 1 May 2004 and that recognition of all member states is a necessary component of the accession process. Thus a stark difference of opinion emerged between the EU and Turkey regarding Cyprus's membership in the EU, which could be traced back to the accession of Cyprus to the EU as a divided island following the rejection of the Annan Plan in the south.

Turkey's accession negotiations to the EU started with the screening process whereby national legislation was analysed with a view to ascertaining the degree of compliance with the EU *acquis* in each of the 33 chapters. Following the screening procedure, the first chapter to be opened and provisionally closed to negotiations on the same day became the science and research chapter on 12 June 2006. No other chapter could be provisionally closed after this one owing to the decision of the Council dated 11 December 2006 not to open eight chapters to negotiations and not to provisionally close any one chapter. The Council stated that Turkey does not fulfil its commitments regarding the full implementation of the Additional Protocol to the Association Agreement without any discrimination and therefore approves the Commission's recommendation not to open eight chapters found to be related to the customs union[2] and not to provisionally close any chapter.

The decision of the Council effectively blocked meaningful progress in the negotiations by making it impossible not to open eight chapters and not to provisionally close any one chapter. Turkey did not comply with the EU's expectation. While minister of EU affairs Egemen Bağış offered a settlement, such as the opening of one port to Greek Cypriot vessels in return for the opening of the Ercan Airport in Northern Cyprus, such offers were not accepted by the EU (Hürriyet 2006). In addition, the accession of Cyprus represented only by the Greek Cypriot government was mostly regarded as an unjust treatment on the part of the EU owing to the fact that Turkish Cypriots were excluded while they were the ones who actually approved the UN Plan in a referendum. This was mostly regarded as the EU violating its own norms. Moreover, the direct trade regulation that was drafted by the Commission as a measure to compensate for the exclusion of the Turkish Cypriot side from membership could not be enacted due to the resistance of the Greek Cypriot government. Thus the overwhelming approach in Turkey to this issue could be summarized as follows: Turkey has made enough compromises in the Cyprus issue and in return was not treated justly and even punished by the EU (Öniş 2009: 7).

The suspension of eight chapters dealt a blow to the accession process. Nevertheless, chapters that were not blocked could still be opened to negotiations on the condition that Turkey fulfils the opening benchmarks. Until 2015, 13 more chapters were opened in addition to the science and research chapter, the last one being regional policy and coordination of structural instruments. The decision not to open eight chapters was reiterated in consecutive Council meetings. Moreover the unanimous decision of the Council in this regard was supplemented by unilateral decisions of member states blocking particular chapters. Sarkozy's France became the first such member state. After Nicholas Sarkozy came to power in

2007, he made it known that he was in principle opposed to Turkey's membership. He summarized his reasoning as follows:

> Entry of a country, whose 98% land is outside European continent, who will be the most populous country of the Union in the coming 20 years, and moreover whose culture mainly carries several aspects of Islam into the EU, will create an overall transformation within the EU, thus will weaken the initial idea of founding fathers of the EU in terms of a political union eventually leading to a chaos.
>
> (Lagro 2008: 72)

While he did not intend to block the process as a whole, he was of the opinion that the negotiations should culminate in a privileged partnership rather than membership. Thus he opposed the opening of chapters which were deemed as relevant for membership, including the chapters on regional policy, economic and monetary policy, agricultural policy, financial and budgetary matters and institutions. Sarkozy was succeeded by François Hollande in 2013, who advocated withdrawing the blockage in some of the chapters on a case-by-case basis.

In addition to France, Cyprus also decided to block six more chapters in 2009 as a further sanction against Turkey (Kambas 2015). Thus the Cyprus impasse became the most obvious obstacle blocking progress in Turkey's accession to the EU. While the EU in general criticized Turkey for its intransigence on this issue, on the part of Turkey it led to a growing resentment and bitterness regarding the EU's handling of the matter.[3]

Factors shaping the EU's approach to Turkey's probable membership

The Cyprus issue was of course only the tip of the iceberg with regard to understanding the obstacles in the way of Turkey's EU membership. The scepticism among some circles and in general public opinion about Turkey being a European country, resentment against Islam and cultural influences that Turkish membership might have for the EU, historical stereotypes about the Ottoman conquests, fears of further migration from Turkey once it enters the EU, doubts about the weight Turkey will have in the EU as a nation of 77 million, potential cost of supporting Turkey's adaptation to the EU *acquis* for the EU budget, and concerns that Turkey's possible membership would bring the EU to the brink of Middle Eastern conflicts could be all considered with regard to evaluating the EU's approach to the matter. Thus Turkey's size, culture, geography, history and level of development all played a part in slowing down the process of accession and the EU's delaying tactics in this regard. As described in the foregoing list of factors, fears, doubts, resentments and so forth were more influential in determining the EU's approach to Turkey than hope and optimism.

How the EU approached Turkey was of course not only shaped by actual facts about or conduct by Turkey. It also reflected the mood the EU was in, its general state regarding the progress of integration and its approach to enlargement. Considered in this manner, the crises the EU experienced – that is the constitutional crisis of 2005 and the financial and economic crisis of 2008 followed by a more general institutional and political crisis of European integration – had a major effect on the general evaluation of further enlargements by the EU and the particular case of Turkey. While on the eve of the ratification of the Constitutional Treaty, the EU's self-confidence was such that it invited the candidate countries to the European Convention drafting the Treaty and also to the signing ceremony that took place in Rome, the rejection of the Treaty in two founding states of the Union led to a sense of disillusionment and ambiguity about the future of European integration. The federal future of Europe was further delayed while the Lisbon Treaty replaced the Constitutional Treaty. Moreover, the majority of 'No' votes in France and the Netherlands was also symptomatic of deeper problems regarding the EU, most prominently the detachment of the citizens from the project of integration, the weakness of the social aspects of integration and the failure of identification with Europe among the general public.

The following crisis of the EU concerned one of its major successes, the Economic and Monetary Union. The European economies were negatively affected by the financial crisis erupting in the US property market. Above all some Eastern European member states, Ireland, and particularly Southern European countries were particularly badly hit by the crisis, leading to serious difficulties in debt repayment and government finances. The crisis necessitated further measures being adopted, including the strengthening of the economic governance aspects of the Union and the rescue funds that could be made available to member states undergoing financial difficulty. Greece's failure to lift itself from the crisis and need for a third rescue package in return for further austerity measures still in 2015 testified to a struggling Union deeply enmeshed in its internal problems. The growth of Eurosceptic parties and growing resentment against the EU in both the right and left of the political spectrum as well as the problems encountered in the foreign policy domain, such as the stand-off with Russia over the crisis in Ukraine and the Arab spring uprisings, were further challenges to the EU's power to attract, shape and transform its own population as well as acting as a model for nearby countries.

These internal and external difficulties led the EU to be much more cautious in its enlargement policy as exemplified by new Commission president Jean-Claude Juncker's statement in the European Parliament (EP) that the EU would not enlarge during his term, which means in the next five years (Pop 2014). Two other factors further fed into the sense of angst about further enlargement. One factor was of course the problematic accession of Bulgaria and Romania in 2007. These countries entered into the Union without fully meeting the Copenhagen criteria and problems especially in the political sphere, such as corruption and rule of law, instigated the freezing of Commission funds for these countries in 2008 and 2012 (Pop 2010). The problems of integration in the case of these countries further decreased the enthusiasm regarding new member states.

The other issue that had a bearing on further enlargement and the case of Turkey's possible membership was migration pressures, both intra and extra-EU. Internal tension between old and new member states intensified regarding the intra-EU migration, mainly from the East to the West of the Union, as exemplified by the extra measures adopted by some member states to limit free movement and some excessive action, such as the expulsion of Roma people from France (BBC News Europe 2010). One major factor regarding these debates was related to the competition for the local labour force that migrants would pose and the burden for social security systems. While such arguments were centred on perceptions and fears rather than facts, cultural considerations and xenophobia were fuelled by economic hardships and ambiguities about what deepening integration would bring to the lives of ordinary people across Europe.

Extra-EU immigration was even a more critical factor impacting on relations with Turkey. On the one hand, control of irregular migration to the EU became one of the major areas of cooperation with Turkey in recent years, leading to the signing of the Readmission Agreement and more recently the joint action plan of 29 November 2015 and EU–Turkey Statement of 18 March 2016 regarding the situation of Syrian refugees (European Commission 2015b). On the other hand, the increasing number of irregular migrants passing through EU's land and sea borders mainly targeting the more prosperous northern and Western European countries and especially the humanitarian crisis in the Aegean and the Mediterranean leading to losses of a great number of lives following the disturbances in the aftermath of the Arab uprisings intensified the security dimension of migratory flows and impacted on the migration sensitivity of the Union. The 2015 Syrian refugee crisis intensified the anti-immigration rhetoric in many EU countries. The series of terrorist attacks in Brussels, Paris and Nice led to harsher security measures, such as the imposition of a state of emergency in France, and fed the view that accepting more refugees and migrants would be dangerous since it embodied the risk of admitting potential terrorists to the country. All these developments had unfavourable effects on Turkey's bid to join the EU since Turkey's membership was evaluated as a factor that would intensify migratory pressures, especially in countries such as Germany (McLaren 2007).

Developments in Turkey impacting on the EU accession process

While the EU was enmeshed in multiple problems, Turkey also was going through major changes and challenges both at home and in the nearby regions. One important challenge was regarding internal political changes under the rule of a relatively new political actor that held power under consecutive governments since 2002. The AKP, coming from an Islamist origin, successfully capitalized on the EU perspective and supported the EU reforms in order to open up the internal political space and fight against opponents, such as the civil and military bureaucracy. While the AKP's predecessor, the Welfare Party, had an anti-EU rhetoric, the AKP voiced its support of the EU process and increased its power base to include liberals and those groups that demanded a reform of the system (Avcı 2011). The AKP and CHP, being the parties representing the majority in the TGNA, acted in unison in passing the harmonization packages through the parliament, making it possible to open accession negotiations. This spirit of optimism and enthusiasm towards the EU perspective diminished since the unresolved Cyprus issue caused a point of contention between the two sides regarding the conduct of accession negotiations. One reason was of course related to the disillusionment in Turkey regarding the EU's approach, which was regarded as unjust and insincere. Other reasons were related to internal developments in Turkey that led to a cooling of EU enthusiasm, a lack of ownership of the EU membership cause, internal political struggles and a changing foreign policy agenda.

The AKP came to power in the 2002 elections with 34.3 per cent of the vote and increased its support, winning 46 per cent of the vote in the 2007 elections and even increasing its share further with 49.95 per cent of the votes in the 2011 elections. The party came with a new agenda in Turkish politics, challenging the mainstream ideology of Ataturkism and established political classes. It portrayed itself as conservative, vied for a place in the centre of politics and depended on previous political movements, such as the Democrat Party of Adnan Menderes and Motherland Party (ANAP) of Turgut Özal, in order to fill up the space in Turkish politics pertaining to the centre right. Its Islamist tendencies were mostly viewed as a threat to the secularist nature of the regime by the bureaucratic elite and hence a case was opened in the Constitutional Court for the closure of the party on the grounds of its anti-regime activities (Hale and Özbudun 2010). While the AKP was saved from the threat of being terminated by a decision of the Court, other Court cases started that had the effect of weakening the military. The cases that started with the confessions of a journalist with links to the intelligence organization and the alleged discovery of illegal weapons in Istanbul began to be tried under the name of Ergenekon as of 2007, followed by the Balyoz (Sledgehammer) cases regarding alleged coup plans by the military. These cases, which had the declared aim of uncovering an underground organization aiming to overthrow the government, turned out to be political trials initiated by Gülenists in the judiciary establishment. The aim in instigating these unfounded trials was to weaken the military and purge it of Kemalist elements in order to fill the cadres with Gülen affiliates. The trials were dropped after nine years, as a result of the judgment of the Supreme Court of Appeal in 2016 on the basis of procedure and principle, and all accused military officials were released without any convictions. The election of the president by the parliament in 2007 also turned into a political stand-off as the CHP contested the quorum necessary for election by referring the matter to the Constitutional Court. At the same time, large-scale protests throughout Turkey under the name of 'Republic meetings' expressed a concern that secularism was under threat.

These political confrontations between the Islamist-oriented AKP and the secularists filled the political agenda in Turkey and led to increasing polarization in the society. In the meantime, EU negotiations were moving towards a stalemate and the perspective of membership was becoming dimmer due to some of the developments in Europe cited earlier as well as changes in the international arena. The EU membership goal was increasingly becoming detached from the concerns of everyday politics while none of the significant political and societal actors engaged in a determined pursuit of this target. The lack of ownership of the EU integration project for Turkey could be discerned in the diminished EU enthusiasm of the governing party, main opposition party, bureaucracy and the major non-governmental actors, such as business organizations. On the part of the AKP, the decision of the European Court of Justice in 2005 on the Leyla Sahin case, finding the ban on the wearing of the headscarf at universities not contrary to the ECHR, led to a disillusionment regarding the extent of protection Europe could provide for religious freedoms and the AKP's causes in Turkey. The main opposition party, the CHP, on the one hand also became disenchanted from the EU mostly due to the EU's approach to the Cyprus issue and what was seen as the EU's application of double standards and support of anti-regime forces in Turkey, such as the Islamist and Kurdish movements (Gülmez 2008). Civil society, on the other hand, could not really apply pressure on political actors in support of the EU process either because they also lost hope that EU membership was a realizable goal for Turkey or because they were also becoming pawns in political struggles between different political forces and factions, such as between secularists and Islamists and also as later on became evident between the AKP and the Gülen movement. Business organizations, such as TOBB and TÜSİAD, that gave full-hearted support to Turkey's EU project before and during the Helsinki European Council and the Brussels European Council of 2004[4] were not able to push forward the agenda in favour of EU integration due to the political atmosphere in Turkey and the stalemate in the negotiations triggered by the EU's doubts about Turkey's eligibility.

The promises of EU membership – that is the expectations of benefits – were no longer sufficient to trigger a neat process of EU harmonization due to factors stemming from both the EU and Turkey. The EU's trials and tribulations owing to its struggle to overcome the crises outlined earlier also led to a weakening of its pull of attraction for countries such as Turkey. Countries such as Ireland and Greece, which were once portrayed as the EU's success stories, were now in the throes of crisis and the EU could not provide a once-and-for-all and clear-cut solution. The depictions by political leaders, media and general discourse regarding the EU deteriorated in this period. Former president Abdullah Gül referred to the EU as 'miserable' in an interview he had during his visit to the UK in 2011 (Dünya 2011). Minister for EU affairs Egemen Bağış criticized Europe on account of being racist and Islamophobic. In a ceremony commemorating the Holocaust in Auschwitz, he expressed his concerns to that effect with the following words: 'It is poignant that the European Union, founded to offset the threats to peace, is today face to face with the danger of being besieged by racist minds that are taking the fascist methods of the 1930s as an example and not even internalizing its own values' (Egemen Bağış 2011).

While the EU context was becoming more fluid and questionable for Turkey, Turkey's aspirations to become a regional power and a model country for Middle

Eastern Arab states grew in this period. In the words of Ahmet Davutoğlu, Turkey would act as an 'order-setter' in the Middle East, especially after the withdrawal of American forces from Iraq starting as of 2007 (Davutoğlu 2008). While Turkey's foreign policy in the republican period was described as passive and cautious, foreign policy under the AKP would be more daring and active, utilizing Turkey's soft power assets, such as its trade and economic links and cultural and historical connections. Turkey should become a 'central power' rather than a peripheral country, projecting its strength to regions surrounding it, such as the Balkans, Middle East, Eurasia and Central Asia (Sözen 2010). This construction of foreign policy under the AKP rule was also relevant for a Turkey on the rise, a model country facilitating the transformation of Arab countries of the Middle East. Although being a candidate to join the EU was very much contributing to Turkey's model country value since it fed into its positive image among the Arab people, final accession to the EU was seen as undesirable since it would limit Turkey's independence in foreign policy (Kirişçi 2013).

One of the best manifestations of this paradox could be observed in Turkey's open visa policy, which was also a factor playing into Turkey's soft power. While especially Prime Minister Erdoğan gave special importance to abolishing visas with several countries in Turkey's neighbourhood as well as in the developing world, Turkey's EU process necessitated an alignment with EU visa policy, which adopted a more protectionist outlook in this regard. Open visa policy was definitely favoured by the government as a means to bolster Turkey's prestige as a destination country, although it conflicted with Turkey's commitments to the EU (Lepeska 2015).

Turkey's foreign policy trajectory in this era ran along a narrative of a central country with a proactive stance in international politics and this conflicted with the stipulations and the mind-set required by the EU accession process. Consecutive AKP governments under Erdoğan prioritized two main challenges, one at home and the other abroad. The former of these struggles was against political opponents within the country and aimed to attain and sustain the party's and leader's power. The latter challenge concerned Turkey's foreign policy ambitions, which brought the country in confrontation with multiple actors, including regional rivals and Western powers, as it aimed to become a regional power, even a global power (Öniş and Yılmaz 2009).

The EU process had at best a pragmatic and instrumental value in this viewpoint in terms of overcoming both challenges. The EU dimension was mostly employed as a factor that could support a critical issue on the political agenda, such as the attempts at a new constitution in Turkey as observed in the 2010 referendum regarding amendment of the Constitution. While the amendments were severely criticized for attempting to increase the influence of the executive over the judiciary by revising the rules of selection and internal conduct regarding the Constitutional Court and the High Council of Judges and Public Prosecutors, the government referred to the EU requirements as legitimating some of the articles in the amendment package. Egemen Bağış, minister for EU affairs, celebrated the positive result of the referendum by noting that it was a sign of the belief of

Turkish people in democracy and human rights, and said that 'we are going to continue with reforms, and we will all take the necessary first steps so that Turkey becomes a country that answers to the European criteria' (Euronews 2010).

Blurring of the membership perspective and Turkey's drift away from the EU

The AKP was able to increase its votes in consecutive elections until the 2015 national elections as outlined earlier. One of the reasons contributing to the AKP's electoral success was the 10 per cent threshold and the election system employed in Turkey, which advantaged the majority party. Recep Tayyip Erdoğan was elected as the president of the country in the first election of its kind, held on 10 August 2014, with 51.79 per cent of the vote. His priority was to change the Constitution and establish a presidential regime. Under AKP rule, Turkey increasingly became a country polarized along the secularist-Islamist and Turkish-Kurdish dimensions. Widespread resentment against the government, especially among urban progressive classes, reached a climax with the Gezi protests that started with opposition to the plan to demolish Gezi Park and led to nationwide street protests (Letsch 2014). After a few days of talks with the leaders of the protests and the government, police force was used against the protestors, leading to loss of lives and serious injuries.[5] Government resorted to media controls and social media bans afterwards, which amounted to a limitation of fundamental freedom in a country that was officially a candidate to join the EU (Paul and Seyrek 2015).

The European Parliament harshly condemned the excessive use of force against peaceful demonstrators, and made a call to the government 'to stop immediately the violence against the demonstrators'. In the resolution the EP noted the 'authoritarian style of governing' of the government, expressed its concern that civil society organizations encountered legal and administrative restraints, and noted the 'social, political, cultural and economic policies' of the government as the reason for the demonstrations (European Parliament 2013). The high representative for foreign affairs and security policy, Catherine Ashton, and the member of the Commission responsible for enlargement policy, Stefan Füle, also made statements expressing their concern about the developments in Turkey and the excessive use of force against the demonstrators and called for a restrained reaction on the part of government and respect for fundamental rights (Füle 2013; Council of the EU 2013).

Füle was in Istanbul for a conference when the events took place and talked about his observations around Gezi Park during his address to the EP, while referring to the young demonstrators as 'typical European youngsters wishing to run their own lives'. He also stressed the need for substantial political reform in Turkey to make advances in Turkey–EU relations possible (European Commission 2013a).

The opinions from the EU were rebuffed by then prime minister Erdoğan, who denigrated the EP resolution, criticizing the EU for supporting the Gezi protests and accusing Commissioner Füle of not being able to provide any arguments against Erdoğan during their meeting but then tweeting behind closed doors.

In a speech he made at a conference, he vehemently criticized the EU's approach towards Turkey:

> Why is Turkey, despite all these improvements, forced to face obstacles put by the Union? Why are standards being invented for Turkey, which have not been enforced on candidate countries ever before? The EU forgets every promise, every signature under every promise. Well, Turkey is not a country that can be forgotten, or kept waiting at the door
>
> (Hürriyet Daily News 2013)

The government, intent on preventing another Gezi demonstration and eager to prevent the public expression of opposition towards the government, continued to bring harsh measures that had the effect of limiting freedom of media and freedom of expression, such as bans on social media networks and revision of legislation regarding the legal decisions on how to ban Internet sites (Akgül and Kırlıdoğ 2015). The process of 17 December that concerned the uncovering of some recordings on the Internet that contained allegations of corruption and mismanagement on the part of political figures was the high point of the falling out and confrontation between the government and the Gülen organization.[6] Policemen, judges, public prosecutors, journalists and so forth were now purged, ousted from their positions and convicted of several crimes regarding an attempt to overthrow the government. The methods used against the Gülen network and the prevention of any legal proceedings against the corruption accusations regarding government figures cast great doubt on the rule of law and democracy in Turkey (Human Rights Watch 2015). At the same time this process also led to the ending of several political cases, such as the Ergenekon and Balyoz cases, and the uncovering of previously ignored cases of fraud at general exams, such as university entry exams. It was found out that affiliates and members of the Gülen organization instigated these cases based on false and fabricated evidence and ungrounded accusations with the aim of weakening the military and ridding it of Kemalist functionaries so that Gülenists could be activated to fill the cadres.[7]

Such irregularities and violations of rights and rule of law principles created concern about the continued fulfilment of accession criteria on the part of the EU. In its 2015 progress report, the Commission noted its frustration at Turkey's regression in terms of the political criteria, especially in the areas of media freedom, freedom of expression and association. For the first time, the term 'backsliding' was used to describe Turkey's situation in three areas under study instead of descriptions such as limited progress or no progress: freedom of expression, freedom of assembly and alignment of public procurement rules (European Commission 2015a).[8]

A very problematic area also criticized in consecutive Commission reports was the condition of the judiciary. Independence, neutrality and efficiency of the judiciary deteriorated as a result of interventions into judiciary independence by the government and legal amendments changing the composition of the judiciary by increasing the clout of the president and government in determining the members of the High Council of Judges and Public Prosecutors and the conditions of appointment and promotion. Arrests of academics and journalists, such as Can Dündar, for reporting about weapons deliveries to Syria, limits brought to social media and the closure of media outlets intensified during the state of emergency declared following the 15 July coup attempt. Turkey's image as a democratizing country which was presented as a model to the Middle East and Muslim world deteriorated, leaving in its place an image of an increasingly authoritarian country. In addition to measures limiting the scope of rights and freedoms in the country, Turkey's foreign policy moves, especially regarding the situation in Syria and Iraq, and President Erdoğan's assertive style and often incriminating discourse against the West altered his perception from a democratizing reformist leader of an EU candidate country to an increasingly authoritarian and populist leader of a country turning away from Europe. This shift in Turkey's international standing and backlash in its democratization process damaged Turkey–EU relations as well as contributed to the extension of the view that Turkey is not likely to complete the accession process anytime in the near future.

As Turkey faced serious problems in terms of its adherence to EU norms and principles, the 'Armenian genocide' debate also created renewed pressure on the country's attempt at EU membership. In 2012 the French Parliament passed a bill making the denial of the Armenian genocide a crime. Turkey tried to prevent the passing of the bill, and when it was adopted by the French Parliament it expressed its resentment at what it saw as an unjust act by the French and, understanding that this was a politicization of history, a violation of the right to express one's opinion. Erdoğan criticized France on this account, reminded French officials of the French committing genocide against the Algerians in their war of independence, and warned that Turkey would review its relations with France. Turkey's ambassador to Paris was called back for consultations, and bilateral visits and any cooperation on joint projects between the two countries within the EU were cancelled (CNN 2012). France, being one of the leading countries in the EU, was also in a position to influence the EU's approach towards Turkey, and this episode regarding the Armenian genocide bill in the French Parliament adversely affected EU–Turkey relations.

In Turkey, although several liberal researchers accept the Armenian genocide claims,[9] the general public is usually averse to the use of the word 'genocide', arguing that both Turks and other ethnic groups suffered during the war, and does not recognize the 1915 events as genocide but as deportation due to the trying war conditions. In recent years discussions on the issue became more open and pluralistic. The approach to how Turkey should deal with such accusations became more humanistic and considerate of the losses of Armenians but at the same time still affected by what kinds of demands Turkey could face if it recognized such claims.

At the executive level, a statement made by the prime minister of the time, Tayyip Erdoğan, reflected a more conciliatory attitude. Erdoğan in the statement he made on the 2014 anniversary of the 1915 events acknowledged the suffering of Ottoman citizens during the last years of the empire and warned against 'constructing hierarchies of pain nor comparing and contrasting suffering'. He also noted that expressing one's opinion on the 1915 events 'is the requirement of a pluralistic perspective as well as of a culture of democracy and modernity' and reiterated the call for a historical commission to investigate the 1915 events. He said,

> Millions of people of all religions and ethnicities lost their lives in the First World War. Having experienced events which had inhumane consequences – such as relocation – during the First World War, should not prevent Turks and Armenians from establishing compassion and mutually humane attitudes towards one another.
>
> (Ministry of Foreign Affairs 2015a)

These words were generally accepted as a positive change in the Turkish state's traditional approach to the issue. The European Commission also noted in its 2014 progress report the prime minister's statement and also stated the existence of 'wide public debate' on the Armenian and Kurdish issues (European Commission 2014a: 4).

The centenary of the 1915 events, 2015, was a critical year for Armenia and Armenian diaspora organizations in terms of voicing more loudly their claims for the recognition of the 1915 events as genocide. The Turkish president Erdoğan sent an invitation to the Armenian president to participate in the ceremonies commemorating the centenary of another event, the epic defence of the Dardanelles by the Ottoman army in 1915. Although the Battle of Çanakkale is commemorated on 25 March annually, this year 24 April was chosen as the date when ceremonies would take place in Çanakkale. The issue was taken up by the European Parliament as well. The EP Report on Turkey's 2014 progress report contained a controversial reference to the EP's resolution dated 15 April 2015 on the commemoration of the centenary of the Armenian genocide, while the European Commission adopted a more neutral stance and referred to the events as a 'tragedy' (Anadolu News Agency 2015). The EP report triggered a stark reaction on the part of Turkey as expressed by the minister for EU affairs, Volkan Bozkır, who found the report unacceptable and sent it to Turkey's permanent representation in Brussels to be returned to EP rapporteur Kati Piri (Hürriyet Daily News 2015a). Thus another point of contention worked to create a new wedge in Turkey's troubled relations with the EU, particularly the EP. The EP had earlier in 1987 adopted a resolution recognizing the 1915 events as genocide and called on the Council to 'obtain from the Turkish government an acknowledgement of the genocide perpetrated against the Armenians in 1915–17' (Official Journal of the EC 1987).

The issue came up again with the adoption of a resolution in the German Bundestag declaring the 1915 events as 'genocide' in June 2016. Turkey called its ambassador back to Ankara for consultations while the government denounced the resolution as 'null and void' (Smale and Eddy 2016). While it was feared by the German government that this resolution could negatively impact on relations with Turkey, particularly the refugee deal made on 18 March, it did not have a lasting influence as following events, such as the terrorist attack at the Istanbul Ataturk Airport at the end of June and the 15 July coup attempt, altered the immediate priorities of the Turkish government.

One of the few areas which witnessed a revitalization of relations has been the migration issue. Turkey's position as a transit country for irregular migration became increasingly critical for the EU in controlling migration flows, especially following the Arab uprisings and the Syrian civil war, which led to an upsurge in the number of refugees fleeing towards Europe. While Turkey rose to top of the global ranking, hosting the highest number of refugees, with close to 3 million Syrians, the irregular crossings in the eastern Mediterranean route across the Aegean increased from 50,830 in 2014 to 885,386 in 2015, a 17-fold increase over one year (Frontex 2016a). While the EU aimed to ease the growing pressure on Greece, which could not deal with the continuous flow of migrants, it turned to the Turkish government for a deal to control the irregular passages across the Aegean to the Greek islands organized by criminal migrant smuggling networks. A joint action plan was agreed by the Turkish government on 29 November 2015, later reinforced with the Turkey–EU Statement of 18 March 2016. Explained in more detail in Chapter 7, this cooperation also provided for an opportunity to revitalize the relations by opening new chapters in accession negotiations, holding bilateral summits and high-level dialogue mechanisms and most importantly accelerating the visa liberalization process.

Turkey–EU relations took a turn for the worse due to several reasons. Firstly the visa liberalization process could not be completed due to five remaining criteria still to be fulfilled by Turkey. Secondly, Turkey's fight against the PKK and involvement in the Syrian conflict intensified, bringing the Turkish state in conflict with both the aforementioned organization and ISIS. This situation contributed to an even more restrictive atmosphere in the country with regards to freedom of expression and media freedom. A third development leading to a further deterioration of relations has been the 15 July attempted coup and the declaration of a state of emergency afterwards. President Erdoğan accused EU officials and leaders of not showing sufficient support and solidarity with Turkey following the coup attempt, while also criticizing the lack of progress in the visa liberalization process despite Turkey's cooperation in the refugee crisis (Şimşek 2016). The fight against the Fetullah organization, seen as the perpetrator of the coup attempt, consisted of the discharging and/or arrests of thousands of bureaucrats, officers, members of the judiciary, police, academics and journalists. The large-scale arrests even reached elected politicians, including the co-chairs of the HDP, a development severely condemned by EU officials. While High Representative Mogherini and Commissioner Hahn issued a statement expressing the concern of the EU regarding the detention of parliamentarians (European External Action Service 2016), the president of the EP described the situation as a rejection of 'values, principles, norms and rules underpinning Turkey–EU relations' (European Parliament 2016) while EP rapporteur Piri called for the suspension of Turkey's accession negotiations.

As the possibility of reintroducing the death penalty began to be debated by politicians led by the president, transition to a presidential regime in Turkey dominated the political agenda. Prime Minister Yıldırım even said that Turkey would face the risk of division unless it shifts to a presidential regime (Babacan 2016). In case the plan goes through and a new constitution is approved by the electorate in a referendum to be held on April 16, 2017, the president will be head of the state and the executive and presidential and parliamentary elections will be held in 2019 unless early elections are called for before this date (Babacan 2016). The EU perspective has weakened further in this process, and striving for eventual membership is no longer a priority for the government and not seen at all likely by the EU.

Notes

1 This formula whereby Turkey would intensify its relations with the Union short of full membership was described as 'customs union plus'. Prime Minister Mesut Yılmaz expressed that Turkey would not accept such a design and insisted on inclusion into the enlargement process in his meeting with German chancellor Helmut Kohl. Sedat Ergin, 'Yılmaz-Kohl İlişkisi Nerede Koptu?', *Hürriyet*, 12.03.1998, http://hurarsiv.hurriyet.com.tr/goster/haber.aspx?id=-9589 (26.01.2014).

2 These chapters are free movement of goods, freedom of establishment and freedom to provide services, financial services, agriculture and rural development, fisheries, transport policy, customs union and external relations.

3 For a wider discussion of the Cyprus issue and its influence on Turkey–EU relations, see Chapter 5 in this volume.

4 Turkey platforms were organized by the İKV, an NGO specialized in EU affairs, and brought together nearly 300 NGOs, including business organizations and labour unions, in 1997, 2002, 2004 and lastly 2011. Strong declarations were published after the meetings that called for enhanced relations between the two sides, putting pressure on the Turkish government to accelerate the reform process and making a call to the EU to open up Turkey's membership perspective on an equitable basis.

5 According to Turkish Doctors Association, 8 people died and 8,000 were injured in the protests, with 104 sustaining serious injuries and 11 losing an eye. See Constanze Letsch, 'A Year after the Protests, Gezi Park Nurtures the Seeds of a New Turkey', *The Guardian*, 29.05.2014, www.theguardian.com/world/2014/may/29/gezi-park-year-after-protests-seeds-new-turkey (05.11.2015). See also Amnesty International, 'Gezi Park Protests', October 2013, EUR 44/022/2013, https://www.amnestyusa.org/sites/default/files/eur440222013en.pdf (05.11.2015).

6 Following the coup attempt on 15 July 2016 perpetrated by Gulenists, the expression 'Fethullah Terrorist Organisation' (FETO) began to be used by the government and media in Turkey.

7 A book titled *Imamın Ordusu (Imam's Army)* was deleted from a computer in a police raid on the author Ahmet Sık's house. He was taken into custody as well as the owners of the publishing house intending to print the book. The book disclosed many details and facts about the clandestine connections the Gulen organization had in the security forces. See Ertugrul Mavioglu, 'İmamın Ordusunda Neler Var? / What Is There inside the Imam's Army?', *Radikal Daily*, 29.03.2011, www.radikal.com.tr/turkiye/imamin-ordusunda-neler-var-1044470/ (22.08.2016).

8 The Commission also noted 'some backsliding in public procurement' earlier, in the 2014 Report on Turkey, but backsliding was noted regarding freedom of expression and freedom of assembly in the 2015 report for the first time. Commission Staff Working

Document, Turkey 2015 Report Accompanying the Document Communication from the Commission to the European Parliament, the Council, the European Economic and Social Committee and the Committee of the Regions, SWD(2015) 216 final, Brussels, 10.11.2015, http://ec.europa.eu/enlargement/pdf/key_documents/2015/20151110_report_turkey.pdf (22.08.2016).

9 See the apology campaign initiated in December 2008 by leading intellectuals signing the following declaration: 'My conscience does not accept the insensitivity showed to and the denial of the Great Catastrophe that the Ottoman Armenians were subjected to in 1915. I reject this injustice and for my share, I empathize with the feelings and pain of my Armenian brothers and sisters. I apologize to them.' www.ozurdiliyoruz.com/default.aspx [accessed:05.11.2015].

4 Transformation of Turkish democracy through EU conditionality

Achievements and limits

Turkey has undergone dramatic democratic reforms since achieving candidacy status in the Helsinki European Council in December 1999. It is no coincidence that this significant democratic transformation has been accompanied by candidacy for EU membership. The prospect of launching accession negotiations generated a strong impetus on Turkey's part to comply with the Copenhagen political criteria and undertake radical reforms for this purpose. However, after launching accession negotiations with the EU, Turkey drastically lost momentum, with the process of transformation in Turkey's democracy and human rights regime nearly coming to a halt. More recently, particularly since the 2011 general elections, Turkish democracy has been going through a quite critical process, which can generally be viewed as regression. This chapter explains this differentiation in Turkey's performance regarding democratization with decreasing effectiveness of EU conditionality along with changing domestic conditions and the interaction between these two factors. In other words, while the chapter emphasizes the importance of effective conditionality and favourable domestic conditions in Turkey's radical democratic transformation after 1999, it shows that weak conditionality, lacking credibility and consistency, and decreasing domestic attachment to EU accession have together played a crucial role in the severe deceleration after the opening of accession negotiations followed by a regression in Turkey's democratization process.

Obviously, conditionality is a prominent EU strategy that is placed at the centre of democracy promotion in candidate countries. The idea that membership, the eventual reward, is made conditional on adopting and implementing the EU's democratic rules and norms lies behind conditionality. The EU has set political criteria in the fields of democracy and human rights as *sine qua non* conditions for opening accession negotiations and ultimately membership itself. Therefore, political conditionality is considered in this chapter as an engine for transforming Turkey's democracy and human rights regime. However, democratization in Turkey is a quite complex process, influenced by both internal and external factors. As the comparative literature on democratization suggests, external influences *per se* cannot generate democratic transition or consolidation in a country. It can play a significantly positive role provided that the underlying conditions for democratic transformation are also favourable (Whitehead 2001). In this sense, the significance of domestic factors and actors are acknowledged but they are examined within their special relationships with the EU. Accordingly, this chapter analyses not only the extent of the impact of EU conditionality on democratization in Turkey but also the conditions and factors, including domestic, which have determined the extent of that impact.

The role of the EU in democratic transformation

Consistent with the significance of the deliberate or active policies of external actors in helping regimes transform themselves towards democratization, the EU has recently been acknowledging its own potential in extending democracy to a wider area. Realizing its success in contributing to the transformation and consolidation of democratic regimes, it has intensified its efforts to be a major democracy-promoting actor in the international arena. In spite of the importance of the impact of EU policies on social, economic and political circumstances within countries, they should not been taken as grand-scale designing but rather as conditioning domestic change by helping those working for the establishment of democratic regimes in their countries.

The EU strives to do this by employing a range of policy tools that can vary from coercive measures, like political isolation, suspension of trade or other economic sanctions, to more positive or incentive-based policy tools, such as granting financial aid and technical assistance to political support and guidance, which rather target the government and public sectors. Acknowledging the crucial role of non-governmental organizations (NGOs) in igniting democratization in authoritarian states and balancing elite power that thwarts domestic democratization efforts, NGO funding has come to constitute an important aspect of European democracy promotion policies.

The EU's commitment to democracy promotion has now become more apparent in parallel with its growing global presence in every field of policy owing to a deeper relationship among EU member states and more closely converged national policies. Deepening of integration is now accompanied by efforts to put democracy and human rights at the core of the EU's external policies and common actions. In that endeavour, a range of EU instruments have been employed so far. However, since the purpose of this chapter is to analyse democratic transformation in Turkey, which started with Turkey's declaration as an EU member candidate at the 1999 Helsinki Summit, the most relevant of the EU's tools for this case is political conditionality, which is the most powerful democratizing tool available to the EU.

Democratic transformation through conditionality

Democratization, which had long been seen as an issue to be dealt only within the realm of domestic politics, has also become an indispensable agenda item in the international arena. The domestic approaches of democratization,[1] based on the view that national structure or actors produce the conditions for the emergence of democracy, were rooted in an assumption of the closed and sovereign nation state, thereby making it difficult to address the global dimensions of democratization (Grugel 2005: 197). As the 1990s progressed, it was understood that such studies, which directed their attention overwhelmingly to domestic factors while ignoring external factors, could not fully explain democratization processes. As Gill (2000: 19) notes, the more a country is exposed to these external factors, the greater the possibility that outcomes will result from an interaction of domestic and international factors, rather than be merely due to domestic factors. That is, external factors may make a considerable contribution to the forces of domestic factors.

In parallel with the rise of democracy as an international agenda item, conditionality has emerged as an important factor in international influence.[2] It is regarded as the most developed of all approaches concerning international factors of democratization and the most visible and proactive policy followed to encourage democratic transformation (Kubicek 2003: 7). Conditionality is defined as a foreign policy instrument that entails 'the linking, by a state or international organisation, of benefits desired by another state to the fulfilment of certain conditions' (Smith 2003: 108). Asking for some conditions to be fulfilled by the recipient state before it can actually receive what it was promised supposes that this state will be sanctioned or deprived of a foreseen reward if it does not comply with the external actors' requirements (Ethier 2003: 100). Therefore, according to some scholars like Baylies (1995) and Carothers (1997), conditionality may take two forms: positive or negative. It becomes positive if it focuses on reinforcing conditions through clearly defined rewards (carrots), whereas it is negative if it uses sanctions (sticks) in the case of non-compliance.

Economic conditionality, which was long used by international financial institutions, like the IMF, was later transformed into political conditionality by other international actors (Pridham 1999: 62). Conditionality has also been increasingly used by states and international organizations to enhance the democratic capacities of a variety of the countries in need of external aid (Spendzharova 2003: 146). Political or democratic conditionality implies that domestic actors or governments are required by external actors to introduce democratic structures or consolidate their democratic regime before receiving a promised reward. The US, as in the cases of Latin American countries, various other developed countries, like Canada, Japan, Britain, Germany, France, the Netherlands and Norway, and international organizations, like the UN and the IMF, have resorted to political conditionality in order to encourage non-democratic countries to accept regime change (Usul 2011: 30).

The EU is one of the major international actors employing conditionality as a standard foreign policy tool to enforce democratic reforms and protection of human rights and minorities in its relations with third countries. As argued by Frank Schimmelfenning et al. (2002), the EU, since its foundation, has made financial and technical assistance and institutional ties first informally and then formally conditional on the fulfilment of its democratic and human rights standards. However, conditionality with a membership perspective, which draws together a wide range of policy fields under a comprehensive accession strategy with a particular focus on democracy, has led to far more influential results. As a regional power, the EU plays a major supportive role in helping an infant democracy in its region to complete its transition and then to be consolidated by a consistent policy of meaningful incentives and disincentives. Conditionality with the prospect of inclusion through membership thus provides a significant impetus for domestic democratic transformation movements in third countries. Indeed, EU conditionality has been regarded as its main source of leverage (Vachudova 2005).

The EU originally established a link between membership and the necessity for each member state to have a democratic regime in 1962 through the Birkelbach Report of the European Parliament. It made Community membership conditional on guaranteeing truly democratic practices and respect for fundamental rights and freedoms. Facing new potential applicants in the early 1990s, the democratic preconditions and the principle of the protection of fundamental rights were incorporated into the Treaty of the European Union and also further elaborated by the Copenhagen European Council in 1993 to be strictly applied in subsequent enlargements. That means that certain democratic requirements have to be met by the applicant states before the EU grants its membership reward (Pridham 1999: 65).

Membership conditionality is generally embodied in Article 49 of the Treaty on the EU, focusing on Europeanness and adherence to key EU values,[3] the famous Copenhagen criteria,[4] the Madrid criterion, as determined in the 1995 Madrid European Council, of effective implementation of adopted norms through appropriate administrative and judicial structures, and the Helsinki criteria, as determined in the 1999 Helsinki European Council, of good neighbourliness and higher standards for nuclear safety[5] (Açıkmeşe 2010: 135–6). The 1997 Luxembourg European Council put the Copenhagen political criteria at the top of the conditionality hierarchy by deciding that compliance with them is a prerequisite for opening any accession negotiations[6] (Açıkmeşe 2010: 136).

The prospect of membership in an exclusive club of democratic societies is seen as a major strength of the EU, which often distinguishes it from other similar international organizations in the competition to be in the vanguard of democracy promotion internationally. Linking membership to the establishment of a functioning democratic regime definitely entails much more than a simple expectation of a democratic transformation in recipient countries in return for economic and aid packages. Indeed, so far, the conditionality employed within its comprehensive membership perspective has proven successful, first in Southern European countries and then in Eastern European countries.

EU conditionality implies an asymmetrical relationship between the EU and applicant countries in which the EU determines and imposes its membership conditions while applicant countries wishing to become members must comply with them. Due to these asymmetric relations, the EU can pressurize applicant countries by threatening to deny their accession if they fail to comply with EU conditions. Vachudova (2005: 109) calls this relationship between the EU and applicant countries 'asymmetrical interdependence'.

EU accession is a comprehensive and highly intense process not only requiring candidate countries to fulfil both democratic and many other preconditions but also encompassing other aspects: deliberate policies, actions and motivations of the EU and its member states; diffusion of ideas, values and practices due to intensive interaction at every level and in every field; and positive and negative responses of a variety of actors within candidate states. Consequently, EU conditionality works hand in hand with the other forms of international influence outlined earlier: contagion, control and consent.

Effectiveness of EU conditionality

The literature analysing the impact of EU conditionality on candidate countries finds that 'size and speed of rewards', 'size of domestic adoption costs' and 'credibility of conditionality' are the most critical mediating factors in explaining how successfully countries comply with the membership requirements and realize democratic reforms (Schimmelfennig and Sedelmeier 2005: 10–17; Schimmelfennig et al. 2006; Schimmelfennig and Schwellnus 2006).[7] In other words, the strength of the commitment of a conditionality recipient depends on an interaction between these factors. More specifically, conditionality is most effective if the calculated benefits of the accession process are sufficiently conditional, credible and high that they exceed the domestic calculated costs of compliance with EU conditions.[8]

The study by Schimmelfennig, Engert and Knobel (2005: 33) on political conditionality showed that the 'credibility of threats and rewards is a core prerequisite of any effective bargaining process', even if this cannot on its own explain the success of conditionality. They emphasize that a credible and conditional membership perspective is a necessary though possibly not sufficient factor for ensuring adoption of initially contested political rules and regulations. Conditionality cannot work effectively without credibility, which means that both the carrot (promise of membership) and the stick (denial of accession) must actually be used according to whether the applicant complies with the conditions (Schimmelfennig and Schwellnus 2006: 3). In other words, the candidate country has to be sure that it will achieve membership if it complies with conditions and that it will be denied accession if it does not adopt the reforms necessary to align with the EU's rules.

An important factor influencing the credibility of conditionality is whether the EU adopts a truly 'meritocratic' approach in its enlargement policy. Asymmetric relations between the EU and applicant countries should be meritocratic to increase the credibility and therefore the effectiveness of conditionality. Meritocracy means that an applicant's place in the membership queue is determined objectively in accordance with the progress it has made towards meeting EU conditions and that all applicant countries are evaluated on the basis of the same criteria on their own merits (Vachudova 2005: 112). Additionally, membership conditionality has to be applied consistently without other considerations playing a role in enlargement decisions. In short, meritocracy and consistency are two important factors strengthening the credibility of conditionality to make it more effective. Similarly, unambiguously stated requirements of democratic reforms increase the effectiveness of conditionality.

If candidate countries are provided with clear, consistent and credible membership conditionality then the size of domestic adoption costs and their distribution among domestic actors determine if they will accept or reject the conditions (Schimmelfennig and Sedelmeier 2004: 674). Since the actors involved in the accession process are assumed to be strategic utility maximizers that are interested in the maximization of their own power and welfare, they prioritize the calculated benefits of the EU membership over the calculated costs of compliance. The EU, in order to have influence, needs to gain the consent of strategic domestic actors to adopt its values and rules. Therefore, the costs of adopting and implementing EU rules for target governments and other strategic domestic actors must not be excessively high.

Democratic reforms in Turkey in the pre-candidacy period and the effectiveness of EU conditionality

How EU conditionality is received by candidate countries is a function of the interaction between the factors 'size and speed of rewards', 'credibility of conditionality' and the 'size of domestic adoption costs', as the external incentives model of Schimmelfennig and Sedelmeier (2004, 2005) suggests. Size, clarity and credibility of the incentive, which have proven to be central to the effectiveness of EU conditionality, have varied in Turkey's case. The EU's conditionality towards Turkey remained generally ineffective until the 1999 Helsinki Summit in providing it with the incentives sufficient to make democratizing reforms.

During the association relationship in the framework of the Ankara Agreement, EU membership incentive was quite weak in terms of speed, clarity and credibility. Although the agreement mainly depends on customs union, it envisages closer and deeper economic integration beyond just free movement of goods. More importantly, Article 28 states the possibility of Turkey's membership and, therefore, includes an ultimate membership objective. However, this does not provide a certain membership perspective since it just states that 'whenever it can fully assume the membership obligations, the possibility of the accession of Turkey will be examined.' The 1993 Copenhagen European Council did not even mention Turkey's membership in spite of its long-lasting associate country status and its 1987 membership application while it decided in favour of eastern enlargement in principle, although the countries concerned had not yet applied. At the 1997 Luxembourg European Council Turkey was again not granted candidacy status while all the other applicants from Central and Eastern Europe were declared as candidates with a decision being taken to open accession negotiations with several.

However, the EU still played a role in mobilizing some democratic reforms before the Helsinki Summit, particularly between Turkey's full membership application in 1987 and the conclusion of the customs union in 1996. Actually, since the EU prioritized security issues over democracy and human rights until the 1980s and accordingly regarded Turkey as geostrategically important, the EU did not put pressure on Turkey regarding its weak democracy and poor human rights record. However, in parallel with its increasing interest in democracy and human rights issues in its enlargement policy and Turkey's full membership application, the EU started to force Turkey to improve in these areas. Indeed, the EU's influence on Turkey's democratization increased since Turkey became more exposed to EU pressures as a country that had applied for membership. In particular, the European Parliament was quite active in pressurizing Turkey to make the necessary reforms, preparing a number of resolutions on Turkey's anti-democratic policies and minority rights, particularly for Kurdish people.

Democratic reforms made during the period of Turkey's full membership application first included recognition of the competence of the European Court of Human Rights to hear individual complaints in January 1987 in order to satisfy the EU's demands in this respect. Second, constitutional restrictions banning former politicians from involvement in politics for ten years were abolished through a referendum in September 1987. The EU (particularly the European Parliament) had always referred to the necessity of accepting the rights of individual application to the European Court of Human Rights and of abolishing restrictions on former politicians for progress in Turkey's democracy and human rights situation. A third important development regarding the consolidation of Turkish democracy in this period was the change in the amendment procedure of the 1982 Constitution in order to make amendment easier.[9] The then prime minister, Turgut Özal, believed it was necessary to make it easier to amend the Constitution in order for democratizing reforms to be implemented quickly (Usul 2011: 90–1).

Turkey continued to introduce political reforms after the European Commission's Avis (Opinion) of 1989 on its full membership application, although the Avis did not offer the prospect of membership, which apparently decreased the EU's democratizing impact. One of the important reforms carried out after 1989 was abrogating Articles 141 and 142 of the Penal Code, related to Communist activities and propaganda, and Article 163, about Islamic activities and propaganda. Their repeal in April 1991 meant that such activities and propaganda would no longer be subject to prosecution.[10] Another reform was the abolition of the law restricting publications in languages other than Turkish (in practice Kurdish), which was not easy to achieve given rising concerns about Kurdish separatism at the end of 1991.

It may be argued that these reforms were carried out because the European Commission's Avis did not officially reject Turkey's application, and even noted Turkey's eligibility for EU membership, although it did not include a proposal for launching accession negotiations either. Thus, the then Turkish government continued to expect accession negotiations to begin in the foreseeable future. Accordingly, the democratizing reforms made after 1989 may still be attributed to Turkey's EU bid, especially considering the Commission's opinion that recent developments in the country's human rights situation had not yet reached the level required in a democracy (European Commission 1989).

However, because Turkey soon realized that the EU would not launch accession negotiations in the near future in response to its full membership application, it started to consider completing the customs union with the EU as a means of achieving its membership objective. As discussed in the first chapter of this book, the Association Agreement of 1963 already envisaged establishing a customs union between the parties as an instrument for fully integrating Turkey into the EU. However, since Turkish policymakers and the governing elite never conceived the customs union as their ultimate objective in relations with the EU, its completion did not constitute an ideal incentive to pressure them to comply with the EU's political conditionality. That is, the customs union was not a rational carrot compared to EU candidacy since, for Turkish decision makers, the costs of compliance exceed what the EU offers as benefits. Any status less than candidacy for full EU membership is an insufficient incentive for democratic transformation in applicant counties. Therefore, in the case of the customs union, the EU's conditionality was not able to offer a favourable cost-benefit analysis to Turkish decision makers. In particular, the objective of completing the customs union could not constitute a strong incentive for decision makers to make political reforms in highly sensitive and, therefore, politically costly areas like the Kurdish issue. Still, Turkey could carry out some democratizing reforms, even if they were limited in scope and nature, since decision makers expected to achieve full membership through the customs union.

While completing the customs union, during the first half of the 1990s, the relations were mainly overshadowed by Turkey's human rights violations, mostly related to Kurdish separatism in addition to other problems of Turkish democracy. When increasing terrorist activities of the PKK – listed internationally as a terrorist organization – led to a military response by the Turkish state, the resulting human rights violations and state suppression in south-eastern Anatolia were harshly criticized by the EU. Relations worsened when the Constitutional Court closed the pro-Kurdish Democracy Party (DEP) in June 1994 and stripped DEP parliamentarians of their political rights. In response to this development, both EU institutions[11] and the troika (Germany, France and Greece) harshly criticized Turkey. Similarly, issues of democracy and human rights were at the top of the agenda of the Association Council convened in December 1994. Finally, the decision on launching the customs union was taken at the Association Council meeting on 6 March 1995, when the EU made any further improvement in relations subject to improvements in Turkey's human rights situation and constitutional amendments. The new troika (Germany, France and Spain) referred to the improvement in human rights situation and democratization as necessary conditions in order to have the customs union enter into force on 1 January 1996 (Usul 2011: 77–80).

The EU then decided to take the Association Council decision on the customs union to the European Parliament for its assent as if it was a trade agreement,[12] while increasing its pressure on Turkey regarding issues of democracy and human rights by warning that the European Parliament would not ratify the customs union if Turkey did not make necessary reforms. Since the then Turkish government was determined to complete the customs union, it was influenced by the EU's conditionality so it needed to do what the European Parliament required to ratify the customs union. The European Parliament's priority was amendment of Article 8 of the Antiterror Law,[13] along with some other constitutional amendments, of which Turkey made 15.[14] Although the European Parliament appreciated these reforms, it still considered them as insufficient, highlighting several times the importance of abolition or amendment of Article 8 of the Antiterror Law to improve Turkey's human rights situation.[15] Indeed, the parliament made its assent for the customs union conditional on abolition or amendment of this article, which was amended on 27 October 1995,[16] after which the European Parliament ratified the customs union 'agreement' (Usul 2011: 80, 94–5).

As discussed earlier, Turkey undertook various democratizing reforms during the pre-Helsinki period in response to EU criticisms and pressure, whose institutions, particularly the European Parliament, frequently emphasized that improvement in Turkey–EU relations was conditional on progress in Turkey's democracy and human rights situation. By making these reforms, Turkey was therefore hoping to persuade the EU to accept its membership application (and also to approve the customs union reward as a functional method towards membership). However, these reforms were insufficient to enable further democratic consolidation. This is because first the EU tried to impose conditionality without presenting a clear and motivating incentive to Turkey as the status of Turkey's application remained undetermined until the 1999 Helsinki Summit. By neither accepting nor rejecting the application, the EU did not clearly react to Turkey's membership bid for membership. Instead, relations were redirected from a membership perspective towards an existing association path within the framework of the Association Agreement through a proposal by the European Commission for the completion of the customs union.

In 1997, at the Luxembourg European Council, Turkey was again not declared as a membership candidate although the other applicants from Central and Eastern Europe were given official candidacy status. Although it restated Turkey's eligibility for membership, the European Council did not offer any strong incentive like candidacy status. In other words, the EU failed to provide Turkey with an accession mechanism, which is the basic incentive necessary to encourage compliance with EU conditionality. Instead, the EU introduced a peculiar formula, the European Strategy for Turkey, which did not include the monitoring mechanism necessary for implementing reforms.

Additionally, as Ali R. Usul (2011: 90, 93, 99 and 104) notes, the nature of the EU's conditionality in the pre-Helsinki period was also ambiguous since the EU's criticisms and conditions were quite general, unclear, conjunctural and unsystematic. Thus, the EU could not present a clear programme for Turkey to follow in order to carry out necessary political reforms. While Agenda 2000 and the first Regular Report in 1998 provided some degree of clarity about EU demands, Turkish decision makers did not take these demands seriously since they saw no light at the end of the tunnel. Consequently, the EU's conditionality had only rather limited effectiveness for Turkey's democratic transformation during this period.

Turkey's democratization process after the Helsinki Summit and the effectiveness of EU conditionality

Following the declaration of its candidacy, Turkey's democratization process under the influence of EU political conditionality can be analysed in three successive periods: 1999–2005, when radical reforms took place; from the opening of accession negotiations until 2011, when Turkey's democratic transformation dramatically slowed; and the period since the 2011 elections when democratization regressed. The chapter explains these changes in Turkey's democratization in terms of the varied application and effectiveness of EU conditionality alongside changing domestic conditions and the interaction between these two factors.

The critical factor in understanding and explaining the radical transformation that Turkish democracy went through after Turkey's candidacy was declared and the drastic slowdown in the transformation process after the opening of accession negotiations is the 'credibility' of EU conditionality. Credibility is a necessary albeit insufficient factor for conditionality to effectively promote the adoption of new and initially contested political rules and regulations. The declaration of Turkey's candidacy status, which carried a credible prospect of membership, constituted an important incentive for it to transform its democracy. However, after accession negotiations opened, the erosion of the EU's credibility regarding Turkey's ultimate membership weakened the power of conditionality to stimulate democratic reforms. In other words, incredible conditionality has negatively influenced the cost-benefit calculations of Turkish policymakers, who are responsible for assessing whether the domestic costs of compliance with EU conditions exceed the benefits. This, in turn, led to the democratization process halting and then reversing.

1999–2005: radical transformation

The 1999 Helsinki Summit was a turning point in relations. Although a membership perspective was already included in the Association Agreement, it only became more concrete and clearer when the EU granted Turkey candidacy status at the summit, which gave Turkey–EU relations 'certainty'. On recognizing Turkey as a candidate state in 1999, the EU introduced a strict conditionality mechanism that linked improvement of Turkey's institutional ties with the EU to compliance with the Copenhagen political criteria. As a candidate state destined to join the Union, Turkey had to sufficiently meet the Copenhagen political criteria to activate the next step towards membership – namely opening accession negotiations. To comply with the criteria, Turkey did indeed engage in extensive and radical political reform, thereby starting a transformation in its democracy.

First, the coalition government formed by the Democratic Left Party (DSP), ANAP and Nationalist Action Party (MHP) approved constitutional amendments in October 2001[17] and three harmonization packages in 2002.[18] On 3 August 2002, the Turkish Parliament abolished the death penalty, increased civilian representation in the National Security Council and granted the right to minority groups to be educated in their mother tongue and to broadcast in it, although the coalition government was clearly divided on these sensitive issues[19] (Eralp 2004: 80). These radical democratizing legislative changes surprised most observers. The costs of adoption of reforms in the areas of abolition of the death penalty and minority rights to which the majority of Turkish society were quite sensitive decreased with the capture of the PKK leader Abdullah Öcalan at the beginning of 1999 and the following ceasefire. Due to the existence of a strong EU conditionality and low political costs of compliance with the EU conditions, nationalist parties of the coalition, the MHP and DSP, could not continue to behave as 'veto points' resisting the EU political reform demands and realized such reforms together with their liberal partner, the ANAP.

On the eve of the Copenhagen European Council in December 2002, these radical decisions created strong expectations in Turkey that the EU would declare a date for opening accession negotiations by the end of April 2004 at the latest. However, the Council failed to meet these expectations regarding a direct date for launching accession negotiations, which led, initially, to a significant sense of disappointment on the Turkish side. However, it did foster a sense of certainty in Turkey–EU relations by including, albeit indirectly, a date. The certainty and perceived strength of conditionality in declaring that accession negotiations could be opened only if the Copenhagen political criteria were sufficiently fulfilled overcame the feelings of disappointment and paved the way for accelerated democratization efforts by the government. Indeed, the new government, which rationally wanted to reap the political benefits of opening accession negotiations, displayed determination to satisfy the political criteria.

This new government, formed by the Justice and Development Party (AKP) after the elections on 3 November 2002, continued the reform process by adopting five more harmonization packages between 2003 and 2004, which aimed at improving the most-criticized aspects of Turkish democracy, such as limits to freedom of speech and expression, and freedom of association, torture and ill-treatment, and the strong influence of the military on domestic politics. In addition to five reform packages, the AKP government also adopted constitutional amendments in May 2004[20] and a new penal code in September 2004, which has had positive effects on a number of human rights areas, particularly women's rights, discrimination and torture. The new press law in June 2004, the Law on Compensation of Losses Resulting from Terrorist Acts in July 2004, the new Law on Associations in November 2004 and the new Code of Criminal Procedure in December 2004 were also adopted. A number of regulations were also issued by the authorities in order to enable the implementation of legislation (European Commission 2004a: 187).

Through these constitutional and legislative reforms Turkey experienced an unprecedented democratic transformation. Indeed, it ensured sufficient compliance with the Copenhagen political criteria for accession negotiations between Turkey and the EU to start on 3 October 2005. Before 1999 it would have been difficult to imagine that Turkey would be starting accession negotiations with the EU. Certainly, the EU's political conditionality has played a crucial role in this transformation. In other words, the need to comply with the Copenhagen political criteria in order to launch the accession negotiations was central to the reform packages that were adopted.

From 1999 onwards, a full-fledged credible accession conditionality was in place since the EU, on the one hand, decided to declare Turkey as a candidate country, but on the other hand refused to open accession negotiations because of

Turkey's non-compliance with the Copenhagen political criteria, which it was required to comply with[21] to start the next stage of the accession process. This strong, clear and credible conditionality forced political and state actors to focus on democracy, thereby stimulating Turkey's democratic transformation.

Additionally, several leading EU officials and politicians, like Gunter Verheugen, the commissioner responsible for enlargement, and Romano Prodi, the president of the European Commission, successfully convinced Turkish policymakers that if conditions were met then accession negotiations would indeed start. As Sinem A. Açıkmeşe (2010: 141) points out, the EU seemed to be committed to Turkish accession, member states were not designing alternatives to EU membership (indicating an intra-EU consensus on rewarding compliance), and Turkey did not perceive double standards in the EU's application of accession criteria and strategies. Turkish policymakers also believed that Turkey would receive the reward only if it indeed fully met the requirements. This credible and certainly conditional incentive thus induced Turkey's policymakers to take radical steps towards democratic transformation.

Another important point regarding the post-Helsinki period is that political reforms did not take place immediately after the 1999 Helsinki decision, which was, as pointed out by Nathalie Tocci (2005: 76), initially mainly a symbolic, albeit important, gesture. Instead, Turkey had to wait till 2001 for a formal framework to be created for its accession process to become more tangible with the adoption of Turkey's Accession Partnership as a road map for accession, along with increased EU financial assistance. After the Helsinki Summit, the EU actively stimulated reforms through the publication of its Accession Partnership Document (APD), announced in November 2000 and approved by the December 2000 Nice European Council.[22] Indeed, the 2001 constitutional amendments constituting a breaking point in the democratic transformation process and the first democratization package paving the way towards the seven other packages were agreed shortly thereafter. This is an important indicator of how important and functional are the certainty and credibility of conditionality for consolidating Turkish democracy. The more the EU is committed to accession, the more credible its conditionality is, hence the more effective it is in transforming Turkish democracy. As Açıkmeşe (2010: 138) puts it, 'This commitment is only apparent in time-tables, calendars, temporal rules, roadmaps and etc. in which candidacy, start of negotiations as well as their progress and final destination of membership are designated.' Similarly, the APD, which has been updated periodically by taking into consideration Turkey's progress in its accession process, along with the Regular Reports that state the EU's criticisms and demands, has provided a monitoring mechanism to check closely changes in the Turkish political system.

Additionally, during this period, the AKP government's consent and commitment were obtained since EU rules regarding greater religious freedoms and civilian control over the military were aligned with its own preferences. The AKP thus appeared as a political party with a strong commitment to EU accession and political reforms, which was not apparent in any other political party, whether right- or left-wing.[23] The AKP claims to be a moderate, centre-right party supporting 'conservative democracy', in contrast to its Islamic predecessors (the Welfare Party and the Virtue Party), which subscribed to the 'National Outlook' (*Milli Görüş*) ideology. To support this claim, the AKP advocated not only religious freedoms but also personal freedoms in other areas. In order to survive in Turkey's secular political context, the AKP needed to adopt a pro-EU reform agenda, particularly concerning civilianization, rule of law and freedoms. This pro-EU reform agenda also gave the AKP's disputed 'conservative democracy' ideology greater legitimacy by demonstrating its compatibility with the EU's democratic norms and values. This allowed the AKP to expand its electoral support base towards the centre in order to increase its vote share (Saatçioğlu 2014: 91). Therefore, the EU was manipulated as a legitimization instrument for policies designed at the national level, but with domestic political priorities in mind.

Accordingly, it may be argued that the effectiveness of EU conditionality to successfully enforce Turkish compliance with EU democratic rules during this period was also facilitated by a liberally oriented government for whom the costs of complying with EU demands were not excessively high. Since the AKP government expected to benefit in domestic politics by adopting and implementing the EU's democratic rules and norms, its compliance costs were low. However, it is also obvious that without a credible EU membership incentive, the government would not have been able to realize the reforms reflecting its liberal preferences in Turkey's existing domestic political setting.

Likewise, the previous coalition government managed to adopt impressive constitutional amendments in October 2001 along with the first three harmonization packages, despite the strongly nationalist position of its two dominant parties (the nationalist-rightist MHP and the nationalist-leftist DSP). Even the coalition's minor liberal centre-right party (ANAP) experienced a significant gap between its leader and the party's rank and file regarding these EU related reforms. The abolition of capital punishment and the essential extension of cultural rights for minorities, which would have been unimaginable only a few years earlier, became a reality in August 2002 with direct implications for Turkish citizens of Kurdish origin (Keyman and Öniş 2004: 185). This was another indication of the causal role of strongly credible conditionality in the Turkish case even in the absence of low political costs of compliance for the coalition government as a facilitating factor.

Both the coalition and AKP governments were convinced that the benefits (moving to the next stage towards membership or, more precisely, a clear and credible membership perspective) would be more than the economic and political costs of compliance with EU political conditionality (particularly, persuading other parliamentary parties to accept the transfer of sovereignty to Brussels). The credibility of the EU's sanctions and rewards also deeply influenced Turkish public opinion, parts of civil society and the market, which put additional pressure on the government to end its resistance to making important reforms in politically quite costly areas, like abolishing capital punishment, allowing broadcasting and education in minority languages, and decriminalizing adultery (Kirişçi 2007: 6).

Additionally, several favourable domestic conditions also affected the preferences of strategic domestic actors (including the government) by reducing their costs of compliance, particularly in the aforementioned politically sensitive areas, with the EU's demands. For instance, in the case of the abolition of capital punishment, Turkey had already maintained a moratorium since 1987, while it was easier to extend cultural rights (i.e. broadcasting and education in mother tongues) to Kurdish people since the PKK had recently abandoned its armed conflict in early 1999.

2005–2011: drastic slowdown

Turkey's important constitutional and legislative reforms cumulatively paved the way to the European Council's decision to open accession negotiations. Since the EU was convinced that Turkey had sufficiently satisfied the Copenhagen political criteria, the European Council decided at its Brussels Summit of December 2004 to open accession negotiations with Turkey on 3 October 2005. The EU welcomed the decisive progress made by Turkey in its far-reaching reform process both in the presidency conclusions of the Brussels Summit and in the Negotiating Framework Document, which was prepared and issued on 3 October 2005 in the same line as the conclusions of the summit. However, it also underlined in Paragraph 18 of the former and Paragraph 4 of the latter that the process was not completed and had to be sustained by Turkey. Additionally, it emphasized its expectations regarding Turkey's efforts to consolidate and broaden legislation and implementation measures, specifically in relation to a zero-tolerance policy in the fight against torture and ill-treatment, and the implementation of provisions relating to freedom of expression, freedom of religion, women's rights, ILO standards, including trade union rights, and minority rights.[24]

However, Turkey's performance dramatically decreased after opening accession negotiations. The only reforms contributing to Turkey's democratization were some minor constitutional amendments in May 2007, some steps taken in relation to the 'democratic opening' initiative, which was introduced by the AKP government in August 2009 to expand cultural rights for the Kurdish minority, and the constitutional amendment package accepted by referendum on 12 September 2010.

The government's objective in launching the democratic opening was to solve the Kurdish problem through democratic measures, efforts and political compromise rather than military means. The AKP started to present the Kurdish issue as a multidimensional political and cultural rather than security phenomenon, although this provoked severe resistance by major opposition political parties and various sectors of the Turkish public. The two main opposition parties harshly criticized the initiative since they feared that it could easily lead to ethnic separation. Within the framework of the initiative, the government made several democratic reforms, such as launching a state television channel broadcasting exclusively in Kurdish on 1 January 2009, allowing languages other than Turkish to be spoken in prisons, establishing a Living Languages in Turkey Institution in Mardin University, easing passage at checkpoints in south-eastern Anatolia and passing amendments to antiterrorism laws on 25 July 2010 to end the prosecution of children solely for taking part in demonstrations. However, several of these initial measures, particularly the last one, faced significant resistance that caused delays. This situation was then aggravated when the PKK restarted its armed attacks in December 2009 after an eight-month-long ceasefire, causing many casualties, thereby increasing the strong resentment in Turkish society, which further weakened support for more reform on the Kurdish issue.

During this period, the constitutional amendment package, which included 30 amendments to the existing Constitution prepared by the military regime following the 1980 coup, was accepted by referendum on 12 September 2010. Although it was presented by the government as an important start for further reforms (Yılmaz 2010: 12), it was subject to intense criticism and opposition from different circles in society, including all opposition parties and particularly prominent constitutional lawyers. Lawyers severely criticized it on the grounds that it would weaken the independence of the judiciary due to provisions to reorganize the judiciary, including the Constitutional Court and High Council of Judges and Prosecutors in Turkey. As Bertil E. Oder (2012) argues, it is highly disputable whether its provisions amounted to a real improvement in human rights protection and democratization in Turkey or whether anti-democratic provisions had been properly replaced by genuinely liberal-democratic values and instruments of constitutionalism. Nevertheless, the amendments were welcomed and regarded as 'a step in the right direction' in the European Commission's 2010 Regular Report on Turkey's Progress.

After accession negotiations began, a massive reversal occurred in Turkey–EU relations which damaged the transformation of Turkish democracy. Turkish public support for EU membership drastically and unprecedentedly fell[25] and the Turkish government seemed to lose its will and drive in support of reforms. Turkey then entered a process that was difficult to reconcile with a candidate country in the stage of accession talks where rule adoption and implementation regarding political criteria were critical. For example, the prosecution and conviction of journalists and intellectuals for expressing their opinions, widespread accounts of excessive use of force, torture and ill-treatment on arrest and while being held in police custody, and overly broad and vague antiterrorism laws[26] that resulted in countless unfair trials and prosecutions of those expressing peaceful dissenting opinions as well as the government's efforts to restrict women's rights by curbing abortion, which would have amounted to a virtual ban,[27] were all incompatible with the Copenhagen political criteria.

During this period, the Turkish public and policymakers perceived that previous certainties regarding eventual membership were severely weakened, partly because negotiations constitute a long and difficult process that necessitates compliance with all the Copenhagen criteria, not just the political ones. More importantly, the credibility of EU conditionality was considerably diminished since the EU did not provide a clear and certain indication that Turkey would definitely become a member if it complied with the criteria. Turkish society and policymakers therefore doubted that the EU would eventually accept Turkey as a full member even if Turkey fully met all the criteria, including the democratic reforms.

In the case of the former Central and Eastern European candidates, Schimmelfennig (2004: 15) argues that the EU pursued a consistent policy of enlargement; that is, it invited those countries to enter into accession negotiations on the same political preconditions, without discriminating against individual countries due to their strategic, economic or cultural features. However, Turkish public opinion was strongly convinced that Turkey was treated differently from Eastern candidate countries, although it was declared as a candidate country on the basis of the same criteria as applied to the other candidate states and, thus, membership conditionality was not applied consistently in the Turkish case. Indeed, as discussed ahead, different considerations to the Copenhagen criteria (specifically, the Cyprus issue) deeply influenced the course of Turkey's accession negotiations, while there were signs that some other conditions (like the Armenian issue) would continue to play a role in the EU's decisions regarding the accession. Another widespread view within the Turkish society was that the EU had implemented conditionality in a more tolerant manner in other enlargement cases, such as Bulgaria's and Romania's accessions. Although they failed to comply fully with the political criteria, they were accepted on the grounds of maintaining stability in the Balkans (Pridham 2007: 453). This non-meritocratic manner favoured the countries concerned, which had not fully met their obligations in particular in the area of rule of law, including judicial reform, corruption and organized crime (Juncos and Perez-Solorzano Borragan 2013: 230–31).[28] In contrast, the EU's non-meritocratic attitude is expected to lead to negative consequences in Turkey's case.

The Negotiating Framework Document, which was prepared by the Commission in line with the European Council decisions of December 2004 as the governing document of the accession negotiation process, contributed to this mistrust since it includes ambivalent statements regarding membership that were not used in previous enlargement rounds:

> the negotiations are an open-ended process, the outcome of which cannot be guaranteed beforehand. . . . if Turkey is not in a position to assume in full all the obligations of membership it must be ensured that Turkey is fully anchored in the European structures through the strongest possible bond.

Turkey perceived the last statement regarding anchoring as an offer of a privileged partnership instead of full membership, which provoked strong displeasure in political and state circles.

Additionally, the document's renewed emphasis on the EU's absorption capacity further damaged the EU's credibility. Although the issue of absorption capacity[29] had taken place as a condition along with the Copenhagen criteria first in the presidency conclusions of the 1993 Copenhagen European Council (under the heading Relations with the Countries of Central and Eastern Europe) and then in the presidency conclusions of the 1997 Luxembourg European Council (in Paragraph 26),[30] it had not been debated in enlargement waves of 2004, 2007 and 2013 as intensively as was in reference to Turkey's membership. Moreover, including such a clause in the Negotiating Framework Document as a potential justification for denying membership was perceived as a sign of the EU's unwillingness to accept Turkey. Evidently, the EU can still decline Turkey's membership by claiming that it cannot absorb it even if Turkey manages to comply with the conditionality.

Other statements regarding the prospect of 'permanent' restrictions (derogations) in areas such as agriculture, structural policies and free movement of persons (Article 12) were again almost unique in the EU's enlargement history (Açıkmeşe 2010: 146). While the EU also applied derogations to the CEECs from membership rights in the area of free movement of persons, these were limited to five plus two years. Moreover, offering membership with 'permanent' derogations might be considered as second-class membership. Consequently, the document was regarded as evidence of double standards towards Turkey and EU reluctance concerning Turkish membership. The ever more stringent, inconsistent and non-meritocratic nature of the negotiations, combined with ambiguity about their end result, played an important role in weakening the motivation of Turkish domestic actors. EU policies were discouraging rather than encouraging. Usul (2011: 164) argues that if the EU had pursued a more constructive pre-accession policy as it had in the case of eastern enlargement then EU conditionality could have been more effective in transforming Turkish democracy.

The credibility of membership regarding whether it would actually be wielded also weakened because of EU policies linking accession to other issues, like Cyprus, which cannot be solved by Turkey's efforts alone. Indeed, the Cyprus issue, which is not directly related to the Copenhagen criteria, has almost completely blocked the negotiations since the European Council decided in December 2006 that the negotiation chapters relating to the operation of the customs union between the EU and Turkey would not be opened and no chapter would be provisionally closed until Turkey met the requirements regarding the extension of the customs union to new members. Turkey–EU relations became heavily preoccupied by the problem of opening Turkish seaports to Greek Cypriot vessels and Turkish airspace to Greek Cypriot air carriers. This shows that the membership reward was made dependent on compliance with specific conditions beyond the Copenhagen criteria, which further weakened the EU's conditionality. The Turkish side started to think that compliance with the political conditions would not play a relevant role in the EU's enlargement decision. Additionally, on the one hand, the EU strictly required Turkey to comply with the Cyprus condition, but on the other hand it inconsistently disregarded this condition while assessing the accession process of Cyprus, the other party in the issue. This inconsistent and, therefore, weak conditionality encouraged Turkey to avoid the economically and politically costly reform process. Since the EU linked its conditionality to the Cyprus issue, which always fosters nationalist sentiments in Turkey as a sensitive question of statehood, the military, political parties and even civil society organizations, whose costs of complying with EU conditionality increased, started to take a rather nationalist position that questioned the legitimacy of EU demands.

The EU, probably for the first time in the history of enlargement, almost lost its credibility with respect to delivering membership. Thus, Turkey is a unique case in terms of the uncertainty over its eventual membership despite being in accession negotiations. In previous enlargements, an accession process, once started, ended with membership unless the candidate countries themselves chose not to join. For example, the membership applications of the last 13 acceding countries and their European credentials were never questioned. Studies of the Europeanization of these countries were based implicitly or explicitly on the premise that they would, one way or another, eventually become EU members (Kirişçi 2007: 2). However, the situation for Turkey started, in this period, to change. It is widely known from regular Eurostat and a number of other agency surveys that a large proportion of European public opinion is against Turkey's membership. According to the Eurobarometer surveys conducted between 2005 and 2010, rates of the proponents of Turkey's membership were 31 per cent in 2005, 28 per cent in 2006, 31 per cent in 2008 and 30 per cent in 2010, while rates of the opponents were 55 per cent, 59 per cent, 55 per cent and 59 per cent respectively (Dagdeverenis, 2014: 7). The possibility of Turkish membership, since the second half of the 2000s, has led to a debate in which a group of European political figures, particularly from Christian Democratic or Conservative parties,[31] has been resisting ultimate membership, particularly due to Turkey's different culture and religion, even though Turkey is an official candidate negotiating accession. Furthermore, both France and Austria have declared that they will put Turkey's membership to a referendum although this is not constitutionally necessary. The constant emphasis on cultural differences and a 'privileged partnership' instead of full membership has generated a general belief in Turkish public onion that the EU is a 'Christian club' that will not let Turkey become a member whatever it does. On the other hand, other EU actors have expressed other non-Copenhagen criteria–based concerns, like Turkey's size, demographic growth and level of economic development, reflecting concerns over Turkish immigration to EU countries, and its location as a neighbour of unstable regions. This ongoing debate on the desirability of Turkey's accession has naturally been perceived by the Turkish government as indicating the lack of a clear, credible and consistent EU conditionality, which has reduced the perceived value of the promised rewards (Tocci 2005: 77).

Turkish policymakers have finally begun to doubt whether the EU is capable or willing to give the eventual reward even if conditions are complied with, which has influenced the cost and benefit analysis of Turkish policymakers since, when calculating the size of compliance costs, they take into consideration the fact that eventual membership is in question. Additionally, increasing Euro-scepticism within Turkish society[32] due to rising Turco-sceptic and Islamophobic tendencies in Europe, embodied in the statements of various influential political figures against Turkey, along with feelings of discrimination about Turkey's candidacy, has raised the costs of compliance. This in turn has discouraged the governing elite from making more radical political reforms and contributed to a drastic slowdown in transforming Turkish democracy, which demonstrates the ineffectiveness of EU political conditionality in ensuring adoption and implementation of EU rules and regulations. Without a credible membership incentive, the power of genuinely reformist forces in Turkey has been extremely weakened so reforms have remained limited, superficial and, more importantly, unimplemented.

In this period, the AKP government started to reinforce its political power after being elected to a second term in 2007 with an increased vote (46.5 per cent). Its enlarged power base and more secure position as a conservative party in a secular political regime due to EU-mandated reforms decreased its previous strong need and, therefore, commitment to EU membership and democratic reforms. This led to an unfavourable cost and benefit calculation for the governing elite in the absence of credible conditionality and strong support for accession within Turkish society. Under these circumstances, the AKP could afford to follow the democratization agenda less strictly and more selectively in accordance with its political interests (Saatçioğlu 2014: 93). Thus, this period constituted a transitionary stage from a radical improvement in Turkey's democratization to regression.

After the 2011 elections until recently: regression

The AKP won the 2011 general elections with an increased vote share that strengthened its dominance of Turkish politics. Being elected to a third term by an overwhelming majority (about 50 per cent) consolidated its electoral hegemony as a mass party, which increased its self-confidence to dominate the political and social realms (Gümüşçü and Keyman 2014: 2). It had already secured its position in Turkey's constitutionally secular political context and diminished the role of the military in Turkish politics through political reforms carried out within the framework of EU political conditionality. While these political reforms strengthened Turkish democracy, they also crucially increased the AKP's political power both in society and against the secularist establishment. This reduced its need to seek and maintain alliances with liberals domestically, and with the EU externally, to pursue its interests. It has lost its strong attachment to EU accession and the political reforms begun during its first term despite maintaining its commitment rhetorically to EU membership. Indeed, Prime Minister Erdoğan did not make any reference to the EU in his 2023 vision speech at the 2012 AKP congress.

Moreover, in the enduring absence of a consistent and credible membership perspective, the role and motivation of EU supporters in the country to get EU membership and political reforms back on track have diminished. The stalling of the accession process and the EU's declining attraction in Turkish society,[33] combined with the further consolidation of the AKP's dominant party position, have led to the governing elite being increasingly reluctant to carry out democratic reforms. The single-party rule with strong self-confidence has paved the way to weakening Turkish democracy in the lasting lack of credibility of EU conditionality. The AKP has followed the EU's political reform agenda with decreasing interest and only selectively to serve its political priorities while also limiting freedom of expression and freedom of the press and ignoring the rule of law to a significant extent to suppress criticism of its policies and consolidate its dominant rule.

There has been a noticeable deterioration regarding freedoms of expression and the press, with antiterrorism laws being frequently invoked to suppress public opposition. Turkey's excessively broad definition of terrorism has led to the imprisonment of many journalists, academics and Kurdish activists, against whom evidence of support for or involvement in acts of political violence has hardly been presented (Tocci and Bechev 2012: 2–3). According to the BIA Media Monitoring Report 2014, 22 journalists and ten distributors began 2015 in prison (Bianet 2014), although this is significantly less than the 104 journalists and 30 distributors/members of the media imprisoned at the start of 2012, when Turkey became the world's greatest imprisoner of journalists (Bianet 2011). Despite this reduction, the number of detentions, censorship and dismissals climbed (Bianet 2014).

Turkey was ranked 149th among 180 countries in the 2015 World Press Freedom Index, rising slightly from 154th in 2014 (Reporters without Borders 2015). Nevertheless, this is still a significant deterioration from its 2005 ranking of ninety-eighth out of 167 countries (Reporters without Borders 2005). In addition, Turkey's rise in the index between 2014 and 2015 'was due above all to the conditional release in 2014 of around 40 imprisoned journalists who nonetheless continue to face prosecution and could be detained again at any time'. Accordingly, 'Turkey's "underlying situation" score –covering such areas as cyber-censorship, lawsuits, dismissals of critical journalists and gag orders – actually worsened, showing that freedom of information continued to decline' (Reporters without Borders 2015). Similarly, the Freedom House (2015a), in its 'freedom of the press' report for 2015, listed Turkey as 'not free', having downgraded it from 'partly free' in 2014. According to this report, freedom of press has further worsened due to new Internet laws adopted to increase the government's power to block websites (like YouTube and Twitter) and the surveillance capability of the National Intelligence Organization (MIT). Journalists and media outlets are also subject to an aggressively used penal code, criminal defamation laws that can be interpreted as a sign of the AKP's intolerance of political criticism and opposition, and the antiterrorism law (Freedom House 2015a). Consequently, self-censorship has become common in the Turkish media. These developments led Freedom House to reduce Turkey's press freedom score to 65 in 2015 (Freedom House 2015a) from 54 in 2011 (Freedom House 2011). Since existing problems remain Freedom House (2016), in its 'freedom of the press' report for 2016, continued to list Turkey as 'not free'.

In the recent period, one of the most striking examples of criticisms regarding violations of freedom of the press was the detainment, in November 2015, of two prominent opposing journalists, the *Cumhuriyet* newspaper's editor-in-chief, Can Dündar, and Ankara bureau chief Erdem Gül. They were charged with revealing state secrets and held in jail for 92 days over a report alleging that the government tried to ship arms to Islamists in Syria (The Guardian 2016a). Arrests of journalists, limits brought to social media and the closure of media outlets intensified during the state of emergency declared following the 15 July coup attempt. In October the editorin-chief and several journalists and columnists of the Cumhuriyet newspaper, a media establishment with a symbolic significance with regard to republican values in Turkey, were detained and arrested for publishing material that was allegedly supportive of the coup attempt. By the end of October 2016, over 170 outlets had been closed and more than 700 journalists had their credentials revoked for alleged links to the Fethullah Terrorist Organisation (FETO), the Kurdish movement, or other antigovernment forces. In December 81 journalists were behind bars in Turkey, the most in any country in the world (Freedom House 2017).

Additionally, political rights and civil liberties, particularly in relation to the principle of the rule of law, have been further worsened. The *Ergenekon* and *Balyoz* (Sledgehammer) cases that started in 2008 and 2010 are important examples in this respect. Hundreds of government critics, including prominent journalists, academics, active and retired military officers of all ranks and civil society organizations, were accused of and many imprisoned for engaging in plans to overthrow the government. These cases were criticized particularly due to their wide scope, excessively long periods of pretrial imprisonment that became de facto punishment without trial and the slow judicial proceedings that breached the rights of the defence (European Commission 2012a: 7). Another concern is the lack of transparency in these cases because investigations expanded rapidly and courts accepted evidence collected by the police alone or supplied by secret witnesses (European Commission 2012a: 7). This led to significant public doubt over the trials' legitimacy. In March 2014, the Constitutional Court ruled in favour of a complaint filed by İlker Başbuğ, the former chief of the general staff, that his legal rights and individual freedom had been violated (Habertürk 2014). Subsequently, Başbuğ, who had been sentenced to life imprisonment, and 52 people convicted in the *Ergenekon* case were released. In June 2014, the Constitutional Court also ruled in relation to the *Balyoz* case that the defendants' rights to a fair trial had been violated since the evidence used was largely manufactured. Ninety-nine people convicted in the *Balyoz* case thereupon were released. The court's judgments opened the way for the retrial of the others (European Commission 2014a: 12). Consequently, defendants of both cases were all acquitted.

Political rights and freedom of expression in Turkey have also been questioned regarding the Kurdish issue. After the 2011 elections, there was a sharp increase in the detention of Kurdish activists, including politicians, municipal representatives, academics, journalists and intellectuals, during the Union of Kurdistan Communities (KCK) investigations. They were arrested under antiterrorism laws, although there was not sufficient evidence of their connection to the PKK's terrorist activities (Tocci and Bechev 2012: 2). Security concerns in relation to the PKK's terrorist activities have always constituted a strong ground since the mid-1980s for invoking antiterrorism laws and suspending democratic rights in Turkey. Therefore, the unresolved Kurdish question is regarded as the main impediment to Turkey's democratization.

At the beginning of 2013, the Turkish government started to refer to a new 'peace process' in order to end the armed conflict with the PKK. For the first time since the beginning of the PKK terrorism in 1984 a Turkish government attempted to deal with this problem through political dialogue instead of using military force. In January 2013, MIT negotiated possible solutions with the imprisoned PKK leader, Abdullah Öcalan. In March 2013, the first stages of the peace process were publicly announced and Öcalan called on the PKK to agree to a ceasefire and withdraw from Turkey into Northern Iraq. The withdrawal lasted until September 2013 with about 20 per cent of PKK members leaving Turkey (Demirel 2013). After the 7 June 2015 general elections, however, the peace process has halted and the security situation has seriously deteriorated as a result of the restarted PKK terrorist attacks. The conflict in Syria has allowed the Syrian Kurdish Democratic Union Party (PYD) to take control of an area extending across Turkey's Syrian border while fighting ISIS. This has changed the conjuncture in favour of the PKK and encouraged it regarding its demands from the Turkish government. The interim government installed until the 1 October 2015 general elections then reacted to the situation in accordance with its highly questionable approach that military force without an accompanying political process can solve Turkey's terrorism problem. If the AKP government had maintained the peace process in a determined way, it could well have successfully resolved the Kurdish question as it was quite close to a successful outcome. This would have removed the main impediment to a more democratic Turkey. Unfortunately, however, the peace process has been abandoned and Turkish democracy is in an increasingly alarming state.

Since December 2015 confrontations between Turkish security forces and the PKK have entered an unprecedented stage. The state has imposed urban curfews to restore public order and deployed heavy weaponry in towns and city districts throughout the south-east, where the PKK engaged in urban warfare through barricades and trenches to prevent the government from retaking full control. By March 2016 more than 350,000 civilians were estimated to have been displaced and at least 250 killed, while 350 Turkish police and soldiers were killed in eight months of fighting (International Crisis Group 2016). Kurdish terrorism also struck Ankara twice in February and March 2016, resulting in 66 deaths, and Istanbul in June 2016, resulting in 13 deaths. Obviously, a merely military way of dealing with the terrorism problem has proved in Turkey's case not to provide an enduring solution.

Moreover, the space for opposition on the Kurdish issue is shrinking and political and human rights abuses increase due to the hardline stance of the government, which is fed by nationalist anger. Indeed, the AKP made a great effort to lift parliamentary immunity from five pro-Kurdish HDP deputies, including its co-chairs, for supporting terrorism paved the way towards the arrests of these deputies on 4 November 2016. This threatens to dismantle a significant legal outlet for millions of predominately Kurdish voters (International Crisis Group 2016). The AKP government has also been criticized regarding violating freedom of expression by detaining academics who signed a petition denouncing military operations against Kurds in the south-east of the country. One thousand one hundred and twenty-eight Turkish signatories from 90 Turkish universities calling themselves Academicians for Peace signed the petition on 11 January 2016. President Erdoğan has severely criticized the signatories and called on the judiciary to act against their alleged treachery. Indeed, prosecutors launched an investigation into the academics over possible charges of insulting the state and engaging in terrorist propaganda (The Guardian 2016b). Four of them who also criticized the government's actions at a press conference in Istanbul on 10 March, reiterating their call for peace, were held in pretrial detention between 15 March and 22 April 2016 (Amnesty International 2016a). Moreover, many universities initiated investigations that have resulted in a wave of dismissals of academics from their posts solely on the grounds that they have criticized the government's policies in the south-eastern provinces. Seemingly, as a result of the breakdown of peace negotiations between the Turkish government and the PKK, the reignition of hostilities in July 2015 and the subsequent spiral of violence, the authoritarian tendency of the Turkish government has been backed by a hardline nationalist stance and therefore increased. The impact of the EU's conditionality on states dominated by a nationalist and/or authoritarian leadership is negligible since the domestic political power costs of meeting the EU's demands are prohibitive. Indeed, the AKP has become a 'veto point' resisting the EU political reform demands or, in other words, differently elaborating EU demands according to the governmental preferences while limiting fundamental freedoms and ignoring the rule of law to suppress criticism of its policies and consolidate its dominant rule.

The Gezi Park incidents in June 2013 and the corruption allegations involving high-level politicians, which emerged in December 2013 following a criminal investigation against several AKP figures, led to several controversial legal and administrative decisions that further damaged Turkish democracy and contributed significantly to turning the recent period into a clear reversal of democratization. The AKP's monopoly of political power and resulting authoritarianism embodied in Erdoğan's personality, which shows little tolerance for opposition and pluralism, combined with his insistence on introducing a presidential system, finally led to wide-ranging societal resistance in June 2013. The AKP responded strongly with increased police brutality and censorship and restricted civil society activism by claiming that the Gezi Park protests represented a 'counter-revolution' against its rule (Gümüşçü and Keyman 2013: 2).

At the end of the same year, on 17 December, a number of AKP officials together with relatives of several ministers were detained due to serious corruption and bribery allegations. In response, the AKP defended itself by claiming that it was faced with counter-forces of the 'parallel state' attempting to remove the legitimate elected government from power. Indeed, the government would then blame the same forces, which would be called FETO, for the coup attempt on 15 July 2016. The AKP government reacted harshly to these accusations from judicial and police circles by taking tough measures which were deemed as being at the expense of democracy and the rule of law. Its administrative decisions and new legal regulations, such as the new law tightening Internet control and the new regulation on the Supreme Board of Judges and Prosecutors (HSYK), restricted freedom of expression, as in the closure of Twitter and YouTube in 2014, and undermined the separation of powers and judicial independence by increasing executive control of the judiciary (Müftüler-Baç and Keyman 2015: 3). The 'freedom in the world' report of the Freedom House reported a downward trend in Turkey due to more pronounced political interference in judicial processes. It rated Turkey as 'partly free', with 3.5 out of 7 in its freedom ranking, 4 out of 7 in civil liberties and 3 out of 7 in political rights (Freedom House 2015b).

The aforementioned developments and the associated measures which totally contradicted Turkey's objective of democratization had important repercussions for Turkey-EU relations. While the European Parliament issued a very critical declaration regarding the Gezi Park incidents, some member states, like Germany, Austria and the Netherlands, objected to the opening of a new chapter in the accession negotiations, and the European Commission also strongly criticized the Turkish government's way of managing the protests. Similarly, regarding developments following the corruption and bribery allegations, Turkey was criticized by EU leaders, like Jose Manuel Barroso and Herman Van Rompuy, mainly in relation to the principles of the rule of law and separation of powers (Soler i Lecha 2014: 3, 4).

Another negative development concerned the drafting of a new constitution, which became the main focus of Turkish politics shortly after the 2011 parliamentary elections. The inter-party Constitutional Reconciliation Commission, with three nominees from all political parties represented in the parliament, was formed to draft a new constitution to replace the problematic 1982 Constitution. However, this process was obstructed because of deep distrust among the political parties and finally came to an end in November 2013. In the following period Turkey experienced quite intensive political competition and challenges due to local, presidential and parliamentary elections at short intervals. Therefore, the political will and consensus necessary for making a new constitution were lacking. Indeed, the new Constitutional Reconciliation Commission could be established in February 2016 only after a long period of time. But this time the commission was dissolved quite early in its third meeting since consensus could not be reached in debates regarding the transition to a presidential system versus maintenance of the parliamentarian system. Obviously, since it is a difficult process to draft a new constitution that matches Turkey's ambitions in the twenty-first century, particularly in terms of democracy and good governance, the process needs both the support of broad circles in society and a consensus in the Turkish Parliament. The political milieu in Turkey immediately after the 15 July coup attempt seemed more appropriate than before in this respect. Joining around a clear common stance against the coup and the resulting decisiveness for eliminating any chance of similar attempts may be regarded as a promising atmosphere for reaching and keeping consensus in the parliament needed for a constitutional reform in this context. Indeed, the post-coup Turkish politics witnessed more conciliatory stances of the opposition parties on the issue of constitutional change that was long called for by the ruling AKP party. However, debates over the constitutional change focused exclusively on the issue of transition to a presidential regime since the government's priority was in this direction. Thus, the promising mood for reaching consensus in the parliament regarding a constitutional reform was quickly lost due to the cleavage between the parliamentary parties over the debated scope of the change. Eventually a constitutional amendment package that proposed by the government and backed by the MHP was passed by the Turkish Parliament on 21 January 2017, with 339 votes in favor.[34] The CHP and the HDP opposed the amendment package enormously strengthening the president's powers. After the President Erdogan approved the constitutional amendment the Prime Minister Yıldırım announced that a referendum on the amendment will be held on 16 April. At the time of writing this book campaigns by 'Yes' and 'No' sides of the constitutional referendum have already started.

All these developments at the expense of Turkish democracy have overshadowed the September 2013 Democratization Package, which was the only important recent contribution to Turkey's democratization in the period after the 2011 elections. The main reforms envisaged by this package relate to rights for Kurdish language–medium instruction in private schools, restoring Kurdish names to villages and provinces, allowing the use of certain letters, like q, w and x, which are especially necessary for Kurdish romanization, greater freedom to wear the headscarf for public employees, laws to protect personal data, elimination of the oath of Turkishness in schools, and measures to enhance freedom of assembly (Kubicek 2013: 8). Regarding the electoral system, the package also proposed to open a discussion about reducing the 10 per cent election threshold for a political party to enter the parliament, to extend financial support for election campaigns to parties that receive at least 3 per cent of the vote and to give parties the right of conducting election campaigns in various languages throughout the election campaign (Demirel 2013). Obviously, some of these reforms that followed the ceasefire and withdrawal of the PKK supported the peace/solution process that came after the democratic opening initiated in 2009. However, the package did not fulfil promises made regarding the Alevi question, Kurdish education in state schools and the issue of freeing imprisoned people under antiterror laws. Therefore, the long-awaited package did not please many circles and led to distrust among others about the government's sincerity regarding satisfactory progress in democratization (Kubicek 2013: 8).

The September 2013 Democratization Package led to some positive developments in Turkey-EU relations. Firstly, the 2013 Progress Report was quite constructive despite the Gezi Park incidents. A few weeks later, a new chapter[35] was finally opened on 5 November 2013 after a three-year break in the accession negotiations. Then on 16 December 2013, the EU–Turkey Readmission Agreement was signed and the EU–Turkey visa liberalization dialogue initiated, through which a visa-free regime between the parties can be achievable. The Turkish government also showed signs of returning its attention to the EU and expected this agreement to further the accession process. However, the subsequent corruption allegations and attendant developments contradictory to the principles of democracy and the rule of law made relations again lose momentum.

The AKP has greatly strengthened self-confidence as a result of its consolidated electoral hegemony and lost its strong attachment to the EU accession and political reforms that existed during its first term. This dominant position over Turkey's political and social realm has made the cost-benefit calculation of making democratic reforms unfavourable for the AKP government given the enduring absence of a consistent and credible membership perspective and strong support for the EU accession within Turkish society. Thus, reforms have been introduced only sporadically in some areas, but with a view to promoting the political interests and priorities of the ruling political elite and with no real reference to the EU (Aydın-Düzgit and Keyman 2012: 2). In some other areas, like rule of law, freedom of expression including media and Internet freedom and freedom of association and demonstration, the democratic transformation process has even regressed, as criticized by the European Commission in its 2015 and 2016 progress reports (European Commission 2015a; European Commission 2016).

Following the 15 July coup attempt and the declaration of a state of emergency already regression in Turkey's democracy has further deteriorated. Through governmental decrees thousands were discharged and/or detained from the military, bureaucracy, judiciary, schools, media, universities and other public institutions due to their links to the FETO, seen as the perpetrator of the coup attempt. At the time of writing, purges of academics, journalists, bureaucrats and other state officials are still continuing, targeting not only the FETO but also those with a critical view of the goverenment, and/or supporting the Kurdish movement. The large-scale arrests even reached elected politicians, including the co-chairs of the HDP, a development severely condemned by EU officials. Even the possibility of reintroducing the death penalty, a crucial aspect of the Copenhagen political criteria and a redline for the EU with regards to the future of the accession talks, began to be debated by politicians led by the president. Apparently, the EU perspective has weakened further in this process, and striving for eventual membership is no longer a priority for the government.

Considering the developments in Turkish politics since 2011 elections, seen as 'majoritarianism with authoritarian tendencies' (Müftüler-Baç and Keyman 2015: 3), and also the 15 July coup attempt and concomitant developments at the expense of Turkish democracy, Turkey needs credible and strong EU conditionality more than ever before in order to mobilize the supporters of liberal democracy and to generate social pressure in the country against electoral democracy. Without a strong EU anchor, Turkey will further deviate from its reformist direction, consolidating the recent tendency towards authoritarian rule. The recent developments in the relations around the agreement on visa liberalization on 18 March 2016 have not provided promising improvement in this respect. This is because the agreement does not propose something further than speeding up the process already started with the Turkey–EU visa liberalization dialogue and Readmission Agreement signed on 16 December 2013. The refugee crisis and resulting increase in Turkey's strategic importance forced the EU to seek a deal with Turkey under the initiative of Angela Merkel in order to slow down the influx of refugees fleeing war and persecution from mostly Syria, Iraq and Afghanistan. The EU demanded that Turkey help secure its external borders. Turkey agreed on a refugee deal after three summits within four months with the EU member states in return for financial assistance, speeding up visa liberalization and opening new negotiation chapters. These developments showed that the refugee issue has recently constituted the main focus of relations. In other words, relations have seemed largely linked to the refugee issue in line with the interests of the parties as the conjuncture forces. Indeed, the issue of illegal immigration, rather than furthering Turkey's membership perspective, has become the priority of the parties. This situation has seriously harmed the EU's consistency and leverage in pushing for democratic reforms in Turkey. For instance, the publication of the 2015 Progress Report, which harshly criticized Turkey's record, particularly regarding political criteria, was delayed to the aftermath of the 1 November elections due to concerns that EU criticism of Turkey's performance would complicate negotiations on the refugee deal. This was considered as a tactical preference of the EU not to affect Turkish politics before the elections at the expense of the government and criticized as being incompatible with the ethics of Europe by the opposing circles.

Last but not the least, opening Chapter 17 on economic and monetary policy on 14 December 2015 after a two-year break in the accession negotiations and more recently opening Chapter 33 on financial and budgetary provisions on 30 June 2016 are noteworthy developments considering the stalled state of accession negotiations. However, there are some other chapters obviously of top priority for Turkey's membership objective: opening Chapter 23, which concerns judiciary and fundamental rights, and Chapter 24, covering justice, freedom and security, would help force the Turkish government to retreat from the restrictions it recently imposed on individual rights and freedoms, and freedom of the press, and to reduce its political interventions in the judicial system. It is challenging regarding the course of the relations that when these chapters can be opened is still uncertain since it is bound by a lifting veto of the Greek Cypriot government.

Consequently, the EU's impact on Turkey's democratization may be expected to remain insufficient considering the fact that its concentration and priority have shifted to internal problems, like the euro crisis and the refugee issue, making its conditionality on the Turkish government weak in terms of monitoring, auditing, pressurizing and encouraging. However, the EU accession process does not have enduring impacts in terms of Turkey's democratization not only because the EU's conditionality is weak but also because internal accommodation is not a priority for the Turkish government.

Notes

1 Most debate regarding democratization processes has been between two internally oriented mainstream approaches, which are structural and agency-based approaches. While the former focused on socio-economic trends and presented democratization as arising from economic modernization or particular changes in social and class structures, the latter claimed that the democratic transitions of the 1980s could be best attributed to the agency of domestic actors (Youngs 2001: 3).

2 In addition to conditionality, contagion, control and consent are conceptualized as international factors in order to understand the complex processes of democratization (Schmitter 2001: 30; Whitehead 2001). The 'diffusion effect' as used by Linz and Stepan (1996: 76) or 'contagion through proximity' as used by Whitehead (2001: 5) occurs when neighbouring countries pursue a process of political learning from the successful steps of each other. Thus, a transformation starting in one country triggers another in its immediate vicinity. While Samuel P. Huntington (1991) describes the same phenomenon as a 'snowballing effect', Jean Grugel (1999: 33–41) employs the term 'socialization'. Whatever the term employed, the concept refers to one of

the possible ways that international factors exert influence over democratization processes through the diffusion of Western values emphasizing individual rights, liberties, pluralism and a liberal market economy. These socialize domestic actors into adopting certain strategies and models invented and developed outside the domestic realm. Another international mode of democratization, 'control', refers to the explicit policies, actions and motivations of external actors to bring democratic regimes to other parts of the world through causing splits within the authoritarian regime and supporting those who are more in favour of change and democratic reform (Whitehead 2001: 8–15). The final international democratization factor of 'consent' refers to the roles and motivations of strategic domestic actors in adopting external values and institutional mechanisms that constitute the core of a democratic regime. To implant a long-lasting and stable democratic regime, the active and voluntary participation and support of a wide range of groups and actors have to be obtained and maintained (Whitehead 2001: 15–16).

3 For example, respect for human dignity, freedom, democracy, equality, the rule of law and respect for human rights of persons belonging to minorities.

4 The Copenhagen criteria consist of three parts: political criteria (stability of institutions guaranteeing democracy, the rule of law, human rights and respect for and protection of minorities); economic criteria (the existence of a functioning market economy as well as the capacity to cope with competitive pressure and market forces within the Union); and adoption of the EU acquis (ability to take on the obligations of membership, including adherence to the aims of political, economic and monetary union).

5 For the Helsinki criteria, see Paragraphs 4 and 7 of the Helsinki European Council Presidency Conclusions.

6 See Paragraph 25 of the Luxembourg European Council Presidency Conclusions.

7 This assumption was put forward as an 'external incentives model' based on rationalist institutionalism.

8 The benefits of membership are generally associated with socio-economic advantages, welfare, security and international legitimacy, while the costs of compliance with conditions may include more limited national sovereignty, revival of ethnic consciousness among some ethnic minorities and economic and financial losses from compliance. Governing elites in candidate countries, while calculating costs, also take into account the costs of exclusion from accession (Schimmelfennig et al. 2006).

9 It was quite difficult to amend the constitution since the original version of the related article (Article 175) required a two-thirds majority of the members of the parliament. In the amended version, the adoption of a proposal for a constitutional amendment requires a three-fifths majority of the members of the parliament by secret ballot.

10 According to Bülent Tanör, 10,949 people were accused of violating these articles between 1982 and 1990 (cited in Usul 2011: 91).

11 At the 1994 Essen Summit, the European Council criticized Turkey and urged respect for human rights after freely elected members of its parliament were sentenced to imprisonment (European Council 1994).

12 Since the Single European Act (SEA), all treaties marking the accession of a new member state and all association treaties have been subject to the European Parliament's assent.

13 Article 8 of the Antiterror Law: 'No one shall, but any means or with any intention or idea, make written or oral propaganda or hold assemblies, demonstrations and manifestations against the indivisible integrity of the state of the Turkish Republic with its land and nation.'

14 These 'amendments removed honourable mention of the 1980 military coup from the constitution preamble and allowed trade unions, associations, foundations, cooperatives and public professional organisations to engage in politics and form links with political parties' (Usul 2011: 94).

15 This article was used as the substitute for Articles 141, 142 and 163 of the Turkish Penal Code, which were repealed in 1991. Its wording was so general that it could be used in a quite broad sense. Over 4,000 people, most of whom were related to the Kurdish problem, had been sentenced under this article since the adoption of the Anti-terror Law (Usul 2011: 95).

16 The amendment removed the phrase 'whatever method, objective and thought' in the first paragraph that had led to the ambiguity and also lowered the prison sentence.

17 The first constitutional reform package included 34 amendments to the country's 1982 constitution, promulgated by a military junta during the last coup-led government. These amendments, inter alia, included shortening pretrial detention periods, limiting the death penalty to times of war or imminent threat of war together with terrorist crimes, making the prohibition and dissolution of political parties more difficult, expanding freedom of association, strengthening civil authority in the National Security Council and abolishing Article 15 of the Constitution, which had banned the constitutional review of acts passed during the National Security Council regime established after the 1980 coup (Aydın-Düzgit and Keyman 2004: 15).

18 Harmonization packages designed with a view to both converting the constitutional amendments into concrete action by bringing Turkish laws into line with the *acquis communautaire* and also introducing further reforms, particularly in the areas of human rights, protection of minorities, freedom of expression and freedom of association.

19 The two dominant parties of the coalition government, the DSP and MHP, which were both characterized by a heavily nationalistic outlook, resisted the political reforms demanded by the EU in these sensitive areas. Only the ANAP, a minor member of the coalition government, appeared to be more supportive of the EU-related reform agenda (Keyman and Öniş 2004: 183).

20 The second constitutional reform package of May 2004, which included ten constitutional amendments, addressed a number of issues related to democracy and human rights: eradicating all remaining death penalty provisions, strengthening gender equality, broadening freedom of the press, aligning the judiciary with European standards and establishing the supremacy of international agreements over internal legislation in the area of fundamental freedoms.

21 The EU has set political criteria in the fields of democracy and human rights that are not part of the acquis, but nonetheless are regarded as a *conditio sine qua non* for opening accession negotiations and ultimately gaining membership itself.

22 Just like the other APDs with the other candidate countries, the APD for Turkey constitutes the key instrument of the pre-accession strategy. It identifies short- and medium-term priorities aimed at the transformation of Turkey in line with the Copenhagen criteria. In response to the APD for Turkey, the Turkish government prepared 'the Turkish National Programme for the adoption of the acquis', which was submitted to the European Commission in March 2001. This was a major attempt to explain how Ankara intended to meet the political and economic requirements laid out in the APD. Turkey's democratization accelerated with these steps, which set the political ground for the reforms. The short-term incentive of opening accession negotiations was thus clear and credible.

23 The AKP government's commitment to the EU membership process and democratic reforms can be explained by both its interests and ideology. For these interest- and ideology-related explanations, see Nathalie Tocci (2005: 80).

24 See European Council (2004) and European Commission (2005).

25 According to the fall 2008 Eurobarometer survey, only 42 per cent of Turkish citizens supported Turkish accession as a good thing (down 7 points since summer 2008; and 19 points since 2005).

26 The Turkish Parliament has made amendments to antiterrorism laws and therefore ended the prosecution of children under these laws solely for taking part in demonstrations. Amendments to the law mean that all children previously convicted under

antiterrorism legislation will have their convictions quashed. However, the new law will not prevent the prosecution of adult demonstrators under antiterrorism laws, allowing unfair trials of people aged 18 and over to continue.

27 The government was reportedly working on legislation to ban the operation after four weeks from conception, except in emergencies. The legislation would have required all abortions, including emergencies, to take place within the first six weeks of pregnancy, down from the ten weeks currently allowed. But the Turkish government needed to withdraw the contentious anti-abortion legislation bill after rising pressure from civil society. If the legislation had come into effect then it would have *de facto* outlawed abortions since, as gynaecologists agree, most women do not learn they are pregnant until after four weeks due to the medical difficulty to determine pregnancy during that period. Indeed, thousands of women and activists have harshly reacted by organizing demonstrations throughout the country to protest the planned ban. In addition, Turkish media published surveys that indicated curbing abortion rights would cause the AKP to lose votes, even among its female supporters. As a result, the AKP government had to drop anti-abortion legislation (Aljazeera 2012).

28 Therefore, the Commission introduced a special cooperation and verification mechanism to continue monitoring progress in these areas and help those countries to address the outstanding problems (Juncos and Perez-Solorzano Borragan 2013: 231).

29 The European Commission replaced the concept 'absorption capacity' with the concept 'integration capacity' in its *Enlargement Strategy and Main Challenges 2006–2007*. For this document see European Commission (2006a).

30 See European Council (1993 and 1997).

31 For example, German chancellor Angela Merkel, former Austrian chancellor Wolfgang Schüssel, former chairman of the Christian Social Union in Germany Edmund Stoiber and former president of France Nicolas Sarkozy.

32 According to the Eurobarometer survey conducted by Eurostat in January–February 2009 only 39 per cent of Turkish citizens supported EU membership as a good thing (Eurobarometer 71 2009: 93). While this rate was 71 per cent in spring 2004 (Eurobarometer 61 2004), it gradually decreased to 28 per cent in fall 2014 (Eurobarometer 82 2014). Although slight increases were seen in some periods, as in spring 2009 (Eurobarometer 71 2009: 93), the rate of Turkish citizens' support for EU membership generally remained under 50 per cent and could never reach the rate of 2004.

33 While 73 per cent of Turkish respondents favoured Turkey's EU membership in 2004, this figure dropped dramatically after 2007 to 45 per cent in 2013. Although support increased in 2014 to 53 per cent, this is not a large change, which shows that EU membership is not as attractive as it was during the AKP government's first term (Transatlantic Trends 2014).

34 Any changes to the Turkish Constitution require the support of at least 367 MPs in the 550-seat Turkish Parliament. If the support of the MPs is less than that but more than 330, a public referendum is needed after the president's approval.

35 It is Chapter 22 on regional policy and coordination of structural instruments.

5 The Cyprus issue

A permanent obstacle to Turkey's accession?

The Cyprus question is an important Turkish foreign and security policy issue. Not only is the island's geostrategically vital location one of the major factors hindering the establishment of a stable, cooperative and trusting relationship between Greece and Turkey, but also the issue has damaged Turkey's relations with the EU since Greece joined the Union. Previously, Cyprus was a four-party issue that was tried to be settled through UN-mediated initiatives and negotiations but later, through Greece's influence, the EU started to be increasingly involved. Most recently, following the EU accession of the Greek Cypriot–controlled Republic of Cyprus, the issue has officially become a five-party issue. This development has harmed Turkey's membership process, resulting in the suspension of several chapters in the accession negotiations. If the current deadlock persists, EU accession negotiations will not be able to proceed as intended, which may mean that Turkey will be unable to achieve its goals from the long, drawn-out process.

This chapter analyses how the EU has become one of the parties to the Cyprus issue, how it has shifted its approach regarding the Greek Cypriot membership from the 'requirement of a political settlement for membership' to 'membership without settlement being a precondition', what role Greece has played in these developments by 'Europeanizing' its Cyprus policy, how the shift in the EU's Cyprus policy and the subsequent Greek Cypriot membership have obstructed Turkey's membership bid, and how the Cyprus issue has impacted Turkey–EU relations.

The overall aim of the chapter is thus to discuss how the Cyprus issue has played the main role in the worsening course of Turkey–EU relations and consider whether it is as responsible for the current deadlock in the accession negotiations as is perceived by many. The chapter concludes that the EU political unwillingness to accept Turkey as a member state is largely responsible for preventing a solution to the Cyprus issue. That is, although the Cyprus dispute does not have a high potential to hinder the accession negotiations, thereby delaying Turkey's membership, the real reason for the current impasse in the negotiations is not the Cyprus question itself but the EU's lack of political will.

The Greek factor and the origins of the issue in Turkey–EU relations

Although Greece has always been an important factor shaping Turkey's policy towards the EC,[1] the long-standing Greek-Turkish conflict only became an issue in

Turkey–EU relations after Greece became an EC member in 1981. Greece began to use its EC (veto) rights as a bargaining tool to pursue its foreign policy interests towards Turkey or to prevent Turkey from achieving its objectives regarding the EU.[2] This situation worsened with the declaration of Turkey's candidacy status in 1999 as Turkey has become subject to extra discriminatory conditionality beyond the Copenhagen criteria, which other candidate countries had to comply with in order to become EU members. Specifically, along with the Copenhagen criteria, accession partnership documents, progress reports for Turkey and presidency conclusions of the European Council regarding enlargement towards Turkey have all addressed the Aegean dispute and the Cyprus issue. Furthermore, the Negotiating Framework Document of 2005, which constitutes the framework for the accession negotiations with Turkey, listed in Paragraph 6 settlement of the Cyprus problem and the concurrent issue of fulfilment of the Additional Protocol, extending the customs union between the EU and Turkey to the ten new EU members, among the requirements for evaluating Turkey's progress in preparing for accession (European Commission 2005b).

It is difficult to argue that the EU has sufficiently resisted Greece's abuses of its membership rights, although it is somewhat understandable given that Greece is an EU member. Actually, until Greece gained membership in 1981, the EC had kept its relations with Turkey and Greece on an equal and balanced basis since their association applications in 1959. However, there are also examples showing that the EU has the capability and instruments, if it has sufficient will, to maintain a balance between the different concerns of the two parties. Therefore, while Greece's potential veto does limit the EU's manoeuvrability, it is also quite clear that the EU sometimes uses this as a pretext against Turkey. The complex relationship between the EU, with Greece as a member, and Turkey has been perceived by the majority of Turkey's political community as evidence that the EU favours Greece, and hence as evidence of the EU's double standard to Turkey's detriment. Moreover, such a perception cannot be eliminated as long as Greece is an EU member but Turkey is not.

Greece's unconstructive manner in the EU over Turkey is closely related to the unresolved Cyprus problem. Since it has proved impossible to reconcile Turkish and Greek interests in Cyprus, the issue has been a major source of conflict between them. As Kramer argues, since joining the EC, Greece has sought to gain the support of its EC partners with respect to its national policy in this conflict with Turkey. Greece first succeeded in preparation for the Association Council meeting of 25 April 1988, at which the EC's opening statement included the claim that 'the Cyprus problem affects EC-Turkey relations.' Although the Turkish side reacted very negatively and boycotted the meeting, the EC consolidated this approach, which established, for the first time, at the June 1990 Dublin European Council summit a connection between the Cyprus problem and EC relations with Turkey. This approach became a point of disagreement between the EC and Turkey since Turkey believed that the Cyprus issue was not linked to EC-Turkey relations. It was thus obvious to Turkey that the EC had abandoned its neutral approach and sided with Greece regarding the Cyprus conflict (Kramer 1996: 217). By doing so, the EC made the Cyprus dispute into an issue between itself and Turkey, when it had previously been exclusively between Turkey and Greece. It therefore lost its political credibility as a mediator for finding a peaceful settlement.

It is significant that the Greek Cypriot government, which is the only internationally recognized political entity on the island, applied for full EU membership on 3 July 1990, following the Dublin European Council summit, which officially stated the EC's position regarding the Cyprus dispute. This application further complicated EC-Turkey relations. The Turkish Cypriot government, supported by Turkey, argued that this application was not only illegitimate but also illegal. It was illegitimate because Turkish Cypriots were not involved in the process although the application was made on behalf of the whole island. It was also argued that, since the Greek Cypriot government is not the 'legitimate government' according to the 1960 Constitution of the Republic of Cyprus, it had neither the right nor the authority to decide or act on behalf of the Turkish Cypriot community, which has been governed by separate, democratically elected governments since 1963. Therefore, some argued that the application contradicted both the 1960 Constitution of the Republic of Cyprus and EU treaties and international law (Tamçelik 2003: 187, 191). The Republic of Cyprus is based on the equality of the two communities on the island within the framework of limitations stipulated in its Constitution. Under this constitution, the Turkish Cypriot community's approval is necessary for critical decisions like constitutional amendments or a full EU membership application, as these can change the island's future.

The application was also illegal under international and Cypriot constitutional law. The 1960 Constitution can be read in such a way that the island, in whole or in part, cannot join the EU without Turkey becoming a member. The Treaty of Guarantee is one of the basic three texts[3] on which the Constitution depends, and stipulates in Article 1 (Paragraph 2) that 'the Republic of Cyprus undertakes not to participate, in whole or in part, in any political or economic union with any state whatsoever' (Mendelson 1997: 139). Greece countered that this paragraph refers to preventing *enosis*[4] rather than joining the EC. Therefore, according to Athens, Turkish argument was not relevant for the time being (Nachmani 2002: 105) as it was obvious that wording of the paragraph referred to *enosis*[5] in order to protect the rights of Turkish Cypriots regarding earlier Greek claims about *enosis*. However, it is also clear that the Greek part of the island has, in effect, participated in a 'political' and economic union with Greece not through *enosis* but within the framework of the EU's mechanisms. This situation can therefore easily be interpreted as illegal under the 1960 Constitution, which currently constitutes the basis of the only internationally recognized political entity on the island, unless Turkey also becomes an EU member. Consequently, contrary to Greece's arguments, Turkey's objections were relevant at the time of the Greek Cypriot's EC application.

In its Avis on the application, issued in June 1993 and accepted by the Council without qualifications in October 1993, the European Commission gave a positive opinion, declaring that Cyprus's EU membership would most likely not pose any special social or economic problems (European Commission 1993). In other words, the Commission accepted that Cypriot accession was possible in principle. However, it also pointed out in Paragraph 47 that 'Cyprus' integration with the

Community implies a peaceful, balanced and lasting settlement of the Cyprus question,' with a view to 'create the appropriate conditions for Cyprus to participate normally in the decision making process of the European Community and in the correct application of Community law throughout the island' (European Commission 1993). The Commission similarly continued in Paragraph 48 that 'as soon as the prospect of a settlement is surer, the Community is ready to start the process with Cyprus that should eventually lead to its accession' (European Commission 1993). Through these statements, as Soysal (2002: 344) argues, it indirectly signalled to the Greek side that solving the Cyprus dispute and compromising with the Turkish side would eliminate all obstacles to the Cypriot membership. Thus, the EU implied that Cyprus's EU membership was conditional on first settling the dispute.

However, the EU soon changed its policy, arguing that the Greek part of Cyprus could join the EU although the dispute had not been resolved. This policy evolved over time, as became apparent in the conclusions of the EU Council of Ministers on 6 March 1995, and then at the December 1997 Luxembourg Summit. Subsequently, it was made explicit in the presidency conclusions of the December 1999 Helsinki Summit. On 6 March 1995, the General Affairs Council of Foreign Ministers reaffirmed the suitability of Cyprus for EU membership and committed itself to opening negotiations with the Greek Cypriot–controlled Republic of Cyprus within six months following the upcoming intergovernmental conference, which took place to reform EU institutions in preparation for its eastward enlargement. It confirmed the EU's will to incorporate Cyprus into the next stage of enlargement that had already been noted in the December 1994 Essen Summit.[6] According to Brewin (2000: 16), March 1995 was a turning point since the Council gave up its condition that the division of the island should be ended before accession negotiations could open. In return, the government of Greece agreed to lift its veto on implementing the customs union with Turkey at the Association Council meeting of the same day.

Brewin (2000: 17) also underlined the significance of the fact that the wording in the conclusions of the EU Council of Ministers referred to 'Cyprus' not to the 'Republic of Cyprus', which had been used by the EU until then. Actually, this change in the wording was a rational result of the aforementioned policy shift regarding the Cyprus issue. The words 'Republic of Cyprus' or 'Federation of Cyprus' would have restored the precondition of a prior settlement on the island because the political entity named as the 'Republic of Cyprus' refers to the 1960 Constitution on which it formally depends, and therefore to the island's bi-communal federal structure. Thus, by using the word 'Cyprus', the EU ignored the divided nature of the island, instead recognizing the Greek Cypriot side as representing the whole island.[7] However, from a Turkish point of view, the Greek Cypriot government had no right to negotiate accession on behalf of the whole island.

The next important indicator evidently demonstrating the EU's shifting policy was the December 1997 Luxembourg Summit. At this summit, Turkey's bid to be included with other applicant countries whose candidate status for EU membership was declared was rejected. The Turkish government reacted indignantly to the EU's proclaimed enlargement outlook. Turkey's resentment was compounded by the EU's decision, under Greek pressure, to open accession negotiations with Greek Cyprus almost immediately, at the end of March 1998, along with the five CEECs, although Ankara had insisted on a prior settlement between the Greek and Turkish Cypriots. Worse, the European Council (1997) in Paragraph 5 called upon Turkey to respect other countries' sovereignty instead of placing responsibility for settling the Cyprus issue jointly on Greece and Turkey. Additionally, in Paragraph 35, while listing the conditions for strengthening Turkey's links with the EU – in other words the conditions for becoming an EU candidate – the Cyprus issue was emphasized and Turkey was required to support negotiations on a political settlement under the aegis of the UN. Thus, the European Council established a linkage between Turkey's candidacy status and the resolution of the Cyprus issue, although the latter was not included in the official membership criteria laid down at the Copenhagen European Council of June 1993. The Luxembourg Summit was the first EU official platform in which political considerations regarding the Cyprus issue (and the Aegean dispute) were referred to as membership conditions.

The Turkish government reacted quite harshly, asserting that Turkey was being treated differently than other applicant countries and declaring that it would suspend political dialogue with the EU. In response to Greek Cyprus's accession, the Turkish government warned that, as soon as the EU launched accession negotiations, Turkey would intensify its integration process with the Turkish Republic of Northern Cyprus (TRNC), which it subsequently did.[8] The Luxembourg Summit thus seriously damaged Turkey–EU relations. However, just two years later, at the Helsinki Summit, relations gained a new impetus with the proclamation of Turkey's candidacy on the basis of the same criteria as applied to other candidate countries.

Although the Helsinki European Council of December 1999 was a new climax in Turkey–EU relations, it was also problematic due to its explicit statement on Cyprus in Paragraph 9 of the presidency conclusions of the Helsinki Summit:

> The European Council . . . expresses its strong support for the UN Secretary-General's efforts to bring the process to a successful conclusion.
>
> The European Council underlines that a political settlement will facilitate the accession of Cyprus to the European Union. If no settlement has been reached by the completion of accession negotiations, the Council's decision on accession will be made without the above being a precondition. In this, the Council will take account of all relevant factors.
>
> (European Council 1999)

The statement makes it clear that the EU would prefer to accept Cyprus as reunified and desires negotiations between the Greek and Turkish sides within the framework of the United Nations to achieve a political settlement. As Soysal (2002: 345–6) argues, the EU thus sent a message to both parties to contribute to resolving the problem. On the one hand, the EU, by emphasizing the role of a political settlement in facilitating accession, has tried to encourage the Greek Cypriot contribution to the solution. If the Greek Cypriot administration does not contribute, then EU membership, to which it has committed itself, may not be realized. On the other hand, it has also pushed Turkey to ensure that the TRNC reaches a negotiated solution as soon as possible. Otherwise, Turkey's full membership process will be suspended. Therefore, Turkey thought that encouraging the TRNC to reconcile with the Greek Cypriot administration constituted a requirement, in addition to the *official* Copenhagen criteria, for Turkey to comply with before becoming an EU member. The Helsinki Summit reaffirmed the linkage between Turkey's full membership and the settlement of Cyprus issue, which had been first established by the Luxembourg European Council. As a result, many in Turkey consider that this issue has become an unstated or unofficial EU membership criterion. Since Turkey had kept the Cyprus issue separate from its relations with the EU, it objected to the EU now assessing its relationship in terms of the Cyprus issue.

It is evident that the messages sent to the two parties through Paragraph 9 of the presidency conclusions were imbalanced. The EU indicated that a solution might not be reached, in which case Greek Cyprus's membership prospects would not disappear. In other words, even if a political settlement cannot be obtained, a divided Cyprus (i.e. the Greek Cypriot–controlled Republic of Cyprus as the representative of the whole island) could be accepted as a full member. Actually, this message had been sent since 1994, as analysed earlier. The Turkish side rightly complained that Greek Cypriots, given that EU membership was guaranteed, would not need to make significant concessions in the inter-communal negotiations conducted under the auspices of the UN. They already felt no motivation to search for a solution, especially after the June 1994 Corfu Summit, the December 1994 Essen Summit, the 1995 EU Council of Ministers Meeting and the December 1997 Luxembourg Summit, when EU membership seemed possible under any conditions, even without a settlement. In contrast, the EU made the Turkish side responsible for making concessions to the Greek side.

Although leaning towards Greece, Paragraph 9 also seemed to aim at mitigating Turkish reactions somewhat by adding the following final sentence: 'In this, the Council will take account of all relevant factors.' This was interpreted as meaning that when the EU decided on membership for the Greek Cypriot–controlled Republic of Cyprus, if there was no political settlement then the situation regarding the Cyprus issue would be considered before making that decision.

The Greek government's statement on the eve of the Helsinki Summit regarding Turkey's candidacy is particularly noteworthy, in that its views on the Cyprus question and the Aegean dispute were largely included in the conclusions of the summit (Aksu 2004: 109–10). This ensured that Greece did not object to Turkey's candidacy at the Helsinki Summit. One can conclude that Greece has efficiently used its advantages arising out of its EU membership in its disagreements with Turkey and become effective in making Turkey subject to additional criteria to comply with before becoming a member. Since Greece particularly emphasized that it could veto the whole enlargement process, other EU member states have needed to take its concerns into account. Thus, Greece has made the EU accept its views on the Cyprus issue in its relations with Turkey, and 'Europeanize' its own policy towards Turkey through a bottom-up process. As Aksu (2004: 109) noted, the Europeanization of Greece's Cyprus policy constitutes an asymmetrical relationship at Turkey's expense or a conditional relationship, with the Cyprus question being another criterion for EU membership. Indeed, the EU's accession partnership documents and progress reports have assessed Turkey in terms of its performance regarding the resolution of the Cyprus question in addition to the Copenhagen membership criteria.

Turkey accepted the Helsinki bid with hesitancy, with some officials recommending to reject the EU's offer of candidate status due to great displeasure about the inclusion of the recourse to the International Court of Justice regarding the Aegean dispute and the statement on Greek Cypriot membership without a settlement being a precondition. However, the view that the benefits of Turkish candidacy and prospective EU membership far outweigh the handicaps posed by these statements prevailed. Meanwhile, to deter the EU from accepting Cyprus prior to a political settlement, Ankara warned that it would strengthen its already close links with the TRNC or even annex it, which would end any hope of reunifying the island (Bahceli 2003: 174–5).

In view of the approaching date of Cyprus's membership and the EU's and UN's clear preference that a reunified Cyprus should join, the last phase of Cyprus's accession process witnessed the most concerted and comprehensive effort by the international community to achieve a settlement since inter-communal talks started in 1974. First, negotiations between the two Cypriot communities, which had been conducted at intervals since 1974, restarted in January 2002 at the invitation of the UN secretary general, Kofi Annan. The Annan Plan, which was a UN initiative providing for reunification on the basis of two essentially sovereign states, was presented to the parties in November 2002.[9] As Kirişçi (2002) reported, there was great diplomatic effort to try to get the plan signed by both parties on the island before the December 2002 Copenhagen Summit of the European Council ended. However, this proved unattainable.

Membership of the divided Cyprus and arising difficulties

The December 2002 Copenhagen European Council took the decision that Cyprus[10] and eight CEECs, except Bulgaria and Romania, would become member states on 1 May 2004 with a view to ensuring their participation in the June 2004 European Parliament elections (European Council 2002). It also declared in Paragraph 12 that 'the application of the *acquis* to the northern part of the island shall be suspended' if no settlement could be reached along the lines of the Annan Plan before 1 May 2004. The decision regarding the accession of Greek Cyprus as representative of the whole island in May 2004, with no requirement of a prior settlement, reduced the probability of a resolution on the basis of the Annan Plan since it created asymmetric incentives at the expense of the Turkish Cypriots. Although the Turkish government declared its commitment to finding a negotiated settlement to the island's problem, it had concerns about whether the Greek Cypriot side would actually be motivated to reconcile with the Turkish Cypriot side given that they were well on the way to becoming a full EU member by May 2004. Subsequent experience in the process towards Greek Cypriot membership in May 2004 clearly demonstrates that the most likely resolution along the lines of the most reasonable UN initiative suffered a major setback at the Copenhagen Summit, as Keyman and Öniş (2004: 187) had predicted.

On 24 April 2004, Greek Cypriots and Turkish Cypriots voted in separate referenda on the Annan Plan, which was the first time that residents had had the opportunity to express their opinion on any peace settlement. The outcome of the twin referenda was a clear 'yes' (65 per cent) from the Turkish Cypriot side, but a resounding 'no' (76 per cent) from the Greek Cypriot side. After the failure of the referendum on the Greek side of the island, Cyprus remains divided into Turkish and Greek parts and in month following the referenda, the divided Cyprus became a member on 1 May, with the *acquis communautaire* suspended in its application to the North, as agreed at the Copenhagen Summit. The admission of Greek Cyprus as representative of the whole island has made the Cyprus dispute much more complicated since the new member now has the chance to bargain for a solution on the status of island on its own terms. For this reason, since May 2004, a peaceful settlement has become less likely.

According to Soysal (2002: 346), until the referendum, the Turkish Cypriots had been continuously accused of taking an uncompromising stance while Turkey had also been criticized for not encouraging the TRNC to reconcile with the Greek Cypriots. From a Greek perspective, Turkey was uninterested in any agreement to reunite Cyprus since it was consolidating control over the TRNC part of the island (Nachmani 2002: 105). However, the Turkish Cypriots' support for the Annan Plan in the referendum has unambiguously demonstrated that the Turkish Cypriots are not the uncooperative or uncompromising side in the dispute. In the same vein, in view of Turkey's determined effort before the referendum to ensure the Turkish Cypriots' constructive stance concerning the Annan Plan, it can easily be concluded, contrary to the Greek view, that Turkey has been sincerely interested in reunification. The Turkish side has become a supporter of the solution along the lines of the Annan Plan, whereas the Greek side has opposed it. The most important reason for the plan's rejection by Greek Cypriots was that they would be in a much stronger situation, with all the instruments necessary to conclude a much more favourable agreement with the Turkish Cypriots, after the island's accession, which was already guaranteed to happen just one week after the referendum. By granting Greek Cypriots EU membership, the EU became a part of the problem and the Cyprus issue got Europeanized.

Once hopes ended for a political settlement for the Cyprus issue, Turkey–EU relations moved into another phase, with the problem of Turkey's recognition of the new member dominating the agenda. On the one hand, Cyprus became an EU member without reaching a political settlement, hence remaining divided. On the other hand, Turkey's EU membership bid and its associated commitments are contradictory to its foreign policy principle of not recognizing the Greek

Cypriot–controlled Cyprus as the representative of the whole island. Turkey's political willingness to recognize it depends only on achieving a political settlement on the island. That is why the Cyprus dispute has also become much more complicated in terms of Turkey's relations with the EU. Improving relations with the EU towards membership had, until Greek Cypriot membership, depended on Turkey's support for the UN secretary general's efforts to settle the issue, which encouraged the Turkish Cypriots to reconcile with the Greek Cypriots. However, after Greek Cypriot membership, the problem of recognition has become the main factor in worsening relations.

At the December 2004 Brussels Summit, the European Council decided to open accession negotiations with Turkey on 3 October 2005. However, this summit also showed how the accession of a divided Cyprus has the potential to block Turkey's membership. At the strong insistence of the Greek Cypriots, the European Council required Turkey to sign the Additional Protocol extending the customs union between the EU and Turkey to the ten new EU members. In other words, the European Council (2004) clearly stated in Paragraph 19 that signing the Protocol extending the customs union to the Greek part of Cyprus where the EU *acquis* is applied was a condition for starting accession negotiations. Turkey had strong doubts about whether its signing of the Protocol regarding the adaptation of the Ankara Agreement to take into account the accession of the newcomers would mean recognizing the Greek Cypriot administration. In order to allay this anxiety, Turkey signed the Additional Protocol on 29 July 2005, but added an official declaration emphasizing that this move did not imply any form of recognition of the Republic of Cyprus and did not change Turkey's existing policy regarding this issue.[11] The Greek Cypriot administration reacted by demanding a response from the EU presidency. In its counter-declaration on 21 September 2005, the EU declared that Turkey must fulfil its contractual obligations regarding the extension of the customs union to the new members; otherwise the negotiation chapters relating to the operation of the customs union would not be opened. The EU decided to observe the issue and evaluate Turkey's implementation of the obligations in 2006. More importantly, through this declaration, the EU and members states referred for the first time to the term 'recognition' of all member states as a necessary component of the accession process in a document which is an integral part of the *acquis*. In view of Turkey's sensitivity regarding the recognition issue, one may argue that the counter-declaration included a harsher and more direct statement in this respect than other related documents. The EU accordingly underlined the importance it attached to the speedy normalization of relations between Turkey and all EU member states.[12]

Signing the Protocol eliminated all obstacles preventing the accession negotiations, which duly opened on 3 October 2005, as decided in the December 2004 Brussels Summit, with the Negotiating Framework Document being adopted on the same day. However, in accordance with the Brussels Summit and the EU presidency's counter-declaration, the Negotiating Framework Document in Paragraph 6 reiterated Turkey's obligation to extend the Turkey–EU customs union to all new EU member states by opening its airports and seaports to them, which thereby included normalizing bilateral relations with the Republic of Cyprus. The Negotiating Framework Document also declared in the same paragraph that Turkey's continued support was required towards efforts to achieve a comprehensive settlement of the Cyprus problem within the UN framework and in line with the principles on which the Union is founded (European Commission 2005b). That is, it obliged Turkey to support a settlement taking these principles into consideration in addition to the UN framework. In this manner, the EU, having officially become a party to the Cyprus question in May 2004 when Greek Cyprus gained EU membership, expressed its will in this respect for the first time.

Because the Turkish Parliament has still not ratified the Protocol, Turkey is only incompletely implementing its customs union with the EU, particularly regarding opening Turkish harbours and airports to Greek Cypriot carriers. The EU, under the Greek pressure, has repeatedly warned Turkey to comply urgently with its responsibilities regarding implementation of the Additional Protocol of 2005 by extending the customs union to all new members. In response, Turkey has declared that it can open its harbours and airports to the Greek Cypriots only if the EU meets its own commitments to end economic isolation of the Turkish Cypriot part of the island. Turkey's policy towards the Cyprus question depends on two major pillars. Firstly, unless a bi-zonal and bi-communal federation based on the political equality of each community is achieved, the Greek Cypriot–controlled Republic of Cyprus cannot be recognized as the sole representative of the island. Secondly, unless economic sanctions on Northern Cyprus are lifted as the EU promised, the Additional Protocol of 2005 will not be implemented.

The clear 'yes' vote for the Annan Plan reversed the negative image of the Turkish Cypriots, who had previously been criticized for being obstructive. Instead, the Turkish Cypriot community started to be seen as the side which was being 'punished' despite favouring the UN solution. Indeed, on 26 April 2004, only two days after the failed referendum, the EU's foreign ministers decided to take some measures (like the Green Line regulation facilitating direct trade with Turkish Cypriots) to ease the Turkish Cypriot community's economic isolation, and to facilitate reunification by encouraging economic development for Turkish Cypriots. Unfortunately, however, this decision was never implemented. In July 2004, the Commission proposed disbursing a package previously approved by the European Council worth €259 million for the North, which had been promised in 2002 if the island was reunified, despite the failed referendum. However, this could not be fully disbursed as the Greek Cypriot government has blocked EU efforts to mitigate the North's economic isolation since it believes such measures serve to consolidate the Turkish Republic in the North as a separate state. The EU's inability to take further steps to remove the economic embargo on the Turkish Cypriots, the suspension of the Green Line regulation facilitating direct (preferential) trade for Turkish Cypriots, and distribution of only €139 million in aid to the Turkish Cypriots due to Greek Cypriot objections have all disappointed Turkey's hopes for resolving the issue. For that reason, the Turkish government emphasizes that future steps towards a settlement must be taken reciprocally, not only by Turkey but also by the EU. In other words, if the EU expects Turkey to meet the EU's requirements for extending the customs union to new members, then Turkey expects the EU to keep its promises to remove the economic embargo against the Turkish Cypriots.

On 24 January 2006 Turkey, with the aim of breaking the deadlock on the issue, published a new initiative proposing to open Turkish seaports to Greek Cypriot vessels and Turkish airspace to Greek Cypriot air carriers in return for the opening of Northern Cyprus's seaports and Ercan airport, the inclusion of Northern Cyprus in the customs union with the EU, and participation for Turkish Cypriots in international sports, cultural and other social activities. Turkey also called on the UN to restart inter-communal negotiations with a view to reaching a peaceful settlement on the island.[13] While the European Commission, the UK and the US welcomed Turkey's new action plan as at least a basis for dialogue, the Greek Cypriots rejected the proposals completely, claiming that Turkey was merely proposing to do what it was already obliged to do as part of its accession process. It was obvious that the Greek Cypriot government thought that the situation favoured it so such an initiative by the Turkish government could not convince the Greek Cypriot side to restart inter-communal negotiations under the aegis of the UN.

The deadlock regarding the unresolved Cyprus issue has undoubtedly become the major impediment to Turkey's accession negotiations. More specifically, Greek Cypriot membership as the representative of the whole island without reaching a political settlement, which has thereby maintained the island's division, has created important concerns for Turkey. First, Turkish concerns regarding the problem of recognizing the Greek Cypriot–controlled Republic of Cyprus have continued to damage Turkey–EU relations and, worse still, the accession negotiations. The European Council of December 2006, 'under pressure from the Republic of Cyprus' (International Crisis Group 2009: 1), endorsed the conclusions on Turkey adopted by the EU Council on 11 December 2006 that eight negotiation chapters[14] relating to the customs union between the EU and Turkey would not be opened, and that the others would not be temporarily closed until Turkey fulfilled its commitments under the Additional Protocol of 2005.[15] The European Council of December 2006 also asked the European Commission to review the situation over the next three years, meaning that, in 2009, Turkey's stance would be reassessed. In December 2009, as Turkish ports remained closed to Greek Cypriot carriers, the European Council decided to maintain the current situation regarding suspension of the eight negotiation chapters. Despite great pressure by the Greek Cypriot government, the European Council did not agree to extend sanctions (e.g. by suspending the opening of new negotiation chapters) in order not to harm the positive atmosphere and promising course of the restarted negotiations between the two communities on the island. However, the Greek Cypriot government reacted by declaring that it would veto the opening of six more chapters,[16] which meant that 14 chapters remained blocked due to Turkey's non-compliance with the Additional Protocol of 2005.

Turkey's second concern, according to Alper Kaliber (2012: 233), is that Greek Cypriot leaders have regarded Turkey's accession negotiations as leverage to exert pressure on Turkey and to obtain Turkey's eventual recognition of the Republic of Cyprus, although this is not a precondition for negotiations to start. However, in their counter-declaration of September 2005 in response to Turkey's unilateral declaration on the issue of recognizing Cyprus, EU member states required Turkey to recognize the Republic of Cyprus as part of its accession process. This proposal was tabled, as can be guessed, by Greek Cypriots, but avoided setting a firm deadline for recognizing the Greek Cypriot government. In short, the Cyprus issue, which has long occupied a central place in Turkey–EU relations, will remain on the agenda during Turkey's accession negotiations.

Following developments: opportunities and challenges for reunification

With Demetris Christofias's victory in the 2008 parliamentary elections in Southern Cyprus, for the first time in the history of the dispute, pro-solution leaders were simultaneously in power in their zones on the island. Mehmet Ali Talat and Demetris Christofias agreed on restarting bi-communal negotiations under the aegis of the UN and in accordance with the basic parameters of the Annan Plan. Negotiations restarted in September 2008 with Turkey's strong support for reunification on the basis of a bi-communal and bi-zonal federation with a single international personality but comprising two constituent states in the North and the South with political equality. However, the election in the North of the hardline nationalist Derviş Eroğlu in place of Talat harmed relations (Kaliber 2012: 234). Although Eroğlu did not leave the negotiation table, negotiations stalled due to a combination of existing problems, like the structure of the federal state, compensation for properties, territory issues and the status of Turkish settlers, which require the parties to compromise, and the current economic crisis in Southern Cyprus.

Worse, the fact that the Greek Cypriots started oil and gas drilling in waters of South Cyprus in September 2011 led to a new crisis with Turkey. The unilateral Greek Cypriot move to extract natural gas and oil led to a fierce reaction and retaliatory actions, like sending the Turkish navy to the region. Turkey claimed that the consent of Turkish Cypriots was required as co-owners of the island. The Greek Cypriots regarded newly found natural gas and oil deposits in the eastern Mediterranean as way to ride out the economic crisis. While the Greek Cypriot government focused on its economic problems, Turkish politicians, like President Abdullah Gül, started to send positive signals, pointing out that reunification would be in the economic interests of both communities, following the election of Nikos Anastasiades on 28 February 2013, who was known for his support of reunification (Tokyay 2013). Similarly, Turkey's foreign minister, Ahmet Davutoğlu, noted that solving the Cyprus problem could also help overcome the economic challenges faced by Greek Cyprus since the most economical and practical way to bring Cypriot gas to world markets was through a pipeline to Turkey (Today's Zaman 2013). According to Davutoğlu, hydrocarbon reserves could be used by both Turkish and Greek Cypriots in a peaceful and economically more beneficial way if they restarted bi-communal negotiations and achieved reunification. While underlining the necessity of determining a timetable of negotiations to settle the dispute as soon as possible, he also pointed out that, if the Greek Cypriots insisted on unilateral exploration, extraction and exploitation of hydrocarbon resources (which means they say the south belongs to them), then a two-state solution could be negotiated (Akgün 2013). Although Anastasiades, who referred to Turkish Cypriots as citizens of the Republic of Cyprus, restated his support for the resumption of the talks, he was not clear about his timetable for restarting negotiations (Morelli 2017: 10). The economic crisis in Southern Cyprus, coupled with the dispute over natural gas and oil in the eastern Mediterranean, raised questions over whether the crisis could be a means to restart stalled talks between the two communities or would lead to a two-state solution.

Until the beginning of 2014, both parties argued over how to restart the talks, although they repeated that they remained committed to restarting the negotiations. Since the parties could finally agree on a joint declaration on 14 February 2014, the talks resumed between Anastasiades and Eroğlu. The joint declaration as the basis of the negotiations envisaged that only unresolved issues would be negotiated since the parties had already agreed on some issues.[17] However, the sides could not agree on how to go forward since their proposals addressing their positions on issues for a future agreement were mutually rejected. Worse, they did a U-turn on several issues as stated by Morelli (2017: 12). Under the influence of the existing problems in the negotiation process, the news about increased interaction among the Greek Cypriots, Greece, Israel and Egypt over energy resources in the eastern Mediterranean pushed Turkey to send its seismic exploration vessel to the southern coast of the island in September 2014 on the grounds that the rights of the Turkish Cypriots were not respected in taking decisions regarding the island's energy resources. Then the negotiations were suspended in October since Anastasiades announced that he would not negotiate for a settlement until the Turkish vessel was withdrawn.

The negotiations remained suspended until some developments providing a positive mood for their resumption took place in April 2015. First, Turkey withdrew its seismic vessel from the island and then presidential elections in the North opened a new horizon for settling the dispute. Mustafa Akıncı, who was the leader of the centre-left Communal Democratic Party (TDP), won the election and expressed its intention of restarting negotiations as soon as possible and reaching an agreement settling the dispute by the end of 2015 (Morelli 2017: 13). Indeed, in May 2015 Akıncı and Anastasiades resumed talks aimed at reunifying the island in an atmosphere seeming to be as optimistic and fruitful as it has ever been. Both sides have agreed to suspend gas drilling in the eastern Mediterranean since any misunderstandings or unilateral acts could hamper the negotiations as previously experienced (Today's Zaman 2015). During the summer and fall of 2015, some confidence-building measures, like agreeing on the opening of a new border crossing at Deryneia and re-establishing electricity connections between the two sides for the first time in 40 years, have been. In accordance with the dominant mood favourable for a peaceful settlement significant progress could be made until the end of 2015 in areas such as economic affairs, EU affairs, and governance and structures. Some steps forward could be achieved even regarding the issues like citizenship of mainland Turks who had settled on the island and distribution of land and property rights where both sides had longheld and very different positions. Despite the internal political developments that made the way to a settlement more complicated, both sides proceeded with the negotiations through 2016 and the atmosphere remained positive and constructive at least among the negotiators who agreed to try to reach a settlement by the end of 2016 (Morelli 2017: 14–16).

Considering the high degree of commitment of the leaders to a settlement the negotiation process seems this time to be more promising, but it still needs to have strong support and more active contribution of the EU to bring it to a successful conclusion, particularly when recalling final frustration despite the similarly hopeful character of the period after Christofias was elected president in 2008 and pro-solution leaders were simultaneously in power in their zones on the island. The EU's role is especially vital to help Anastasiades and Akıncı overcome long-established obstacles to a settlement that prevented the parties from reaching a resolution in the past. Indeed, the issues of territorial adjustment and the right of guarantorship[18] as sticking points of the negotiations constitute main setbacks in the process towards reaching a peaceful settlement as experienced in Mont Pelerin, in November 2016 for the former issue and in Geneva in January 2017 for the latter issue. Serious differences on a rotational presidency, territory, and security guarantees remained wide enough to prevent an actual agreement from being achieved during those sessions (Morelli 2017: 15–17). As the Independent Commission on Turkey[19] argues, a resolution in Cyprus will not only revive Turkey's accession to the EU but also benefit the EU, which has been troubled by recent problems, such as a massive influx of migrants and the repercussions of the Greek economic crisis (Today's Zaman 2015). 'At a time when headlines are dominated by talk of Greece or the United Kingdom leaving the EU, knocking down the last remaining wall in Europe would remind all Europeans of the importance and necessity of integration' (quoted in Today's Zaman 2015).

Notes

1 For example, this can be clearly shown with regard to Turkey's decision to apply to the EC for association in 1959 following Greece's application. For this example, please see Birand (1996: 47–55).

2 For instance, Greece had blocked for years the proper application of the EC-Turkey Association Agreement and the Additional Protocol of 1973 by repeatedly vetoing the release of financial aid that the EU agreed to provide to Turkey as a part of the Association relationship. For a detailed analysis see Stephanou and Tsardanides (1991). This is just one example of Greece's continuous attempts to obstruct any new action in EC-Turkey relations by highlighting the Cyprus dispute and Turkey's unsatisfactory human rights situation.

3 The others are the Treaty of Alliance and the Treaty of Establishment.

4 It is the Greek word used to express unification of the island with Greece.

5 The Greek foreign minister commented on this paragraph in 1959 that 'the wording was specifically designed to exclude possible Greek devices in the direction of enosis' (Mendelson 1997: 139).

6 According to Nugent (cited in Brewin 2000: 16–17), the Corfu Summit under Greek Presidency in June 1994 is sometimes hailed as the first time the question of Cyprus's accession had not been linked to a resolution of the Cyprus problem.

7 The EU started to reuse the term 'Republic of Cyprus' in its official documents after the Greek Cypriot–controlled Republic of Cyprus became a member in May 2004.

8 For example, the first meeting of the Association Council between Turkey and the TRNC took place on 31 March 1998, the day that accession negotiations with Greek Cyprus opened. The Association Council was set up with the task of framing measures necessary to bring about economic and financial integration, and partial integration in matters of security, defence and foreign policy. Turkey also began to include Turkish Cypriots in Turkish delegations and missions abroad. Following the Luxembourg Summit, Turkey's position on solving the Cyprus problem changed from obtaining a bi-zonal, bi-communal federation, supported for nine years, to creating two independent states on the island (Süvarierol 2005: 60).

9 In more detail, the Annan Plan is a proposal on the reunification of Cyprus as a loose confederation of two constituent states, the Greek and Turkish Cypriot states. These states are to be joined together by a minimal federal government apparatus, resembling the Swiss confederation model. From a Turkish point of view, the plan sufficiently assures bizonality and political equality, the respect of ethnic diversity and human rights, and the existence of an independent sovereign state with a single international personality (Sözen 2005: 69, 70).

10 It is, in Turkish terms, 'the Greek Cypriot administration', which is the only entity on the island recognized by the EU as representative of the whole island.

11 The declaration states that 'The Republic of Cyprus referred to in the Protocol is not the original Partnership State established in 1960. Turkey will continue to regard the Greek Cypriot authorities as exercising authority, control and jurisdiction only in the territory south of the buffer zone, not representing the Turkish Cypriot people, and Turkey will treat the acts performed by them accordingly. The signature, ratification and implementation of this Protocol did not amount to any form of recognition of the Republic of Cyprus referred to in the Protocol; nor prejudice Turkey's rights and obligations emanating from the Treaty of Guarantee, the Treaty of Alliance, and the Treaty of Establishment of 1960. Turkey's existing relationship with the Turkish Republic of Northern Cyprus will remain unchanged' (Seyrek 2005: 117).

12 For the counter-declaration of the EU on 21 September 2005 please see www.eu-un.europa.eu/articles/en/article_5045_en.htm.

13 For details regarding the action plan, see the press statement by the then Turkish foreign minister at http:www.mfa.gov.tr/new-initiative-by-turkey-on-cyprus.en.mfa.

14 Eight negotiation chapters: free movement of goods, right of establishment and freedom to provide services, financial services, agriculture and rural development, fisheries, transport policy, customs union and external relations.

15 For these conclusions see Council of the European Union (2006: 8–9).

16 These six chapters are freedom of movement for workers; energy; judiciary and fundamental rights; justice, freedom and security; education and culture; foreign, security and defence policy.

17 For the text of the joint declaration, see Cyprus Mail (2014).

18 The 1959 Zurich and 1960 London treaties provided Turkey, Greece and the UK with rights of guarantorship over Cyprus for maintaining its independence, territorial integrity and security. While, the Greek side demands the removal of any rights of guarantorship since it thinks guarantees are unnecessary in an EU member state, the Turkish side desires to keep Turkey's protection.

19 The Independent Commission on Turkey (ICT) is a group of distinguished European policymakers who have formed an independent commission to examine the challenges and opportunities presented by Turkey's possible membership in the European Union. The Commission is made up of former heads of state and government, foreign ministers and European commissioners, and other Europeans who have previously held high positions in public office.

6 The EU's integration capacity

An escape clause for the EU or the actual impediment to Turkey's accession?

The prospect of Turkey's EU membership has been a controversial issue among the EU elite and public opinion alike, with important repercussions for the enlargement and ultimate borders of the Union. In a way it could be compared to the British accession to the EU, which had been delayed due to the unilateral French veto exercised twice by President Charles de Gaulle. Despite many differences between the two countries, it may still be deduced that accession of a relatively large country with a distinctive international identity may be quite difficult since it may cause uneasiness in some member states regarding the effects on the balance of power and influence in the Union. Turkey's relations with the EU go back to 1963 and for over 50 years it could not be crowned with membership. Opposition to Turkey's accession to the EU can be seen both at the elite and public opinion levels in EU member states. According to Eurobarometer data, support of Turkey's EU membership among member states varied between 28 and 31 per cent between 2005 and 2010, while opposition was higher, between 55 and 59 per cent, during the same period. While Turkey is depicted as the candidate state least supported by EU citizens, new member states are generally more supportive of Turkey's EU accession and countries with sizeable Turkish populations tended to oppose Turkey's accession to the EU at a higher rate than others (Dagdeverenis 2014: 7).

While some member states, such as Austria, Germany and France, are generally known to have a sceptical attitude towards Turkey, political party families, such as the Christian democrats, tend to object to Turkey's membership in the EU on cultural and religious grounds. Recently we have witnessed changes in some prominent member states' preferences regarding Turkey's accession to the EU: in Germany, while the Schröder government had been pro-Turkish membership based on the fulfilment of accession criteria, its successor government under Angela Merkel adopted a policy of privileged partnership. In France, the same happened in reverse order – that is while the incumbent government under President Hollande did not outright reject Turkey's suitability for EU membership, the previous administration under President Sarkozy vocally questioned Turkey's European vocation.

The issue of Turkey's probable membership in the EU has been a prominent topic during the campaigns before the British referendum on EU membership. While the 'Leave' campaigners manipulated the issue by posing Turkey's membership as a threat, stating 'Turkey with a population of 76 million is joining the EU,' Prime Minister Cameron tried to assure the electorate that this would not take place at least until 3000 (Parker 2016), while the influential newspaper *Financial Times* in its editorial column allayed fears about Turkey's entry into the EU in the following words: 'Turkey has as much chance of joining the EU as Istanbul being renamed Constantinople' (Financial Times 2016). This rhetoric created a real confusion since Britain had been one of the few supporters of Turkey's EU membership. Following the coup attempt in Turkey and the declaration of a state of emergency, criticisms about Turkey's suitability as a candidate country intensified. Austrian prime minister Christian Kern suggested ending Turkey's accession talks (Reuters 2016), while a member of the CDU in Germany, Roderich Kiesewetter, said that the aim of Turkey's EU negotiations is not accession but to prevent Turkey from allying with Russia and China (n-tv 2016).

The instability in Turkey, deterioration in rule of law and human rights and the recent crisis following the coup attempt all led to a further decline in Turkey's image in the EU as a suitable candidate country. Moreover, in and of itself the EU public opinion has grown more sceptical of EU enlargement and European integration in general. The increasing refugee flows and the deal reached with Turkey to stem irregular migration have been widely criticized as a concession to the Turkish government and Erdoğan despite Turkey's intransigence in fulfilling EU political conditions. The increasing support for populist parties and leaders in the EU has testified to the strengthening of xenophobic and ultra-right-wing tendencies among the EU public. Under these conditions, it became more difficult for EU leaders to support Turkey's EU accession and for Turkey to convince Europeans that its accession would be a good thing for the EU. The already distinct and differentiating traits Turkey had vis-à-vis other European countries have been even more noticeable in the recent period as Erdoğan's Turkey began to be portrayed more and more as an authoritarian and anti-Western country in the media and political discourse. Although problems in Turkey regarding respect for basic freedoms and rights may have justified the 'othering' of Turkey, a constant vilification of Turkey, which also had condescending tones, did not help with the EU's approach towards Turkey, in the sense of developing a coherent, consistent and realistic policy. When taken into account together with the stalemate in the accession negotiations, growing opposition to Turkey's membership and the consecutive crises the EU faced, the EU anchor began to lose its power to instigate change and reforms in Turkey. This pitfall in the EU's approach to Turkey led it to overlook Turkey's importance as an emerging economy and regional player as well as its undeniable vocation in Europe and waste an important opportunity to extend the European zone of freedom, rights and prosperity to include Turkey.

Opposition to Turkey's EU membership may be related to complex and multifaceted root causes emanating from objective factors regarding Turkey and perceptions about Turkey, as well as conceptions about the EU and Europe in general. Since opposition to Turkey's EU membership is closely related to debates about Turkey's Europeanness, one's view of Turkey's place in Europe is mutually constitutive of conceptions about Europe and the current integration project. As a country lying on the outskirts of the continent and forming a barrier or bridge to other continents, Turkey is often depicted as the other of Europe. Agreeing to integrate such a country as a full member into the Union would entail a much different versatile understanding of what Europe means and where its borders lie. Simply put, support for Turkey's EU membership – on the condition that it fulfils the Copenhagen criteria – would coincide with an understanding of Europe as an open space having the possibility of regenerating itself, based on common ideals of human rights and democracy, while opposition to Turkey's membership on grounds of culture and religion would mean an understanding of Europe as a civilizational entity specified by common cultural and religious roots. At a technical level, considerations about a probable Turkish membership in the EU are closely intertwined with ideas about the future path of European integration. It may be assumed in this respect that those propagating a deeper Union – that is federalists – would be apprehensive about Turkey's accession due to its propensity to slow down further integration, while those for a looser form of Union – that is intergovernmentalists – would most probably also view Turkey's membership as a factor that would work in their favour.

This chapter aims to dwell on the various assessments about Turkey's probable membership in the EU by linking them with the question of the 'integration / absorption capacity' of the Union. Thus the chapter aims to decipher how decision makers and governments view Turkey's accession from the viewpoint of the EU. Integration capacity is a useful concept which sums up the whole range of considerations about Turkey's EU membership and depictions about the impact a probable Turkish entry would have on the EU and its member states. Although this concept is a general term that is applied to the enlargement policy of the EU and thereby involves all candidate countries, the case of Turkey is particularly striking from the perspective of debates about integration capacity. Several aspects regarding Turkey set the country apart from all the other present candidates to join the EU. These aspects, such as impact of Turkey's membership on the institutional balances in the EU, cultural and religious differences, Turkey's geopolitical neighbourhood, level of socio-economic development in the country and potential burden on the EU budget, imbalances between Turkey's regions, and speculations about migratory movements from Turkey, all form the substance of evaluations about the EU's integration capacity regarding Turkey. These issues will be discussed in the chapter in connection with their relation to evaluations of the EU's capacity to absorb Turkey after taking a look at the trajectory of the concept of absorption/integration capacity.

EU enlargement debates and integration/absorption capacity

The integration/absorption capacity of the EU entered into the vocabulary of the EU institutions in the 1990s together with the far-reaching eastern enlargement process. The European Council in Copenhagen in 1993 explicitly mentioned the absorption capacity of the EU with regard to its enlargement process: 'The Union's capacity to absorb new members, while maintaining the momentum of

European integration, is an important consideration in the general interest of both the Union and the candidate countries' (European Council 1993: 13). Although the term's usage is more recent, considerations regarding the effects of accepting new members on the state of the integration process go back much earlier to the first enlargement of the Communities. French president Charles de Gaulle's words regarding the British membership in the EEC in 1963 could be taken as a concern about Britain's compatibility with the existing member states of the Community and hence an early consideration of integration capacity on both sides (Giauque 2002: 185):

> England in effect is insular, she is maritime, she is linked through her exchanges, her markets, her supply lines to the most diverse and often the most distant countries . . . [T]he question . . . [is] whether Great Britain can now place herself like the Continent and with it inside a tariff which is genuinely common, to renounce all Commonwealth preferences, to cease any pretence that her agriculture be privileged, and, more than that, to treat her engagements with other countries of the free trade area as null and void – that question is the whole question.

Considerations about Greece's application to the EC of the time were also closely related with the probable impact such accession would have on the EU. Hence, the Commission's opinion on Greece's application to the EC included a statement to that effect, without naming it as 'integration/absorption capacity': 'A quite different issue raised by the prospect of Greek membership is that implied by any enlargement of the Community, namely its effect on the working methods and the future development of the Community' (EC Commission 1976: 4).

A new member state, especially a large, poor or diverse one, incorporated the potential risk of disrupting the balances of the EU and led to adjustment pressures on the common policies and institutional mechanisms. Such concerns were exacerbated with the big bang enlargement of 2004 and 2007 since it pertained to the accession of 10+2 states, most of which quite recently made a transition from socialism to liberalism. In the case of eastern enlargement, the Union devised a well-tailored enlargement strategy, including extensive assistance and monitoring on the part of the EU, with a view to preparing the countries for accession. The reference to the absorption capacity of the Union in Copenhagen could be evaluated as an additional condition of membership to the famous 'Copenhagen criteria'.

The debates surrounding the Constitutional Treaty and the ensuing rejection in the French and Dutch referenda heightened the sense of apprehension about further enlargement of the EU. The conclusions of the June 2006 European Council devoted a quite long section to this concept and noted the importance of making sure that 'in future the Union is able to function politically, financially and institutionally as it enlarges, and to further deepen Europe's common project'. A 'special report on the EU's capacity to integrate new members' embodied an approach to enlargement that was outlined as 'ensuring that Union can maintain and deepen its own development, in terms of policies and institutions, while pursuing an enlargement agenda' (European Commission 2006a: 17). The report noted that absorption/integration capacity is a 'functional concept' since it is related to the capacity of the EU to 'take in new members at a given moment or in a given period, without jeopardizing the political and policy objectives established by the Treaties' (European Commission 2006b: 17). The report also added that the Commission was to prepare an assessment of an applicant country's potential impact on EU institutions and policies upon receiving an application of membership as it did with regard to Turkey's accession and also in the Agenda 2000 document.

Until the end of the Cold War, the EC enlarged with six new member states over a period of 31 years. In the period since 1989, it enlarged with 16 countries over a period of 26 years. Thus the enlargement process in the recent era involves a much larger number of countries over a shorter period. In addition to that, the accession of Central and Eastern European countries that just recently came out of socialist regimes with little experience in democracy and market economy proved to be a major challenge to the EU. The EU instigated a pre-accession process in which to prepare these countries and also other applicants for the process of integration with EU norms and standards. The pre-accession strategy may be seen as one way to make sure that newly acceding countries will not exceed the EU's integration capacity and that the EU institutions and policies will continue to function effectively. But despite all the precautions, it is no secret that the EU's cohesiveness and integrity have been strained in a Union of 28 member states with cultural, economic and social differences. Hence, one can deduce that especially after the difficulties involved in the 2007 enlargement with regard to the management of EU funds and alignment to EU norms in terms of good governance and rule of law, the EU now approaches new candidates very cautiously and thinks twice before accepting a new member state. The challenge is all the more prevalent when the candidate country is a populous, middle-income, developing country in a difficult part of the world, such as Turkey.

The EU's integration capacity and Turkey

Though the EEC of the time was quite receptive to signing an association with Turkey in 1963, Turkey's integration as a member state was a different issue. In response to Turkey's application for membership in the EC in 1987, the Commission noted in its opinion that accepting a new member state was not contemplated until 1993. The EC's priority at the time was implementing the provisions of the Single European Act and achieving the single European market by the 1992 deadline. Any enlargement, let alone with Turkey, would constitute a serious risk to the deepening of European integration and effective functioning of the EC. In this understanding a deepening EC would have to think twice before accepting a new member state due to the potential effects on its integration process and the difficulties a newcomer might have since membership involves greater responsibilities (EC Commission 1989: 1):

> The implications of any position the Community adopts concerning a further enlargement of the Community of Twelve will be greater than those of the positions adopted with regard to previous applications for accession, on

> account both of the new ambitions of European integration resulting from the Single Act and of the increased rights and obligations which now apply to the status of Member State.

According to the Commission, 'the question will be whether the Community can adapt its institutional operation in such a way as to enable it to welcome within its fold new members without running the risk of weakening its management and decision-making capacity' (EC Commission 1989: 3). The Commission also noted the special difficulty Turkey's integration would pose owing to the country's high level of population and low level of development. Evaluating Turkey's condition, the Commission concluded that the economic and political situation in the country was not adequate for adjustment to the EC in the medium term (EC Commission 1989: 4).

When the Union unanimously agreed to open accession negotiations with Turkey in 2004, similar considerations about Turkey's suitability for membership and the EU's capability to integrate Turkey as a member were discussed at both the EU and member state levels. The Commission prepared a report on Turkey's likely impact on the Union, accompanying its recommendation to start accession negotiations with the country. Titled as 'Issues Arising from Turkey's Membership Perspective', the report analysed the probable effects of Turkey's accession to the EU regarding the geopolitical, economic, trade, regional, institutional, sectoral and free movement dimensions. In the introduction to the report, the Commission noted that the topics examined were pertinent to the 1993 Copenhagen European Council's emphasis on the 'capacity of the EU to absorb new members' (European Commission 2004b: 3). Faced with multiple challenges to Turkey's membership prospect among the member states and political groups, the Commission saw the need to prepare such a report that would evaluate the impact of a possible Turkish membership in the EU. Since most of the issues that are proposed to justify Turkey's exclusion from the Union are based on general statements that are not always supported by factual evidence, more detailed research on these considerations about Turkey's membership perspective was most appropriate.

The Commission noted in its report that whether Turkey would actually become a member of the Union depended on various factors, such as the evolution of the EU itself and changes in Turkey and in the international context. Thus the report did not embody a definitive tone with regards to eventual membership of Turkey but discussed the relevant issues based on the present reality. The Commission outlined the unique nature of Turkey's bid to join the EU: 'Turkey's accession would be different from previous enlargements because of the combined impact of Turkey's population, size, geographical location, economic, security and military potential, as well as cultural and religious characteristics' (European Commission 2004b: 4). The report considered the impact all these different factors would have on the EU, ranging from the size of the Turkish economy, proximity to regions such as the Middle East and Caucasus, democracy, regional economic disparities, the high number of Turks living in the EU and the extra-migratory pressure with membership, management of external borders, energy routes, adaptation of Turkish agriculture and representation in EU institutions. After discussing these possible effects in detail under separate headings, the report concluded that Turkey's membership was likely to make a significant impact on the EU and its institutions. However, the financial cost of integrating Turkey could not be calculated beforehand and it would be up to the member states of the EU to decide on Turkey's membership based on what they 'are prepared to accept' (European Commission 2004b: 48). Turkey's membership, according to this view, is not a settled issue but will be finalized along the way, depending on how the negotiations unravel and how the determining factors evolve in the meantime. The Commission, as is appropriate, left the political decision of whether to accept Turkey's bid for membership to the Council representing the member states. The account in the report amounts to a recognition of the political nature of the enlargement process – that is that it is not only a matter of technical calculation whether a candidate country complies with the membership criteria but also very much determined by the interests and approaches of the political actors on both sides.

The Negotiating Framework Document also underlined the importance of integration capacity in the case of Turkey's probable accession to the EU: 'Every effort should be made to protect the cohesion and effectiveness of the Union' (European Commission 2005b: 1). The Commission was assigned the task of monitoring whether this condition was met during the negotiation process – that is to warn the Council when and if the impact of Turkey's accession to the EU became so disturbing that it would damage the institutional balance and operation of the Union. Thus from the start of negotiations, Turkey's size, geographic location, culture and economic condition created question marks in the minds of EU decision makers who were anxious that Turkey's entry could seriously disturb the balance and integrity of the EU.

Turkey's integration into the EU presents some dilemmas and second thoughts for the EU.

Culture and identity

Some of the first considerations that come to mind when considering the issue of the integration capacity of the EU in terms of Turkey's membership are identity and culture. Does Turkey belong in Europe? Is Turkey fit to become a member of the EU in terms of having European traits and values? Will Turkey's membership in the EU dilute the European nature of this project? Despite the fact that Turkey's formal application to become a member of the EU in 1987 was accepted by the Council and Turkey was regarded as a country that is eligible but not yet ready to become a member of the EU, the question of Europeanness is still a point of contention. This situation is tied to two important factors: first that Europeanness is a constantly shifting and changing phenomenon which acquired a renewed relevance in the aftermath of the Cold War (Delanty 1995), and second the evolution and deepening of European integration and the growing importance attached to a common identity.

Turkey's Europeanness was actually celebrated by the then president of the European Commission, Walter Hallstein, in 1963 when he declared that 'Turkey is a part of Europe' during the signing ceremony of the Ankara Agreement (Rehn 2008). Three decades later, Europe and European were defined differently under the light of contemporary developments and necessities of the integration process. The ending of the Cold War and eastern enlargement led to a reconsideration of Europe's borders and a re-evaluation of what constitutes Europe and separates it from other geographies owing to the fluidity of borders in the east and south-east. The issue of borders was closely related to debates about European identity since how the 'other' was to be defined constituted the demarcations of one's idea of self. In this sense, a common European identity could be defined with reference to commonalities that differentiate Europeans from the 'other'. The changing borders of Europe also led to a reconsideration of what Europe means and what brings together Europeans – that is a common past, common belief, common values and so forth. Europe could mean many things. According to Diez, EU Europe meant an othering of a past of wars and enmities between European peoples (Diez 2004). Derrida and Habermas viewed it as a specific political and cultural construct marked by respect for international order and based on the Kantian tradition of perpetual peace (Habermas and Derrida 2003), while others saw Europe mostly based on a more essentialist viewpoint. In all these denominations, there lay a latent other, whether it be Islam, Asians, state of war, autocracy or American type of market capitalism, and international unilateralism.

While debates on European identity intensified in the post-1989 era, Turkey also became a relevant issue in such considerations. That Turkey as a country in the south-east of Europe was regarded as European as may be evidenced in the acceptance of its application for EC membership in 1987. Yet there was also a vagueness, what may be defined as 'liminality', in its identification as part of Europe. Its geography, culture, religion, politics and level of development were among the considerations that resulted in 'contested Europeanness'. For Europeans Turkey's membership in the common European space could mean more difference than what could be tolerated in terms of values, lifestyle and world view.

One of the most apparent oppositions to Turkey's EU bid on the grounds of identity came from the Christian Democratic Parties of the EU in 1997; speaking on behalf of the European People's Party, Wilfred Martens, former prime minister of Belgium, said that the EU is a civilization project and Turkey has no place in it' (Economist 1997; Dahlman 2004). Another important politician who voiced his antagonism to Turkey's EU membership was Valerie Giscard d'Estaing, former president of France and president of the European Convention, in charge of drafting the Constitution of Europe. Giscard d'Estaing noted in an interview that Turkey is not European and that its membership would be 'the end of Europe' (BBC 2002). What he was referring to could be inferred as a conviction that the EU does not have the capacity to integrate Turkey for the reason that Turkey is not and will never be part of Europe. Another veteran European politician, this time from the left of the political spectrum, Helmut Schmidt, also voiced his concerns over Turkey's EU bid and said that Turkey should never be allowed to become a member of the EU. He was reported as saying that due to predominant religion in the country Turkey is part of Asia rather than Europe and that it should not be allowed into the EU because of the size of its population (Bağcı 2000). In another panel he is quoted as underlining the importance of the Enlightenment for Europe and saying that 'the Enlightenment has never reached Turkey and will never reach Turkey' (Hürriyet Daily News 2001).

Angela Merkel is one of the most prominent figures in Europe who voices her idea of proposing a privileged partnership to Turkey rather than membership. In an article she wrote in 2004, she based her argument on a lack of compatibility with regard to values. According to her, the EU is 'based on a value system that has historical roots' (Kylstad 2010: 5). Apparently, fulfilling the Copenhagen criteria would not be sufficient in the case of Turkey since there is no way that history may be rewritten, and thus Turkey does not share these common values that Europe shares in its history (Kylstad 2010: 4–5).

Whether the EU possesses the capacity to integrate Turkey in terms of culture and identity is a debate that is likely to continue. Being the candidate country the accession of which is least supported by the European public, it is to be expected that Turkey's membership will be linked to debates about identification with European culture. Despite the fact that many EU countries host sizeable Muslim populations, the entry of a 77-million-person country with a predominantly Muslim population raises eyebrows in terms of compatibility with EU culture and values. It may be the existence of Turkish and/or Muslim populations in countries such as France and Germany that is exacerbating doubts about Turkey due to problems of integration and perceptions of a misfit between Islam and European culture. According to Moisi, 'for the average Frenchman a Turk is an Arab,' and is associated with difficulties in integrating Muslim immigrants in the country (Barysch 2007: 4). In the depictions about Turkey in the media, those aspects that are striking and different are mostly highlighted. According to a journalist, 'In the newspapers, a "secular state with a predominantly Muslim population" gets edited down to "a Muslim country" ' (Barysch 2007: 1), stressing difference from other European countries.

Turkey's continuity with the Ottoman era and link with Ottoman conquests in Europe came to be voiced more often in the European public space in terms of portraying Turkey's bid to join the EU as a threat to European integrity. A member of the European Commission expressed his concerns in this regard by linking Turkey's EU membership to the siege of Vienna and remarked that if Turkey joins the EU, then 'the defeat of Turks in Vienna more than 300 years ago could turn out to have been in vain' (Gow and MacAskill 2004). References to a past of enmity rather than alliances and cooperation were a mechanism of othering. While the wars and enmity between the members of the EU were now diminishing in importance and lines of demarcation were becoming more fluid, differences and antagonism were being exacerbated when it comes to Turkey. Referring to historical phases, it was also another point of difference that Turkey did not go through the specific periods of history that Europe experienced, such as Renaissance and

Enlightenment (Merkel 2004, cited in İnal and Yeğenoğlu 2005). In this way, a specific essentialist approach to history was also being used in deciding about Turkey's place in Europe.

Former president of the Commission Jose Manuel Barroso expressed the open-ended nature of Turkey's EU accession in his address on the formal start of negotiations: 'Of course the road towards Turkey's accession will be long and difficult. Accession, as for every country, is neither guaranteed nor automatic.' He also made a connection with the lack of knowledge or misinformation about Turkey in the European public and drew attention to the need for Turkey to make itself more known and appealing to the EU citizens: 'Europe must learn more about Turkey. And Turkey must win the hearts and minds of European citizens. They are the ones who at the end of the day will decide about Turkey's membership' (European Commission 2005a).

Impact on the EU in terms of institutions

Another consideration linked with the integration capacity of the Union is the issue of institutional representation. The level of representation in the EU institutions was a major issue of controversy before the 2004 enlargement and could be arranged only with the Treaty of Nice that entered into force on 1 February 2003. Although most of the acceding countries had quite small populations other than Poland and Romania,[1] the entry of 10+2 countries was bound to have a significant effect on the institutional balances and decision-making mechanisms in the EU. With the accession of a country with 77 million inhabitants, the issue of institutional representation is to acquire an even greater salience. One of the overriding concerns is that Turkey will have an important bearing on the decision-making process especially in the Council and have a dominating presence in the parliament with at least an equal number of MEPs as to those coming from Germany. As transmitted by the European affairs editor of Reuters, a German politician replied, '100 MEPs' when he was asked why he opposed Turkey's membership in the EU (Barysch 2007: 4). The population weight will undoubtedly reflect Turkey's influence in the overall governance structure. This will both provide for the entry of an important player into the balance of power among the member states and challenge the present influence of leading countries in the EU.

If we simulate Turkey's representation in EU institutions based on the present rules of representation in accordance with the Treaty of Lisbon, Turkey would impact on the voting mechanism, representing about 13.26 per cent of the EU population,[2] hence constituting an important share in the 55 per cent voting majority and/or blocking minority, as well as in the 65 per cent of EU population criteria.[3] Similarly, Turkey would elect at least 96 representatives to sit in the European Parliament, based on the present representation of MEPs from Germany. The same simulation could be conducted for the other institutions, such as the Economic and Social Committee and Committee of the Regions.

While institutional representation is negotiated right before the accession of a new member, Turkey's representation would anyhow be quite substantial in case of membership, based on the present logic of proportionality. This would make it more challenging for present member states of the EU to accept Turkey's membership, especially the larger ones, which would see it as more of a threat to their established positions. Hence, the integration capacity argument would also include such a consideration based on the difficulty of absorbing a large country as a member state of the EU.

Alternatively, while larger member states may see Turkey as a contender for their power in the EU, medium-sized or smaller member states may see Turkey as a 'balancer' against the overbearing influence of larger member states and as a potential ally in triggering a change in decision-making in the desired direction. Thus, Turkey's potential entry into the EU may be viewed differently by the present member states depending on their ideas about power and influence in the institutional mechanism. For example, it has been stated that one of the reasons why Spain supports Turkey's accession to the EU is related to 'its possible contribution to the strengthening of the Mediterranean axis' in the Union (Soler i Lecha and Garcia 2010: 58–9).

A second factor that may influence member states' calculations about Turkey's influence on institutions and decision-making would be their expectations about Turkey's approach to integration. Is Turkey expected to be a member state that is pro-integration or a Eurosceptic country not keen on sharing its sovereignty (Müftüler Baç 2004: 33)? Based on the present situation, it would appear that Turkey would be included in the second category – that is more like the United Kingdom than Germany in its support for an integrated Europe. France, a forerunner of European integration, would not really like to see another large member state with Eurosceptic tendencies in the EU. However, it should be taken into consideration that Turkey will not become a member of the EU in its present state but would need to go through considerable transformation that might also influence its approach to Europe and idea of European integration.

Finally, a third factor which may impact on the potential influence of Turkish membership on the EU's institutional structure would be the political ideologies of ruling parties in the member states. Two typical cases have been observed in Germany and France. The positive approach of the Red-Green coalition under Gerhard Schröder in Germany towards Turkey's EU accession was replaced with a preference for a privileged partnership under the Christian Democrat chancellor Merkel. Similarly, President Hollande in France showed a more lenient approach to Turkey's EU membership, lifting the veto on regional policy and structural funds chapter in Turkey's negotiations. An ideological outlook about what kind of an EU a politician or government wants to materialize would also influence evaluations of Turkey's EU membership.

Economic and budgetary implications for the EU

Turkey, a middle-income country with regional imbalances and development problems, has been regarded by many in the EU as a potential burden on the budgetary resources. Especially for countries which are net contributors to the

EU budget, Turkey is usually evaluated as a country that would receive more than it contributed to the budget. For other countries that are net receivers, Turkey would be regarded as a competitor for funds. Going back to the discussions about the reallocation of budgetary funds prior to the eastern enlargement of the EU and how several member states and regions no longer qualified for funding after the entry of less well-off members to the EU, the potential membership of a sizeable country like Turkey would surely create more controversy. It would also be regarded as one of the foremost considerations in the integration capacity debate. Turkey's size, overall level of development and regional problems have been mostly evaluated as barriers against its membership in the EU.

Despite being a middle-income country whose GDP per capita equals 53 per cent of the EU average, Turkey surpasses that of Bulgaria and is equal to that of Romania, both current member states (Eurostat 2015a). Still, it can be predicted that Turkey's lesser-developed regions would qualify for substantial sums of EU funding under the structural funds, thus lowering the levels of assistance to existing member states (Oskam 2005). Based on the present principles, Turkey's regions would qualify for funding from the budget, since 70 per cent of these funds are allocated to regions with a per capita GDP lower than 75 per cent of the EU average (European Commission 2014b). As in the case of institutional representation, budgetary allocations would have to be redefined and a phasing-in mechanism applied pending Turkey's probable accession to the EU.

Turkey's agriculture would also need support under the EU funds to be able to be integrated into the Common Agricultural Policy. Turkish agriculture displays some misgivings in terms of adaptability to EU agriculture, such as low productivity, small size of farms, fragmented nature of agricultural land, insufficiencies in irrigation, persisting plant diseases and lack of coherence of agricultural statistics (Eraktan 2013; Kilit 2014: 1). Thus the costs of adaptation to EU standards and the support of agriculture once Turkey becomes a member of the EU are expected to place a substantial burden on the EU budget.

According to a study conducted by Derviş et al., potential transfers from the EU budget to Turkey will be an important factor that will have a decisive impact on Turkey's membership in the EU. While Turkey most probably would be ready to accept transition periods until it fully qualifies for transfers under the EU budget as was the case in previous enlargements, the fact that it would nevertheless receive a large portion of EU funds could affect the approach to its accession prospects. Moreover, fairness of budgetary allocations in comparison with present member states, especially those that recently acceded to the EU, would be a major concern for Turkey (Derviş et al. 2004: 1). The study aimed to find out the net contribution/allocation under the EU budget were it a current member of the EU – that is in 2004 – and calculated that it would receive a net sum of €16 billion. The study also forecasted that Turkey's net benefit from the budget in an enlarged Union in 2015 would amount to 0.20 per cent of EU GDP (Derviş et al. 2004: 4). If we take the figure for the EU total GDP in 2014, which is €13.92 trillion, this would mean that Turkey would receive nearly €28 billion after the ending of the transition period. According to a study by Harry Flam, based on the current rules, Turkey would receive a net transfer of €12 billion from the EU budget (Flam 2005: 349). However, any simulation regarding Turkey's net benefit from the EU budget runs the risk of being erroneous since budgetary rules will certainly be renegotiated before Turkey's entry into the EU. In the meantime, the two most important items in the EU budget, agriculture and structural funds, are frequently being reformed, making any forecast no longer tenable.

Regarded from a different perspective, Turkey as a fast-growing country which is among the 20 leading economies of the world could also contribute to the EU's economic dynamism and growth. It could contribute to the industrial potential of the EU, act to bring dynamism with its leading sectors, such as automotive, tourism, and construction, and act as a hub for channelling European business and investment in third markets in its vicinity. Thus what can be regarded as a burden on the budget could work in the other direction as a contributor to EU growth and prosperity.

Foreign policy and security implications

Turkey provides for a critical case of enlargement from the foreign policy and security viewpoint as well. Its geographical location near non-democratic and unstable regions is depicted as threatening for European security, and Turkey's membership is regarded as carrying the EU border to such unstable geographies. The European Commission assessed this situation as follows: 'Turkey's accession would extend the EU's borders to countries which are presently a source of tensions, and bring problems of the region higher onto the agenda of the EU's external relations' (EC Commission 2004: 7). Turkey, a NATO member and staunch frontline state for European security during the Cold War, was now evaluated as a security- consumer rather than a security-provider in the post–Cold War era (Üstün 2010: 169).

Viewed from a different perspective, Turkey continues to maintain its critical role for European security. Much of the EU's security problems, from control of weapons of mass destruction and fight against terrorism to control of irregular migration, could not be handled without the effective participation of Turkey. Turkey could and does contribute with its military assets as well as its diplomatic and peace-building initiatives to CSDP missions and operations. More importantly, Turkey's location and state identity are particularly critical for Europe since Turkey is situated as a bulwark against any threats that may emanate from instability, radicalism and authoritarianism in the Middle East and the Mediterranean region. Turkey's participation in EU operations and cooperation within the framework of high-level foreign policy dialogue are signs that European security would benefit to a great extent from Turkey's contributions. In the first report prepared by the Independent Commission on Turkey, the authors noted the positive contribution Turkey's accession would have on 'stronger EU policies on the South' and argued against the view that Turkey's membership would drag the EU into the problems of the Middle East. The report contended that 'Turkey, with its pivotal position at the heart of the Eurasian region and as a Western pillar of the wider Middle

East, can be of indisputable benefit to European action in this area.' Turkey is also evaluated as a valuable contributor to the European Security and Defense Policy due to its location and military capacity (Independent Commission on Turkey 2004: 18).

Turkey's geographic location in the intersection of continents, regions and cultures is a source of both strength and vulnerability. It may contribute to an active engagement in adjacent regions and benefit the country in terms of political clout, economic prosperity and cultural influence. At the same time, it may expose the country to multiple risks and threats and pose the challenge of achieving a balance between the needs and priorities for each region. Turkish foreign policy displays a duality in terms of its Western and Eastern dimension and it is 'the story of succeeding and failing to find and make use of a balance between the two' (Yavuz 2004: 236). The changing security threats after the ending of the Cold War, such as terrorism, weapons of mass destruction, state failure, radicalization, security of supplies, and irregular migration, led to the emergence of new challenges for Turkey emanating from the south and east of its borders. Since these new threats also imperilled security and stability in the European area, the EU viewed Turkey as a valuable partner and ally, as well as a country that could act as a forward station and/or a buffer zone which would insulate Europe against the spread of such threats. In this conception, Turkey should be kept at arm's length in extensive cooperation and collaboration with the EU. However, it should not be given full membership since such an occurrence would carry the borders of Europe further east into the conflict-prone regions.

Especially the increasing instability, geopolitical shifts and conflict in the aftermath of the Arab spring exacerbated this approach towards Turkey. The prolongation of the Syrian civil war fuelled terrorism and radical groups, such as ISIS, and led to an unprecedented exodus of people from the region amounting to more than 4 million refugees fleeing to neighbouring countries and to Europe via Turkey. Thus Turkey became even more critical for the EU for containing the flow of refugees and migrants and preventing the threat of terror reaching European capitals. In 2015 the foreign fighters problem became a controversial issue between several EU countries, such as Britain, France and Germany, and Turkey regarding which effective cooperation, especially in the area of policing and intelligence gathering, was needed.

In the geopolitical risk environment that is proving more testing for European security each day, Turkey's own struggle with democracy, slowdown of reforms, Kurdish problem, foreign policy disputes and growing polarization in the country make it a less than appealing candidate for EU membership. Turkey's growing involvement in Syria and Iraq and allegations of support to radical groups, such as ISIS, also raise eyebrows concerning Turkey's potential contribution to European security and defence. The decreasing level of alignment with EU declarations in the area of foreign and security policy is also criticized by the EU, as most prominently displayed in Turkey's lack of alignment with the EU's decision to apply sanctions to Russia following the Ukrainian crisis.

Turkey's impact on the foreign policy and security dimension of European integration constitutes one of the critical factors constituting the integration capacity of the EU. Turkey's geopolitical position, its involvement in the Middle Eastern conflicts and its own security problems may prove to be challenging for the EU to take in. Hence it may be rational for EU decision makers to prefer some sort of an enhanced dialogue with Turkey in this area as an important partner rather than a member state. Whether this is a plausible policy option for Turkey is another question. The Independent Commission on Turkey in its 2014 report contends that foreign policy cooperation with Turkey can be effective only within the scope of a credible membership perspective: 'Without a credible accession process, Turkey will not feel bound to cooperate and align itself with the European Union.' The report recommends the opening of Chapter 31 in Turkey's accession negotiations and notes that only a revitalized accession process can motivate Turkey to comply with EU CFSP statements and work with the EU in pursuit of common aims (Independent Commission on Turkey 2014: 44).

Migration and free movement

Migration and free movement may be considered as one of the primary subjects in considerations of integration capacity when it comes to the case of Turkey. The negotiation framework for Turkey referred to long transition periods, derogations, specific arrangements or permanent safeguard clauses in the case of free movement of persons (European Commission 2005b).

Related to the presence of around 4.6 million Turks living in Western Europe (Ministry of Foreign Affairs 2011), the opening of borders to Turkish citizens is regarded as a process that would trigger further migration from the country. Studies have been conducted on the level of expected migration from Turkey to the EU in the event of Turkey's accession and the results mostly showed that the estimated flow is not as high as expected. The Commission staff working document accompanying the second report on visa liberalization also calmed anxieties about an influx of Turks into the EU once the visa requirement is lifted, owing to an increase in income (European Commission 2016a: 46).

> Turkish citizens are since many years not so inclined to international migration. Although the unemployment rate is slightly above 10% and many Turkish citizens have relatives and friends within the EU and some of them may be tempted to join them with any possible mean (including irregularly), nevertheless the overall level of welfare in the country is no longer as low as it used to be.

The increasing levels of unemployment in several EU member states and stagnation of growth in the aftermath of the global financial crisis would make the EU a less than attractive target for job-seekers who can more easily find jobs in the Turkish labour market due to a higher rate of growth.

Moreover, transit migration through Turkey, which has particularly intensified in recent years, calls into question Turkey's integration into the Schengen Area, which especially under the present circumstances of rising migration to the EU is considered as a major stumbling block on the way to Turkey's accession. Considering transit migration through Turkey, it is a fact that control of irregular migration cannot be handled only by way of strengthened borders but needs a comprehensive approach to the issue, including dealing with the political and economic problems in countries of origin. Although there is a definite need to act in unison with Turkey in its border policies and control of migration, the issue necessitates a much broader focus and international cooperation beyond Turkey and the EU. Nevertheless the refugee deal agreed by the EU and Turkey on 18 March 2016 delivered results in terms of controlling irregular migration through Turkey to Greece on the eastern Mediterranean route. While around 1,740 migrants passed daily from the Turkish coast to the Aegean islands, this number decreased to 47 after 1 May (European Commission 2016b: 2).

While Turkey figured prominently in the EU's strategy of cooperation with transit countries in stemming irregular migration flows, the issue was closely linked to freedom of entry for Turkish citizens to the Schengen Area for short-term stays. The prospect of visa liberalization for Turkish citizens has been on the agenda in Turkey for some time now, linked to cases adjudicated by the European Court of Justice, such as the *Soysal* and *Demirkan* cases regarding the legality of the visa requirement, and more recently the visa liberalization dialogue. The recently started visa liberalization dialogue between Turkey and the EU is based on a roadmap including 72 criteria that need to be fulfilled by Turkey. The dialogue started to function as of the signing of the Turkey–EU Readmission Agreement on 16 December 2013.

Among the criteria, which are divided into four sections, including document security, migration management, public order and security as well as fundamental rights, the implementation of the Readmission Agreement is particularly significant. Targeting Turkey as a major route for migration to the EU, the signing of the agreement was made into a condition to start the visa liberalization dialogue by the EU. The successful implementation of the agreement would necessitate effective coordination with Turkish and EU authorities on the exchange and return of irregular migrants, Turkey's preparation for building the capacity to host migrants, effective protection and monitoring of borders as well as fighting against illegal trafficking networks.

The Commission's third report on progress in the visa liberalization dialogue was announced on 4 May 2016 and recommended the lifting of the visa requirement for Turkish citizens. The Commission made this recommendation based on its expectation that Turkey would complete all of the 72 criteria, 5 of which remained to be fulfilled. One of these five criteria – that is the revision of Turkey's antiterror legislation with a view to narrowing its application – was challenged by the Turkish president and government officials in view of the current fight against PKK in the south-east of the country and several terror attacks by ISID in large cities. Hence, the target date of June 2016 for the lifting of the Schengen visa for Turkish citizens could not be achieved. The impending terror attacks in Belgium,

France and Germany increased the anxiety about security and turned a greater percentage of the population in EU countries against an open policy in migration. This growing scepticism about migration and open borders prevailing in Europe and the manipulation of the issue by populist parties may be a factor which could make it more difficult for the EU to lift visas for Turkish citizens. On the other hand, Turkey made it clear that it would not implement the Turkey–EU Readmission Agreement unless visa liberalization goes through. In an interview he gave to *Le Monde*, President Erdoğan stressed this issue (Ayad 2016):

> The EU does not behave in a sincere way with Turkey. There are currently 3 million refugees in Turkey, and the only concern of EU member states is that those refugees do not reach their territories. The EU suggested that we accept the readmissions (of migrants coming from Turkey) in exchange for visa liberalization for Turkish citizens. The readmission agreement and the visa liberalization were to come into force simultaneously on June 1. It is now August and the visa liberalization is still pending. If our claims are not met, we will have to stop readmissions.

President Erdoğan expresses the dissatisfaction he felt with the EU's handling of the issue and clearly links the readmission process with the fulfilment of the visa liberalization promise. It remains to be seen whether the two sides will come to an agreement and visas will be lifted in the following days.

Faced with increasing tides of migration towards the EU from conflict-ridden regions, it would not be difficult to conclude that migration and free movement will figure prominently in considerations of integration capacity in the years to come. Turkey would clearly pose a difficult case in this regard owing to the size of its population, developing country traits, problems with internal stability and geographical bridge position. Membership with derogations in the case of free movement of persons would not be feasible since free movement is a vital component of the internal market and the Area of Freedom, Security and Justice. Membership without free movement rights would not be acceptable for a country aiming at integration with the EU, a country which already has a customs union with the EU and is about to start negotiations on the modernization and expansion of the customs union to include new sectors, such as services.

A successful conclusion of the visa liberalization process would lift hopes for the future of Turkey–EU relations since it would mean that Turkish nationals travelling in the EU would no longer be regarded as a threat. At the same time, since visa liberalization necessitates the implementation of the Readmission Agreement, it would also mean that several problems related to transit migration would have been solved by then with highly protected borders in the east and south-east of the country, an effective system for managing migration and a working system of cooperation with EU authorities. Still the difficulties in surveillance of the sea borders between Turkey and the EU remind one that control of irregular migration is not such a straightforward issue and whether in or out of the Union would necessitate the EU and Turkey to work in liaison.

Alternatives to membership

The insufficiencies with regard to the capacity of the EU to integrate Turkey are related to the aforementioned factors. On the other side of the equation, Turkey also displayed delays and inconsistencies in terms of adaptation to the EU *acquis* due to the interruption of the negotiations for political reasons, decline in support for EU membership and conflict with political interests, as we have witnessed in the case of public procurement or social policy areas. Leaders of two leading states of the EU, Angela Merkel and Nicholas Sarkozy, have been pioneers of an alternative path for Turkey–EU relations: privileged partnership. The idea was first proposed by the German Christian Democrats in 2004. Karl-Theodor zu Guttenberg, a German politician who later became minister of the economy, prepared a report outlining the contents of this proposal. According to zu Guttenberg, the Turkey–EU customs union would be extended to new areas, such as agriculture and services, institutional cooperation would be enhanced within the framework of the Association Council, and Turkey would be represented in EU institutions as an observer and participate in EU defence, security and foreign policy mechanisms, while also gaining full membership in the decision-making process for these policy areas. Zu Guttenberg drew attention to the risks that would emanate from the collapse of negotiation process and to the need to devise alternative scenarios for the management of Turkey–EU relations (Guttenberg 2005):

> We must have alternative models up our sleeves that would guarantee Turkey the 'strongest possible bond' to the European Union during the negotiating process. If we do not, a failure of the entry negotiations would constitute nothing less than the final rejection of Turkey – the worst case scenario. Options other than full membership for Turkey are of vital strategic necessity for Turkish-European relations – especially now that the entry negotiations have started. The negotiating framework clearly implies scenarios under which Turkey would not actually join the European Union. We need to take the utmost care to avoid the possibility of Europe rebuffing Turkey completely.

A second proposal outlining what is meant by 'privileged partnership' was prepared by the European People's Party in 2005 and included eight points proposing Turkey's participation in trade policy, full judicial cooperation, control of immigration, cooperation in maritime security, development aid, defence, foreign policy and cultural and educational projects (Euractiv 2009). In short, this formula would involve extensive cooperation between the two sides, building on the Association relationship without giving Turkey membership status. Thus the EU side would enjoy benefits from working together with Turkey on issues related to trade, foreign policy, energy and so forth without sharing their decision-making powers with Turkey. For Turkey this formula would be unacceptable since with the customs union based on the Association Agreement Turkey could already be deemed as a partner of the EU and the only meaningful improvement of this relationship would be membership with the rights it would entail.

Other proposals included a gradual integration plan aired by the Party of European Socialists in the European Parliament. This formula would entail Turkey's participation in all EU institutions, and policy debates without the right to vote would help Turkey's alignment with the EU, finally paving the way to its membership. Although different from the privileged partnership proposal in rhetoric, this alternative did not specify the conditions for the final transition to full membership status and thereby effectively foresaw a gradual progression of the Turkey–EU relationship towards a vague target of accession. One important difference would be that gradual integration kept the option of membership alive since Turkey's eligibility for accession according to Article 49 of the TEU was recognized per se (Karakaş 2013: 1069).

Although alternatives to full membership were rejected outright by Turkey, the stagnation of the accession negotiations necessitated alternative ways to manage Turkey–EU relations. During Stefan Füle's term as the commissioner responsible for enlargement and European neighbourhood policy, the 'Positive Agenda' was aired as a new mechanism to provide for a revitalization of Turkey–EU relations. Launched in May 2012, it involved the establishment of working groups on issues of mutual interest, such as judiciary and fundamental rights, energy, foreign policy and counterterrorism, to aid Turkey's alignment with the EU. It was specifically mentioned that the Positive Agenda was not intended to replace the accession process but rather to complement and support it (European Commission 2012b). Unlike initial expectations, the Positive Agenda could not breathe fresh air into the process due to the existence of multiple hurdles which could not be overcome by such a limited endeavour. More recently, the high-level dialogue mechanisms on energy, economics and political dialogue aimed to bring the parties closer with the aim of cooperating for the resolution of common problems. The rift grew between Turkey and the EU as criticism on the part of the EU regarding the situation of rule of law, democracy and human rights in Turkey intensified and resentment and disillusionment with the EU became deeper and more visible in the country.

The most pressing issues in the relations – that is modernization of the customs union and visa and free movement questions – were dealt with under parallel and separate processes. The respective chapters in the negotiations – that is chapters on external relations, judiciary and fundamental rights, and justice, freedom and security – could not be opened to negotiations in the accession process since the first one was blocked by the 2006 decision of the EU Council while the opening of the latter two was vetoed by the Greek Cypriots. Hence the pressing need to arrive at some form of new arrangement in these issue areas brought about the commencement of separate negotiations and agreements. While the Readmission Agreement and visa liberalization dialogue kicked off a process of alignment and reform with respect to migration and borders, problems in the functioning of the Turkey–EU customs union were to be resolved and its remit enlarged to include new sectors in a modernization process, the negotiations for which are expected to begin in 2017 (European Commission 2015d). Intensified cooperation between Turkey and the EU to ease the refugee flows from Syria led to a renewed effort to 're-energize' the relations by the opening of new chapters in the negotiations, holding of regular summits and acceleration of high-level dialogue mechanisms mentioned in the earlier paragraph (European Council 2015).

The stalemate in accession negotiations necessitated the adoption of alternative mechanisms formally intended to complement and aid Turkey's accession to the EU. However, as all the critical issues in Turkey and EU relations are now managed outside the accession framework, negotiations themselves have been stripped of relevance in terms of bringing Turkey closer to the EU. It is also true that the efforts Turkey had already undergone in complying with the visa liberalization requirement and the further alignment to the EU law of the economy, which would be facilitated by the customs union modernization, would aid Turkey's integration into the EU in terms of norms and standards. The final decision about membership will depend on both Turkey's resolve to fulfil the criteria and the EU's will to welcome a disparate country, such as Turkey. Unless these conditions are met and political will materializes on both sides, the separate and specific areas of cooperation and convergence outlined earlier will pave the way for a special kind of relationship between Turkey and the EU short of membership. The Brexit vote to leave the EU also brought about the possibility for Britain to act as a model for countries like Turkey which find it difficult to accede to the Union as a full member due to political and cultural reasons (Nas 2016a).

Notes

1 The lowest population being in Malta with around 425,000 and the highest in Poland with around 38 million inhabitants. See EU Website, EU Member Countries, http://europa.eu/about-eu/countries/member-countries/ (05.11.2015).

2 This is based on a simulation of EU population as the present 28 member states plus Turkey. In such a simulation Germany constitutes 13.85 per cent of EU population, slightly above Turkey's share.

3 See Eur-lex web page for a description of the voting rules at the Council of the EU: http://eur-lex.europa.eu/legal-content/EN/TXT/?uri=uriserv:ai0008 (27.08.2015).

7 Readmission and visa liberalization

Two sides of the same coin?

Visa and readmission emerged as critical and sensitive issues in Turkey–EU relations in the recent period. Turkey signed a Readmission Agreement with the EU on 16 December 2013 and concomitantly started a visa liberalization dialogue. Until then, Turkey's insistence on the lifting of the visa requirement for short-term visits to the EU was met with scepticism on the part of the EU. EU officials mostly regarded Turkey as a potential country of emigration and more importantly as a country of transit migration to the EU. Turkey's liberal visa policy in recent years meant that citizens of countries requiring a visa to travel to the EU could enter Turkey freely and could then seek ways to make a further passage to the EU. The visa requirement was seen as a necessary measure in order to control the movement of people from or via Turkey. On the other hand, the visa requirement for Turkish citizens and the strict procedures for visa application created a sense of frustration, exclusion and discrimination among the Turkish public. Since Turkey was the only candidate country whose citizens required a visa to travel to the EU after December 2009,[1] EU member states' reluctance to lift the visa also fuelled the perception that the EU's policy was unjust and discriminatory, adding to the already existing sense of double standards being applied by the EU towards Turkey. The stalemate in the accession process further intensified the problem, since free movement and migration could not be managed and resolved within the framework of accession negotiations. Chapters of the *acquis* related to migration – that is Chapter 24, on freedom, security and justice – could not be opened to negotiations due to the Greek Cypriot veto.

The priorities of the parties – that is a readmission agreement on the part of the EU and visa liberalization on the part of Turkey – were finally reconciled and a new process started whereby both parties expected to achieve their aims. Turkey and the EU agreed to link the start of visa liberalization process for Turkish citizens to the precondition of the signing of the Readmission Agreement, negotiations for which had commenced in May 2006, broken off in 2006, initialled by the parties on 21 June 2012, finally signed on 16 December 2013 and entered into force on 1 October 2014. In this new phase, effective cooperation and burden-sharing between Turkey and the EU were needed in order to manage irregular migration and to realize visa-free travel for Turkish citizens. Upon implementation, the Readmission Agreement would result in the return of nationals of Turkey and EU member states, and also third-country nationals and stateless persons who have transited through the territories of Turkey or the EU on their migration route and who are illegally residing in Turkey or the EU member states (Zoeteweij-Turhan 2015: 147).

The story of visas for Turkish citizens

Germany became the first EU country stipulating a visa requirement for Turkish citizens on 5 October 1980, followed by France, Belgium, Netherlands and Luxembourg (Groenendijk and Guild 2011: 80). This was a reaction to the military coup d'etat in Turkey and the resulting increase in the number of asylum-seekers to European countries, especially Germany (Groenendijk and Guild 2011: 53). Although several member states had already made bilateral visa abolition agreements with Turkey dating back to the 1950s and were signatories to the 1957 Council of Europe Agreement regulating movement of persons (Groenendijk and Guild 2011: 22–4),[2] European countries adopted a restrictive stance on this issue starting with the 1970s. What was regarded as a transitory arrangement continued to this day, emulated by other Western European countries and the new member states of the EU following their accession to the Union. The visa requirement for short-term stays in EU countries was also integrated into the *acquis communautaire*, with EC Regulation 539/2001, listing Turkey as a country whose citizens require a visa to travel to the EU (Official Journal of the EC 2001b). Turkey had already been on the blacklist of EU member states adopted under intergovernmental cooperation in the ad hoc group on immigration, as early as 1987 (Groenendijk and Guild 2011: 53). Due to the establishment of the Area of Freedom, Security and Justice originating from the Schengen Convention of 1990, the management of borders and the visa issue are no longer in the sole preserve of national governments but constitute an area of shared competence with the EU. Thus even newly acceding states to the EU, such as Croatia, a country which did not require visas from Turkish citizens, adopted the visa requirement right before its entry to the EU in the process of alignment to the EU *acquis*.

Turkey fought for the lifting of the visa requirement, basing its argument on Article 41(1) of the 1970 Additional Protocol. According to this article – that is the standstill clause – Turkey and the then EC were barred from bringing any new restrictions to the freedom of establishment and freedom to provide services between the parties (Official Journal of the EC 1973). Thus if a member state did not implement any visas on Turkish citizens travelling to the EU with the purpose of engaging in services and/or establishment, that member state would not be able to stipulate a visa requirement after the entry into force of the Protocol. For the existing member states this date would be 1973, and for the later-acceding countries, it would be the date of entry into the EU. Eleven EU member states did not apply a visa requirement for Turkish citizens before the entry into force of the Additional Protocol or at the time of their accession, and therefore bringing about a visa requirement for the provision of services after that date is a breach of EU law (Groenendijk and Guild 2011: 80).[3] This was also the opinion of the European

Court of Justice, which ruled in a case involving lorry drivers from Turkey travelling to Germany – that is the *Soysal* case of 2009 – that Turkish citizens travelling to Germany for the purpose of delivering a service could not be required to obtain a visa (Kaya 2014: 134). Since international agreements entered into with third countries constituted a primary source of EU law, the Schengen Regulation on the requirement of visas, which listed Turkey as a country whose citizens required a visa to travel to the EU – that is the Schengen black list – actually contravened a primary source of EU law.

The *Soysal* judgment lifted spirits in Turkey with the hope that it would lead to an annulment of the visa requirement regarding the provision of services by Turkish nationals in the EU. However, most member states were reluctant to immediately follow up the ECJ judgment with effective action. Only two countries engaged in a rule change following the *Soysal* judgment, Germany and Denmark. In Germany, some groups of Turkish nationals were removed from the visa list, such as 'lorry drivers, workers servicing installations, important artists, researchers and sportsmen' (Groenendijk 2011: 33). However, people belonging to these specified groups had to still apply to the German consulates to obtain a visa exemption document. Thus in effect, the procedure stayed the same while only the nature of the document applied for changed. Denmark also specified those categories of Turkish nationals that would be exempt from visas – that is 'who are resident and employed (or economically active) in Turkey and have been designated as a service provider' (Groenendijk 2011: 33). A Turkish service provider travelling to Denmark for that purpose would be subject to control at the border. In both countries, the rule changes following the *Soysal* case did not lead to any actual improvement in the situation of Turkish citizens travelling to the EU. For the other nine countries that should have also acted to revise visa exemption rules for Turkish nationals, no rule change took place (Groenendijk 2011: 35). Still, the *Soysal* judgment provided a legal path for Turkey to follow and seek improvement in the conditions of travel to EU member states.

In EU law, freedom to provide services is interpreted as a two-sided action between the provider and receiver of services and should be enjoyed by both the provider and receiver of services as stipulated in Article 1(1) of Directive 64/221 and consolidated by ECJ case law (Groenendijk 2011: 20).[4] When applied to the case of the Turkish Association Law, this would mean that Turkish citizens travelling to the EU not only to deliver but also to receive services should not require a visa since this would be within the scope of freedom to provide services. A Turkish citizen travelling to the EU as a tourist, student or person in need of medical help would not need a visa since they would be the recipient of services. Thus the next step from the *Soysal* judgment would be a second judgment regarding a Turkish citizen travelling to the EU with the purpose of receiving services. Such a judgment if it ruled the visa requirement to be unlawful would open up a new opportunity for Turkey and would make the continuation of visas much more tenuous. Such a model case came in 2011 when Ecem Demirkan, wishing to travel to Germany with the aim of visiting her family, opened a case against German authorities. The case referred for preliminary ruling was decided in 2013 amid strong pressure by member states. The ECJ ruled that travelling to the EU as a receiver of services would not be contrary to the visa requirement, thus bringing about an effective end to what Turkey could gain on the judicial front.[5] This judgment clearly showed that the visa was a very sensitive and highly politicized issue. It would be difficult to lift the visa for Turkish citizens, who between 2009 and 2014 paid a total of €235.6 million to EU consulates to apply for a C-type Schengen visa (Economic Development Foundation 2014). The existence of about 4 million Turkish-origin residents and citizens living in Western Europe (Ministry of Foreign Affairs 2015b), the lack of legal migration policies on the part of EU countries, and the continuing influx of irregular migration to the EU can be seen as reasons preventing the lifting of visas for Turkish citizens.

Whether the visa is an effective tool to control irregular migration is another issue. Those entering the EU with a short-term visa could overstay the allowed period and continue to reside in the EU informally. Following the visa liberalization in Western Balkan countries, the EU was faced with an increasing number of asylum-seekers from these countries who actually did not qualify for international protection but wanted to benefit from the asylum opportunities in some Western European countries (European Stability Initiative 2015). While this may be a problem, it is better tackled by revising asylum systems so as not to create a pull factor for bogus claims and cooperating with countries of origin and transit in hindering such flows. The visa by itself is not an effective tool to fight against unwanted migration. Those people who are denied a visa could strive to enter the EU by other means, as witnessed recently in the influx of refugees from Africa, and particularly Syria. Besides, most of the unwanted migration involving Turkey is transit migration through the country. Turkey, with higher levels of growth than many EU member states, became not only a transit country but also a destination country for migrants. The most effective way to tackle unwanted migration in a humanitarian way would be to align Turkey's visa policy with that of the EU, strengthen border controls, fight against migrant smuggling, improve facilities for hosting migrants, and establish mechanisms to distinguish valid political asylum claimants and relocate them in developed countries.

Reflecting on the positive effects of visa liberalization for the Western Balkans, European Stability Initiative, a non-governmental organization working extensively in Eastern Europe and on the visa issue, notes the following (European Stability Initiative 2011):

> The visa liberalisation process for the Western Balkans was a great success. It was a win-win-win game: the EU has gained in security by turning its neighbours in the Balkans into partners that help protect its external borders. The Western Balkan governments had gained in internal security. Their citizens had gained visa-free travel.

While the visa since 1980 became an entrenched practice of EU consulates in Turkey, it also triggered a whole sector of activity involving the consulates and agencies that handle the application process. Once such an entrenchment takes place, creating vested interests, it becomes more difficult to let go of the practice, especially in an atmosphere of economic crisis and migrant-scepticism in Europe.

The EU's troubles with irregular migration and the role of Turkey

Europe can be viewed as a continent of migration, having witnessed consecutive waves of migration since its early history. While in recent centuries migration was mostly from Europe to other regions, mostly to colonies and the New World, in search of freedom from religious or ethnic persecution, wealth and better opportunities, the post–World War II era witnessed a large influx of immigrants and refugees to Europe from Asia, Africa and Latin America. After World War II, major European economies, such as Germany, needed additional labour forces in an effort to reboot their production and revitalize their war-torn economies. The so-called Gast Arbeiter came from Southern Europe and also from countries such as Turkey. The slowdown of Western European economies and emergence of structural unemployment in the 1970s, especially after the oil shock of 1973, terminated the demand for labour migration. Family reunions became one of the persisting sources of legal migration to Europe, coupled with the high numbers of asylum-seekers finding refuge in Europe, while irregular migration from east of Europe increased, especially following the ending of the Cold War. While the already existing migrant communities in Europe acted as bridges to their home countries, contributing to further migration, political and economic crises in source countries, facilitation of transport and communication with technological revolution and the attraction of the European life acted as stimulating factors contributing to further migration. The generous asylum provisions in Western European countries also acted as stimulants, triggering a pull factor for migration to Europe (Castles et al. 2013).

In the EU, the communitarization of migration started with the informal Trevi group in the 1970s and followed with the Schengen Agreement, Schengen Convention and the codification of the intergovernmental 'Justice and Home Affairs' pillar in the Maastricht Treaty, later embodied in the 'Area of Freedom, Security and Justice' with the Treaty of Amsterdam. In this process, the policy areas regarding migration, protection of external borders, visas and asylum, and fight against transborder crime became issues handled jointly by the member states under the EU. While the EU communitarized the issue of mobility of people within the Union, it also aimed to harmonize policies dealing with the protection of external borders and movement of people across these borders. For member states which viewed migration flows as a destabilizing process, full coordination between countries that were regarded as targets of migration within the EU and those that more often acted as gateways to these countries was essential for the effective functioning of the Area of Freedom, Security and Justice.

Following the fall of the Berlin Wall and demise of Communist regimes in Central and Eastern Europe, East-West migration intensified. With the accession of CEECs to the EU, this migration became intra-EU migration after a transitory phase of five years (Fihel et al. 2015). People from Eastern Europe were moving into Western European countries in search of jobs and better life opportunities. Migration of Roma people to Western Europe also triggered quite fierce measures by some member states, as we have seen in the case of deportations of Roma people from France in 2013 (France 24 2013). The rise of radical right parties in Western Europe since the 1980s fuelled anti-immigrant rhetoric. Migration became a highly securitized issue linked to the presentation of migration as a threat to cultural integrity and stability of EU societies. The continuing influx of irregular migrants began to be viewed as being 'invaded by foreigners' who would not fit into the cultural identity and would pose a burden on labour markets and welfare state provisions. This securitization of migration also compelled the EU and its member states to take action to control migratory flows and prevent economic refugees from claiming political asylum.[6]

Europe hosted people fleeing from war, ethnic strife and oppression during and after the Cold War years. The refugees fleeing the one-party regimes of Eastern Europe were followed by people fleeing from war and ethnic strife in the Balkans and post-Soviet space. At the same time, with the lifting of the strict Cold War division in Europe, migration from East to West also assumed an economic character. The generous asylum policies of some Western European countries during the Cold War years now gave way to a more cautious approach since most of migration was due to the search for jobs and a better standard of living. The EU hosted an increasing number of asylum applications in 2015, going up by 85 per cent in the second quarter of 2015 compared to the same quarter of 2014. Among the asylum-seekers Syrians, Afghanis and Albanians were the most numerous nationalities among a total of 213,200 (Eurostat 2015).

In its search for an area of free movement protected by common external borders, the EU aimed to harmonize visa and asylum policies while it strengthened its outer boundaries. In the absence of a comprehensive policy for legal migration coupled with the pull factors that Europe presented, the pressure from irregular migration intensified. The number of irregular migrants crossing EU borders increased from 104,000 in 2009 – declining to 72,000 in 2012 – to 283,000 in 2014 (European Parliament 2015). The number of irregular migrants reached a climax in 2015, with nearly 885,000 migrants crossing EU borders in 2015 (Frontex 2015). Faced with the Syrian refugee crisis, the EU turned to Turkey and Western Balkan countries in order to deter further migration, aiming to engage in a joint process of burden-sharing and increasing the capacity of these countries to host refugees.

On the EU side, Turkey was viewed as a major transit route for irregular migration to the EU, and greater cooperation for the protection of borders and fight against illegal migration were called for. Turkey was involved as a transit country in two migration routes destined for the EU, the eastern Mediterranean and the Western Balkan routes as defined by Frontex. The eastern Mediterranean route goes through Turkey via Greece, southern Bulgaria or Cyprus. According to Frontex figures, this route has become the second most-often used route to the EU, witnessing an increase from 52,300 migrants to 57,000 in 2011, later dropping to 50,830 in 2014 (Frontex 2016a). Due to the frequent illegal passages through the River Evros/Meric along the Greek-Turkish border, additional measures were implemented by Greek and EU authorities. In November 2010, Rapid Border Intervention Teams (RABIT) were deployed by Frontex along the border following a call for help by Greece. Greece also stepped up cooperation with Turkish authorities and intensified its border control, including the construction of a fence along a 12.5-kilometre area of the north-eastern town of Orestiada. Increasingly, migrants resorted to alternative routes, shifting their paths to the Aegean islands and the Turkish-Bulgarian land border. In 2014 and 2015 Aegean islands, such as Rhodes, Kos, Samos, Chios and Lesvos, saw an unprecedented influx of refugees on their way to the EU, mostly fleeing the Syrian War, which forced the capacity of these islands to host migrants to the extreme. The numbers of illegal border crossings along this route rose from 50,830 to 885,286 between 2014 and 2015, a huge increase of 17.4 times (Frontex 2016a).

The Western Balkan route going through the Turkish-Greek and Turkish-Bulgarian land or sea borders through Macedonia and Western Balkans into Hungary has witnessed increasing numbers of migrants. According to Frontex statistics, the number increased from 3,090 in 2009 to 43,360 in 2014. As a result of the upsurge in refugees due to the Syrian War and rising instability in the wider region, the number of illegal border crossings along this route rose to 764,038 in 2015, a 17.6-fold increase, similar to the eastern Mediterranean route (Frontex 2016b). Migrants and refugees increasingly used this route as a way to reach EU borders. After they reached Hungary, they were able to file for an asylum application, after which they were transferred to open centres. Most migrants left those centres to travel further west (Frontex 2015). The ongoing migration along the Western Balkan route came to a halt with increasing border controls and closing of borders by states along the border, such as Macedonia, Hungary and Austria, as of March 2016. Faced with a continuing influx of refugees and migrants, countries increasingly leaned towards unilateral emergency measures rather than a Union-wide stance. With border controls reinstated also in the west of the EU between France, Germany, Denmark, Sweden, Austria, Norway and Poland (European Commission 2016c), one of the aims of the Commission became to reconfirm the Schengen Area and make it function again until the end of the year. The EU clearly saw that one of the primary successes of the European project, the Schengen Area, could become a thing of the past, if effective measures to protect the external borders could not be enacted and implemented soon.

Turkey was often accused of not doing enough to fight against illegal migrant smuggling networks, preventing migrants from leaving for Europe, and keeping the geographical limitation of the 1951 Geneva Convention (Zoeteweij-Turhan 2015: 155). However, the increasing migration to and through Turkey creates an undue pressure on Turkey's migration management system which cannot be handled by the country alone. While Turkey is seen mostly as a transit country, it has also become a destination country, hosting migrants from Africa, Asia and Eurasia. As a country at the crossroads of continents, Turkey hosted refugees fleeing Nazi persecution during World War II, from Eastern Europe, the Balkans and the Caucasus during and after the Cold War. Since the crumbling of the Ottoman Empire, Turkey also hosted many Muslim and Turkic immigrants from the Balkans, as well as Eurasia. Between 1923 and 1995, Turkey hosted more than 1,686,163 immigrants who settled in the country (Kirişçi 2003: 82). According to the latest figures published by the Directorate-General of Migration Management, the number of irregular migrants in Turkey increased from 29,426 in 1998 to 58,647 in 2014, reaching a peak of 94,514 in 2000, totalling 961,018 between 1998 and 2014. In 2014, the top nationalities were Syrians, followed by Afghanis and Burmese. As of 1 October 2015, a total of 2,066,601 Syrian refugees are registered in Turkey, nearly 87.5 per cent living outside hosting centres. The official status of Syrian refugees is defined as being under temporary protection. Turkey continues to adhere to the geographic limitation of the Geneva Convention of 1951, under which it grants only temporary protection to refugees from the East (UNHCR 2015). The geographical limitation is a right recognized by the Geneva Convention and necessitated by Turkey due to concerns about the capacity to host an increasing number of asylum-seekers from Asia (Kirişçi 2014: 8). The visa liberalization roadmap lists the lifting of the geographical limitation as one of the conditions for visa-free travel to the EU. In the annotated roadmap, Turkey notes that this condition may be met only upon membership in the EU (Turkish Ministry of Foreign Affairs 2013).

Another criticism directed to Turkey concerned its liberal visa policy towards many Middle Eastern and African countries, which was regarded as increasing the pull effect for migrants to travel freely to Turkey and then seek passage through the foregoing routes to the EU. The liberalization of Turkey's visa policy was mostly associated with Turkey's active foreign policy during the 2000s, and its wish to increase its international clout while also facilitating cultural and commercial exchanges with Asian, African and Eurasian countries. Since almost all of these countries were on the Schengen blacklist, Turkey's policy of open borders actually conflicted with its status as a candidate to join the EU and its commitments to align its legislation with that of the EU. On the other hand, the stalemate in Turkey's EU negotiations and the blocking of Chapter 24 on freedom, security and justice by the Greek Cypriots effectively meant that the EU lost any leverage that it may have on Turkey's alignment to the EU *acquis* in this field. The visa liberalization reintroduced the conditionality component, which has weakened in the accession process. Turkey implemented almost all the 72 criteria embodied in the roadmap save for 5 of them until the end of April 2016, mainly owing to the acceleration of the process and the adoption of a clear target date for the lifting of the visa.

The Turkey–EU Readmission Agreement and the visa liberalization roadmap

The EU has signed readmission agreements with third countries following the conferral of competence to the Union bodies in this area with the Amsterdam Treaty provisions – that is according to Article 73k (Zoeteweij-Turan 2015: 148) – as a tool to manage irregular migration by returning illegal migrants depicted while crossing EU borders or inside countries to the transit or source country. The negotiations for a readmission agreement between Turkey and the EU were started in 2005, which stalled for a long time and was finally signed in 2013. Turkey was reluctant to sign the agreement because of the common apprehension at both elite and popular levels about the burden the implementation of this agreement would create. The major questions causing this anxiety were first whether Turkey would be able to host a huge number of migrants returned by the EU and resend them to their countries of origin and second how the two sides would agree on proof of transit through Turkey for illegal migrants depicted in the EU. The cost and burden involved in hosting returned migrants, many of whom would not be able to be sent back, and the potential problems involved in the implementation of the agreement coupled with the already widespread feeling that the EU was not just and sincere in its approach to Turkey led to the perception that Turkey was now regarded as a dumping ground for unwanted migrants by the EU.

The other pressing issue regarding mobility of Turkish citizens in the EU was the visa requirement and Turkey's demands for its abolishment. As outlined earlier, what started as a temporary measure assumed a permanent character and increasingly caused a resentment in Turkish society. While only about 10 per cent of the population hold passports in Turkey, the number is rapidly increasing, with Turkish people travelling more and more abroad for touristic, business, educational and other reasons. The visa constitutes a psychological factor fuelling the already widespread sense of being rejected and isolated by the EU. It is depicted as a 'paper wall' creating undue procedures in the application process. The length of the application, the number and types of documents demanded and the ordeal involved in going through the process are frustrating especially if you are rejected at the end or given a very short-term visa ending the day after your planned return.[7]

Demands for the lifting of the visa were first and foremost voiced by civil society, especially by specialized organizations, such as IKV, and business organizations, such as TOBB. The visa was seen as creating a barrier to human contact and also infringing fair competition in the Turkey–EU customs union since business people from the EU were able to travel to Turkey freely[8] while Turkish business people had to apply for a visa. For some time, Turkish organizations were hopeful that visa could be abolished as a result of the case law of the ECJ which would declare the illegality of the visa based on Article 41(1) of the Additional Protocol. The *Soysal* judgment gave further hope to this expectation; however, the *Demirkan* case brought an end to optimism regarding the legal process. The issue was too politicized to be resolved by court judgments only.

The EU tied visa liberalization to the signing of the Readmission Agreement, and finally the signing and ratification of the agreement opened up a new process whereby Turkey would need to implement the requirements of the agreement and visa roadmap in order to enjoy visa-free entry into the EU. The Readmission Agreement signed in December 2013 and entered into force in October 2014 necessitates both parties to accept both their own nationals, stateless persons and third-country nationals 'who do not, or no longer, fulfil the conditions in force for entry to, presence in, or residence on the territory of the requesting Member State'

(Official Journal of the EU 2014). The return of third-country nationals coming from countries with which the parties have not signed readmission agreements will be realized only three years after the entry into force of the Turkey–EU Readmission Agreement. Return of illegal migrants will be based on mutual consent of the EU and Turkey based on sufficient proof showing that the migrant passed through the territory of the party concerned, such as a train ticket, receipt of purchase, doctor's prescription and so forth.

The visa liberalization roadmap included 72 criteria for Turkey to realize in order to qualify for visa-free travel. The Commission would oversee Turkey's track record in fulfilling these conditions and, based on a positive evaluation regarding the fulfilment of the criteria, would present a proposal to amend EC Regulation 539/2001, transferring Turkey from the negative list to the positive list of countries whose citizens do not need a visa to enter the Schengen Area. The proposal would then be voted on by the EP and the Council of the EU by qualified majority.

The 72 criteria foreseen in the visa liberalization roadmap for Turkey were grouped under four blocks: documents security, migration and border management, public order and security and fundamental rights. The roadmap stipulated the fulfilment of these criteria, among which the following may be highlighted: full and effective implementation of the Readmission Agreement, issuing of biometric passports, strengthening border surveillance with deployment of trained border guards and technological devices so as to decrease the number of irregular migrants entering Turkey and existing for the EU, aligning Turkey's visa policy to the EU, lifting the geographical limitation to the Geneva Convention of 1951, establishing an effective migration management system, establishing a mechanism for the monitoring of migration flows and expulsion of illegal migrants, strengthening the fight against organized crime, terrorism and corruption, improving judicial cooperation in criminal matters with the EU, strengthening law enforcement agencies, adopting legislation on the protection of personal data, ensuring freedom of movement for Turkish citizens without any discrimination, improving the conditions of the Roma population, and revising the legal framework in the area of organized crime and terrorism and improving implementation of related agencies with regards to rights to liberty and security, the right to a fair trial and freedom of expression, of assembly and association (European Commission 2013b).

The first assessment report regarding Turkey's progress in fulfilling the requirements of the roadmap was published in October 2014 (European Commission 2014c). The report was in general quite moderate in its evaluation, including a positive recognition of the reforms Turkey had carried out by then. Turkey in an effort to modernize its migration management system and take steps in the direction of alignment with the EU *acquis* started a process of reforms, such as the adoption of the Law on Foreigners and International Protection. The law streamlined and embodied all provisions for foreigners in Turkey, including visa requirement, right of residence, and work, as well as conditions of expulsion and international protection. The law also provided the legal basis for the establishment of the Directorate-General of Migration Management under the Ministry of the Interior.

One of the most contentious issues with regard to the visa liberalization criteria is related to the EU's condition of lifting the geographical limitation to the

1951 Geneva Convention relating to the status of refugees. Turkey's recourse to the geographical limitation meant that Turkey was to apply the provisions of the Convention only to refugees from Europe and not from other geographies.[9] The geographical limitation to the Geneva Convention is maintained to this day, owing to an apprehension about security threats that inflows of refugees from the East would create. This differential treatment of refugees resulted in a 'two-tiered asylum policy' (Kirişçi 2003: 83). While refugees from Europe enjoyed the rights embodied in the convention and were granted refuge in Turkey to be relocated to more developed countries, refugees from non-European countries, such as Iran or Central Asian Republics, were permitted to reside in the country unofficially without a defined legal status. Some were allowed to stay on, benefitting from some legal provisions granted to persons from Turkish descent to settle, work and apply for citizenship in the country, while others moved on to settle in third countries (Kirişçi 2003: 84). Turkey was also criticized for deporting some refugees to unsafe regimes and thereby infringing the non-refoulement principle (Kirişçi 2003: 87).

The start of accession negotiations with the EU carried the issue to the agenda since Turkey also had to adapt to the EU *acquis* on asylum. While the related Chapter 24 could still not be opened to negotiations due to the Greek Cypriot veto, Turkey's geographical limitation to the Geneva Convention was included in one of the conditions of the visa liberalization roadmap. Under the part on international protection, Turkey was requested to

> Adopt and effectively implement legislation and implementing provisions, in compliance with the EU acquis and with the standards set by the Geneva Convention of 1951 on refugees and its 1967 Protocol, thus excluding any geographical limitation, so as to ensuring the respect of the principle of non-refoulement.
>
> (European Commission 2013b)

While Turkey also accepted being bound by the roadmap, in the annotated version the Turkish side noted that the lifting of the geographical limitation would be realized only upon membership in the EU. Considering that the EU would demand to see all the criteria mentioned in the roadmap fulfilled in order to qualify for visa-free travel, this issue will likely cause another point of contention between the parties. While, it is imperative that Turkey should modernize its asylum policy and correct such inconsistencies as the two-tier system, it is also true that hosting an ever-increasing number of migrants and refugees is a major challenge for the country.

The EU refugee crisis and Turkey–EU relations

The summer of 2015 witnessed an unprecedented influx of refugees to EU borders, mostly Syrian and Iraqi refugees fleeing war and terror. According to figures published by the International Migration Organization, 710,000 refugees travelled to the EU in the first nine months of 2015. Refugees mostly followed the Aegean or Western Balkan route, passing to Aegean islands from the Turkish coast and/or passing through the Turkish-Greek and Bulgarian borders through Macedonia and Serbia to Hungary. Hungary felt the need to close its borders while Germany and Austria reinstated border controls. While Germany adopted a more hospitable approach to refugees and agreed to host 800,000 of them, several member states rejected hosting refugees, arguing that they did not have the capacity or were anxious about problems of integration of Muslim migrants. EU leaders debated the problem, the quota of migrants that the EU would accept and ways to cope with it in consecutive meetings of the Council. It was agreed in May and September 2015 to relocate 160,000 refugees over two years from Italy and Greece, which hosted the largest numbers of refugees in the EU. However, this quota could not be fulfilled due to widespread resistance shown by some member states, such as Hungary, which organized a referendum on 2 October 2016 to decide whether to accept any more refugees to the country (BBC News 2016). As of 29 August 2016, only less than half of the 160,000 refugees agreed by the EU could be relocated in member states (European Commission 2016d).

Searching for the effective solution to this problem which apparently would continue in view of the grave situation in Syria and Iraq, the EU turned to Turkey, proposing a refugee deal. Commission vice-president Timmermans, related members of the Commission and chancellor of Germany Angela Merkel travelled to Turkey to debate the issue with the prime minister and president (Bölinger 2015). Turkey became Merkel's only hope for controlling the inflow of migrants and refugees along the Western Balkan and eastern Mediterranean routes. The draft joint action plan proposed by the EU was published on the website even before an agreement was reached on the issue between the parties.

The draft action plan published by the Commission on 6 October 2015 (European Commission 2015c) aimed to accelerate Turkey–EU cooperation to deal with the refugee crisis, offering Turkey some rewards in return for stepped-up cooperation and coordination with the EU. The aim of the EU was mainly to prevent further irregular migration through Turkey to the EU by supporting Turkey's capacity to host refugees and prevent further migration to Turkey and exit towards the EU. The EU envisaged a high-level cooperation on migration with Turkey, offering three important rewards to convince Turkey: first, increase funding, which is expressed as 1 billion in the draft action plan but has been increased to €3 billion in further deals between the parties; second, promise to open further chapters in Turkey's EU accession negotiations, such as Chapter 17, on economic and monetary affairs, followed by others that are currently blocked by Greek Cypriots; and third, accelerate the visa liberalization process. The joint action plan was adopted by the EU and Turkey in their summit meeting of 29 November 2015. The EU's increased need for Turkey's cooperation due to the refugee crisis could be evaluated as a window of opportunity in Turkey–EU relations, contributing to an acceleration of the accession negotiations and visa liberalization process. The action plan promised to provide an impetus that would place the relations on a new level of cooperation in dealing with a common problem.

The 18 March deal between Turkey and the EU and the future of cooperation on visas and migration

The deal struck at the 29 November summit created a great deal of controversy both in Turkey and in the EU. While several human rights and migrant organizations protested the deal for failing to take into account the rights of refugees for protection under international law and engaging in a violation of their rights by aiming to send them back to a country, such as Turkey, with human rights problems, many in Turkey were anxious about the burden Turkey would have to face when migrants started to be returned under the Readmission Agreement (Paçacı Elitok 2015). The leader of the chief opposition party, Kemal Kılıçdaroğlu, said, 'Let us give 6 billion euros to the EU so that they will take in all the Syrian, Afghan and Pakistani refugees' (Başaran 2016). Although several of the provisions of the joint action plan rested on earlier commitments by the parties embodied in the Readmission Agreement and visa liberalization dialogue, the EU's urge to stem ever-increasing numbers of refugees and migrants crossing the Aegean and Turkey's expectations regarding visa-free travel to the Schengen Area brought about an urgency for their swift and effective implementation.

The first months of 2016 witnessed some but limited progress on the implementation of the agreement on both sides. The ultimate objective of the plan, which was to bring down the number of migrants and refugees passing through Turkey mainly towards Greece and further into the EU, could not be achieved. According to the implementation report published by the European Commission in February 2016, the number of migrants and refugees arriving via Turkey decreased considerably; however, figures recorded for January regarding daily irregular passages are still high for winter circumstances – that is 2,186 in January compared to 6,929 in October and 3,575 in December. Despite measures taken by the Turkish government, such as opening the labour market to Syrians and requiring visas from Syrians arriving to Turkey via third countries, the Commission insisted that Turkey should focus more on stopping irregular transits from the Turkish shore to the Aegean islands (European Commission 2016e). Hence further need emerged for the EU to cement the ongoing cooperation by way of a new and more detailed deal with Turkey which would strengthen the mechanisms to control the irregular crossings of migrants and refugees across the Aegean.

The new and strengthened deal agreed by the parties rested on nine points agreed at the 18 March summit. According to the statement published following the summit, 'all new irregular migrants crossing from Turkey into Greek islands as from 20 March 2016 will be returned to Turkey' (Council of the EU 2016). In exchange for each Syrian returned to Turkey, the EU commits to resettling a Syrian refugee from Turkey. Asylum applications by refugees arriving in Greek islands will be processed swiftly in hotspots aided by staff from EU agencies and member states. Turkey is expected to build sufficient reception centres for returned migrants and respect the principle of non-refoulement for Syrians. Turkey's proposal to bring forward the target date for visa liberalization to June 2016 was accepted by the EU leaders, subject to Turkey's fulfilment of the 72 criteria embodied in the roadmap. Turkey and the EU agreed to open one more chapter to negotiations during the Dutch term presidency of the Council of the EU – that is Chapter 33, on financial and budgetary provisions. Hence, the deal between Turkey and the EU also entailed an acceleration of the accession negotiations. The Turkey–EU statement did not refer to the chapters blocked by the Greek Cypriots, such as energy, judiciary and fundamental rights, freedom, security and justice, education and culture and foreign, security and defence policy. However, it was also added that preparations for the opening of further chapters would proceed – 'without prejudice to Member States' positions in accordance with the existing rules' (European Council 2015: item 4).

The agreement arrived at on 18 March, complemented the Turkey–EU Joint Action Plan of 29 November and solidified the deliberations between the parties on the 7 March meeting in Brussels. Turkey and the EU entered a new phase of intense cooperation on the struggle against irregular migration. It is yet to be observed whether the deal will be effectively put into implementation since a number of hurdles and discrepancies exist, such as the unwillingness of several member states in accepting the resettlement of refugees and the insufficient resources of Greek authorities for managing the return of irregular migrants and asylum applications of refugees. The deal is criticized for disregarding refugee rights under international law since collective expulsions are prohibited. It was also reported in the press that Turkey expelled refugees back to Syria regularly since January 2016 and thus could not be deemed as a safe country for Syrian refugees (Amnesty International 2016). Turkey's application of the geographical limitation to the Geneva Convention continues. Turkey granted international protection to Syrian refugees on an indefinite basis, which was regarded as sufficient by the EU. The EU's demand from Turkey for issuing work permits for Syrians was also carried through in January 2016. EU funds amounting to €3 billion in total started to be allocated for the basic necessities of the nearly 3 million refugees in Turkey, such as food, shelter and education. Hence a working relationship has been already underway between Turkey and the EU.

The success of this refugee deal also depended on whether the concomitant process of visa liberalization would be realized in due course. The second report prepared by the Commission evaluated the level of progress Turkey has made in fulfilling the requirements for visa liberalization and stipulated 46 points Turkey had to carry out in order to qualify for a visa-free regime (European Commission 2016f). The EU–Turkey statement following the 18 March summit required Turkey to engage in the necessary steps for the fulfilment of the roadmap until the end of April so that the Commission would evaluate Turkey's progress in May and submit to the Council and Parliament a proposal to lift the visa requirement for Turkish citizens regarding short-term trips to the EU. Visa liberalization has been one of the most prominent aspects of the deal for Turkey since the promise of visa-free travel motivated the government to proceed with cooperation with the EU regarding the refugee crisis. The popular repercussions of visa liberalization would be a great advantage for the government since it would be regarded as a success in Turkey's EU process. The government already passed the Data Protection Act through Parliament at the beginning of April and submitted a package of proposals, including the establishment of a Human Rights and Equality Institution, adopting relevant Council of Europe Conventions and strengthening the border management system and reforms embodying progress on major aspects of the visa liberalization roadmap's conditions (European Commission 2016b). Hence the weakening of the political conditionality mechanism in Turkey–EU relations was reignited again within the framework of the visa liberalization process.

The Commission published its report on 4 May in which it recommended the lifting of the Schengen visa for Turkish citizens despite the fact that Turkey had not yet fulfilled all the 72 criteria. The remaining criteria included the signing of an operational agreement with Europol, ensuring judicial cooperation with EU member states, effectively following up on the Council of Europe's Group of States against Corruption (GRECO) recommendations, revision of the Data Protection Law, which was not fully in line with EU standards (Ceran 2016), and lastly, revision of antiterror legislation with a view to narrowing its applicability to crimes directly linked to terror acts. There were also two other criteria which Turkey would fulfil given sufficient time – that is the issuing of biometric passports and the full implementation of the Turkey–EU Readmission Agreement, which was expected as of June 2016. The Commission justified its recommendation to lift the visa requirement in the following words (European Commission 2016b):

> On the understanding that the Turkish authorities will fulfil as a matter of urgency and as they committed to do so on 18 March, the outstanding benchmarks of the Roadmap, the Commission presents together with this Report the proposal to amend Regulation 539/2001 to lift the visa requirement for Turkish citizens holding a biometric passport in line with EU standards.

The Commission showed good will and recommended the lifting of visas on the understanding that Turkey would swiftly complete the fulfilment of the remaining criteria. In doing so, the Commission was also acting in full cognizance of the time strain involved in the deal. Turkey could have retracted from its plan to fully implement the Readmission Agreement and stop cooperation with Greek authorities regarding the implementation of the 18 March agreement and the readmission procedure between the two countries.[10] The Commission's recommendation had to be approved by the European Parliament and the Council acting by qualified majority in order to be adopted. Parliament's LIBE committee met on 9 May to discuss the issue and concluded that Parliament would not debate or vote on the issue until all the criteria were fulfilled by Turkey. The MEPs argued that Turkey should not receive discriminatory treatment from the EU and described the 18 March agreement as a 'shady deal' (European Parliament 2016).

Turkey's reaction was also quite indignant while President Erdoğan and the minister for EU affairs of the time, Volkan Bozkır, accused the EU of creating obstacles in front of visa liberalization and not fulfilling its promise, although Turkey fulfilled the criteria stipulated in the roadmap (Toksabay 2016). The war of words from both sides quickly evolved into an impasse. On top of it all, the architect of the Turkey–EU refugee deal on the Turkish side, Prime Minister Ahmet Davutoğlu, was forced to resign due to discordance with the president. This situation made the successful conclusion of the process even more difficult. Prime Minister Davutoğlu was the person who convinced the EU to bring forward the target date for visa liberalization from October to June. He worked at every stage of the process together with minister of EU affairs Bozkır. The fact that he was no longer in office meant that the deal was weakened due to lack of ownership on Turkey's side and its successful conclusion was in doubt. President Erdoğan was also quite ill at ease with the deal and the visa liberalization process, criticizing even the adoption of an earlier target date for the lifting of the visa requirement. He also warned the EU that the €3 billion promised by the EU was not forthcoming (Kroet 2016). President Erdoğan and minister for EU affairs Ömer Çelik also made it clear that Turkey had already done enough to fulfil the criteria for visa-free travel to the EU and would under no circumstances revise the antiterror law, which was one of the five criteria still to be completed (Nielsen 2016).

The coup attempt by a faction of the Turkish military that took place on 15 July in Turkey was averted due to resistance by the president, the government and the parliament as well as thanks to the civil initiative displayed following the plea by President Erdoğan broadcast via FaceTime on a private TV channel, when people went out on the streets to block the operations of the military personnel. Following the coup attempt, a state of emergency was declared and thousands were discharged and/or detained from the military, bureaucracy, judiciary, universities and other institutions due to their links to the clandestine Gülen organization. Under these circumstances the visa liberalization process was forgotten and lost importance. In the meantime, no progress has been made in the fulfilment of the remaining five criteria. The implementation of the 18 March EU–Turkey statement continued without interruption as the numbers of illegal crossings from Turkey to Greece remained at low levels (Nas 2016b). According to the latest figures available, a total of 2,635 persons arrived to Greece via the sea route in October 2016, compared to 211,663 during the same month in 2015. The numbers had decreased from a total of 67,415 monthly arrivals in January to 1,554 in June (UNHCR 2016).

The refugee deal and the visa liberalization process emerged as two critical and dynamic issues in Turkey–EU relations in the recent period. The two issues were interlinked with the signing of the Readmission Agreement in 2013. The upsurge in refugee flows to the EU in 2015 created a de facto situation whereby the EU needed the cooperation of states on EU borders, such as Turkey and the Western Balkan countries, in order the suppress the inflow of refugees and migrants. Visa liberalization together with financial assistance and the facilitation of the EU process was a motivating factor that the EU promised in return for signing and implementing the Readmission Agreement. Taking into account the continuing targeting of EU countries by migrants and refugees mostly from Asia and Africa, and the increasing apprehension felt by the public and spurred by far right parties in several EU countries, it could be concluded that cooperation on fending off irregular migration will be one of the prominent issues in Turkey–EU relations in the years to come.

Notes

1 Albania, Macedonia, Montenegro, Serbia and Turkey are the candidate countries to join the EU. Visa liberalization for Macedonia, Montenegro and Serbia took place in December 2009, and for Albania in December 2010. Bosnia Herzegovina, which is a potential candidate country, has also been granted visa-free travel in December 2010.

2 The title of the agreement is 'European Agreement on Regulations governing the Movement of Persons between Member States of the Council of Europe'. It was signed in 1957 and entered into force as of 1 January 1958. Sixteen states were bound by the agreement as of March 2010, including Turkey and 12 EU member states (Groenendijk and Guild 2011: 24).

3 The first group includes original member states of the EU, Germany, France, Belgium, Netherlands, Luxembourg and Italy. The second group includes later acceding countries – that is UK, Denmark, Ireland, Spain and Portugal.

4 Article 1(1) states that 'The provisions of this Directive shall apply to any national of a Member State who resides in or travels to another Member State of the Community, either in order to pursue an activity as an employed or self-employed person, or as a recipient of services.' Council Directive 64/221/EEC of 25 February 1964 on the co-ordination of special measures concerning the movement and residence of foreign nationals which are justified on grounds of public policy, public security or public health, Official Journal 056, 04/04/1964, 0850–0857, http://eur-lex.europa.eu/LexUriServ/LexUriServ.do?uri=CELEX:31964L0221:EN:HTML (08.11.2015).

5 See Infocuria, Judgment of the Court (Grand Chamber) of 24 September 2013, Leyla Ecem Demirkan v Bundesrepublik Deutschland, Case C-221/11, Reference for a preliminary ruling: Oberverwaltungsgericht Berlin-Brandenburg – Germany, http://curia.europa.eu/juris/document/document.jsf?text=&docid=142081&pageIndex=0&doclang=EN&mode=lst&dir=&occ=first&part=1&cid=53399 (08.11.2015).

6 For an account of securitization of migration in the EU, see J. Huysmans, 'The European Union and Securitization of Migration', *Journal of Common Market Studies*, Vol:38, No:5, December 2000, 751–77.

7 For a full account of the complaints of Turkish citizens about the visa application process see Zeynep Ozler, M. Ozsoz, *Visa Hotline Project: Final Report*, Economic Development Foundation Publications, No: 231, Istanbul, 2010.

8 Citizens of 11 EU member states are required to have a visa to enter Turkey, which can be attained through an e-visa system.

9 See UNHCR, 'Reservations and Declarations to the 1967 Protocol relating to the Status of Refugees', www.unhcr.org/4dac37d79.html (08.11.2015).

10 The Readmission Agreement between Turkey and Greece went back to 2001, although it was not properly implemented until recently. The 18 March agreement between Turkey and the EU rested on the implementation of this agreement with a view to the return of irregular migrants from Greece to Turkey.

Conclusion

Relations between Turkey and the EU are going through a critical and tumultuous period. The recent rapprochement between Turkey and the EU over the issue of stemming refugee flows promised progress in the relations. The 29 November Turkey–EU refugee action plan and the 18 March refugee statement envisaged greater Turkey–EU engagement not only in the area of fending off irregular migration but also in other areas of Turkey–EU relations: visa liberalization for Turkish citizens based on Turkey's fulfilment of 72 criteria, opening of new chapters in the accession negotiations, high-level dialogue mechanisms, revision of the customs union, and holding of regular Turkey–EU summits. The 18 March refugee agreement produced concrete results as may be evidenced by decreasing numbers of migrants using the Turkey-Aegean route and hence diminishing pressure on Greece and the EU. Turkey engaged in extensive reforms during April with a view to fulfilling the 72 criteria envisaged in the visa liberalization roadmap. Turkey's enthusiasm in this regard created hope for the lifting of the Schengen visa requirement for Turkish citizens, which was hoped to make a considerable contribution to the building of good will and trust between the parties.

However, two developments, the second much more dramatic than the first, brought about uncertainty and dubiousness once again in the relations. The first development was the resignation of Prime Minister Ahmet Davutoğlu and the formation of a new government by Binali Yildirim. Davutoğlu together with the minister for EU affairs, Volkan Bozkır, was one of the architects of Turkey–EU cooperation since the eruption of the refugee crisis. He developed a working relationship with EU leaders, especially Merkel. The nearly six-hour meeting he had with Merkel and Mark Rutte, the Dutch prime minister, just before the 7 March Turkey–EU summit in Brussels was of key importance for shaping the fundamentals of the refugee deal that would be cemented at the 18 March summit. He was the person who insisted on bringing forward the target date for visa liberalization to June 2016 and devised the 1:1 exchange scheme whereby the EU agreed to resettle one Syrian refugee from Turkey for each Syrian returned to Turkey from the Aegean islands. With his resignation he was out of the picture and President Erdoğan filled the void with his quite antagonistic comments and accusations towards the EU. He criticized the refugee deal, questioned the haste in the visa liberalization process and protested the EU's insistence on the revision of the antiterror legislation as part of the visa liberalization criteria. Although technical negotiations continued between Turkey and the EU, the close cooperation and amicable mood were replaced once again with adversity. The June 2016 deadline for the visa liberalization and implementation of the Turkey–EU Readmission Agreement could not be met, although the refugee deal continued to be implemented and the numbers of migrants using the eastern Mediterranean route continued to remain low. At the time of writing of the book, the October deadline for visa liberalization was already missed and Turkey's minister for EU affairs, Ömer Çelik, made a statement in his Athens visit that if visas were not abolished by the end of the year, Turkey would stop the readmission process and scrap the refugee deal (Habertürk 2016).

The second and more dramatic development was an unprecedented event that took place in Turkey. On 15 July 2016, a faction in the Turkish armed forces connected with the Gülen organization started an operation to take over control of the state and government. Tanks and troops were mobilized to strategic positions, including the Bosphorous Bridges, TGNA, the presidential palace, state radio and television and other TV channels, such as CNN Turk, the intelligence organization and police special operations centre. A team was sent to seize the president from a hotel where he was vacationing in Marmaris. The coup attempt was averted thanks to an appeal by the president which was broadcast on CNN Turk through a FaceTime call to citizens to go out on the streets and resist the putschists, the resolve of all political parties against the coup attempt, civil resistance of citizens on the streets, and the opposition shown by several elements of the military who refused to collaborate with the FETO faction. By the early hours of the morning, it was apparent that the coup attempt failed and putschist soldiers were one by one arrested. A state of emergency was declared for three months on 20 July and the European Convention of Human Rights was suspended until the end of the state of emergency. Several measures were adopted by governmental decrees aiming to restructure the military establishment and eliminate all traces of Gülenist plotters from the military, bureaucracy, judiciary, schools, universities, media and other public institutions. At the time of writing, purges of academics, journalists, bureaucrats and other state officials are still continuing, targeting not only the Fetullah Terror Organisation but also those with a critical view of the government, and/or supporting the Kurdish movement. The turn of events in Turkey increased the rift between the two sides further in terms of mutual trust and understanding. While political figures in Turkey and the mainstream media described the events following the coup attempt as a victory of Turkish democracy, prominent figures in Europe and European media tended to perceive it as a move away from democracy towards authoritarianism.

At the time of writing this book, the state of emergency is still ongoing, having been renewed again for a three-month period. The last two developments in the chain of events have been the detention and arrests of the editor-in-chief and several journalists and columnists of the *Cumhuriyet* newspaper, a media establishment with a symbolic significance with regard to republican values in Turkey, and the arrests of members of HDP, including the co-chairs of the Party. These were regarded by EU officials and leaders as a further deterioration of Turkey's democracy and human rights, leading to denunciations and condemnations. The EP in a resolution adopted on 24 November 2016 called for a suspension of accession talks. Hence Turkey and EU relations have become increasingly strained following the coup attempt and the declaration of the state of emergency. While drastic measures taken by the government against those accused of involvement with terrorist organizations or aiding and abating them by criticizing the government endangered the recently declared aim of 're-energizing Turkey–EU relations', the stalemate in the visa liberalization process also threw the future of the refugee deal into jeopardy.

In the aftermath of the attempted coup, EU representatives, such as the chair of the European Council, Donald Tusk, president of the European Commission Jean-Claude Juncker, president of the European Parliament Martin Schulz, and high representative for foreign and security policy Federica Mogherini, condemned the coup attempt and showed their solidarity with Turkish people. However, following the coup attempt, the declaration of the state of emergency, adoption of severe measures with the aim of eliminating the Gülen organization, and allegations of torture and ill-treatment of those arrested after the coup raised eyebrows in many European capitals not only Brussels. EU leaders warned Turkey against a shift towards authoritarian methods and called for respect for rights and freedoms. There were even calls to cut off Turkey's EU accession process amid reports about a certain shift of axis for Turkey as Turkey's ties with Russia showed signs of recovery after going through a crisis in recent months. Germany's chancellor, Angela Merkel, tried to placate sceptics, and a member of the ruling party, Roderich Kiesewetter, gave an interview on the n-tv channel, stating that the goal of Turkey's EU negotiations is not membership but to prevent Turkey from allying with Russia or China (n-tv, 2016). Reintroducing the death sentence began to be debated in Turkey after the failed coup and President Erdoğan noted several times that if Parliament passes such a resolution, he would readily ratify it (Ayasun 2016). A definite redline for the EU, several prominent figures, such as Juncker and Merkel, said that reintroduction of the death penalty would definitely bring the end of Turkey's EU perspective. Lastly, President Erdoğan warned the EU that the refugee deal would not be continued unless visa liberalization goes through. The doubts expressed by EU leaders about the measures taken in Turkey and the lukewarm support given to Erdoğan were also severely criticized by several governmental figures and perceived as the EU and the West leaving Turkey alone in its struggle against the Gülen organization. This understanding fed a sense of indignation and resentment towards the EU and the West in general, observed in the statements of the president, prime minister and several ministers. An example was the issue of bringing back the death penalty, an important aspect of the Copenhagen political criteria and a redline for the EU with regards to the future of the accession talks. The referandum to be held on April 16 aiming to amend the Turkish Constitution and change the system to an "executive presidency" also proved to be a straining factor in the relations fueling crises over the attempts of Turkish politicians to hold rallies in EU States such as the Netherlands.

No matter what shocking events unravelled in Turkey, the interdependence between the two parties is a fact of life. The EU needs Turkey's cooperation in dealing with vital problems, such as migration and foreign policy, energy and security issues. For Turkey the EU plays a vital role as an anchor for political and economic reforms and is a key trade partner and a source of foreign direct investment. From this perspective, it would be wise to expect a revitalization and a 're-energizing' of Turkey–EU relations in the near future. Membership may not be in the cards for some more time; however, the continuation of Turkey's EU negotiations is still strategically important for both sides. For Turkey, it is a reassurance of Turkey's European perspective and a guarantee of Turkey's relative stability. For the EU, it is a tool to ascertain Turkey's cooperation in dealing with Europe's problems and to prevent Turkey from venturing into new and rival partnerships. There is always a risk that Turkey may expose the hypocrisy of the EU's approach and declare an end to negotiations; however, based on the current state of Turkey–EU economic relations this does not seem very likely.

The refugee deal and the joint action plan between Turkey and the EU started a process of close cooperation and coordination of efforts with a view to stemming the flow of migrants towards the EU. Turkey plays a significant role in the search for a solution to one of Europe's existential problems – that is keeping the Schengen Area intact. It is to be seen whether the enhanced cooperation within the framework of the refugee deal will spill over into other areas of Turkey–EU relations and provide a boost to Turkey's accession process. One thing is for certain. Based on common expectations and growing interdependence, Turkey and the EU will enjoy the benefits of working together, which can form a working pattern in their relations in the years to come.

Notwithstanding the developments in Turkey–EU relations in recent years, the legal basis of the relationship still depends on the 1963 Association Agreement. The Ankara Agreement is one of the earliest association agreements of the EU that also contain a membership perspective. Indeed, it has been the only existing example – since Greece's membership in 1981 – where the membership perspective is clearly provided for by a separate clause, Article 28. The model on which it depended and the framework it provided all show that everything was designed with a view to integrating Turkey into the EC. In reality, the association has envisaged more than what a customs union is in theory, coming close to introducing a common market between the parties. This indicates very well that the parties did not intend to bring the association to an end with the establishment of the customs union. The Ankara Agreement also provided a highly structured relationship and a high level of political dialogue in order to ensure the objectives of the association.

In spite of all these institutional facilities and design, the association relationship was not able to proceed as intended, falling far short of its declared objectives. The transitional stage, in which the parties were required to comply with various commitments to establish customs union, failed to result in a progressive integration as envisaged in the Ankara Agreement and the Additional Protocol. Among the reasons behind this failure, the non-fulfilment of the obligations by the parties comes first. The structural character of the Ankara Agreement and the

Additional Protocol that have general provisions needing a further act in order to be implemented has contributed to this non-fulfilment. The Association Council needs to take decisions providing detailed rules, procedures and timetables in order to implement their substantive provisions. Since the Association Council could not take such decisions due to socio-economic or political reasons, some important pillars of the association, such as free movement of workers and services, could not be realized.

Turkey's incapacity and the EC's reluctance to meet their commitments regarding the customs union might be regarded as the leading factors responsible for the malfunctioning of the association. The disparity between the parties regarding their understandings about, and interpretation of, the objectives of the association constituted another important reason for the failure of the agreement. While Turkey mainly focused on its long-term political objective of membership, the EC was almost exclusively motivated by the shorter-term economic objectives of the association, and so ignored its declared ultimate objective. The EC had important reservations about Turkey's membership bid and tended to regard the association as an instrument for strengthening relations with an important strategic partner, rather than a potential member, whose political stability was important for the EC's interests and could be secured by ensuring its economic development. Indeed, the EC was reluctant to diminish the negative impacts of its enlargement processes and its policies towards third countries on relations with Turkey, so it could not improve the instruments of the association by taking the needs of Turkey into consideration in that respect. Therefore, not only the incapacity of Turkey to meet its commitments arising from the agreement but also the lack of political will on the EC's side, which is essential for achieving the objectives of the agreement, may be regarded as responsible for the failure of the association in serving as a preparatory stage to Turkey's membership.

Current relations with the EU are quite comprehensive, depending on a two-track experience since the declaration of Turkey's candidacy in 1999, comprising association based on a customs union on the one hand and candidacy in the process of accession negotiations on the other. Therefore, they range from the issues covered by the customs union to cooperation in areas like fighting illegal migration and defence and security. It should be noted that this massive and complicated way of interdependence between the parties could be best managed by accepting Turkey as full member. Therefore, Turkey can participate in the decision-making procedure of the EU and become a direct implementer of the EU's policies. Before this could be realized, effective means of cooperation like enhanced dialogue and joint action should be used in order to eliminate the problems arising from the asymmetric nature of the relations.

The customs union has been a major tool of integration of the Turkish economy into European and global markets, resulting in a trade volume growth from \$67 billion to \$389 billion between 1996 and 2012. Statistics show that trade and investment linkages between the EU and Turkey have deepened through the customs union. But its asymmetric structure arising from the fact that while Turkey needs to align its trade policy with that of the EU, it cannot be involved in the

EU's policy-making mechanism in this respect because it is not an EU member leads to important problems for Turkey. As long as Turkey's situation of having a customs union relationship with the EU without being a member of it protracts and the parties do not take any measures to deal with these structural problems, even its positive effects on the Turkish economy may be counterbalanced and it will get more difficult to regard the customs union as a true device for accession.

The EU was based on a customs union after all, and the Ankara Agreement took the EEC Treaty, the founding treaty, as model to integrate the Turkish economy into the EEC. Thus, in every opportunity during the establishment process of the customs union Turkey drew the EU's attention to the clear and direct correlation between the customs union and Turkey's membership as constructed by the Ankara Agreement. As a matter of fact, Turkey expected that EU membership would be reached in a quite short period of time. Therefore, Turkey did not consider its non-involvement in the policymaking procedure in which it could have the opportunity to influence trade policymaking in the EU as a major problem. But still in the absence of a well-defined and strong membership outlook after a long period of the customs union relationship, this situation constitutes a major problem because it complicates the operation of the customs union itself. In order to consider the customs union as a true device for Turkey's accession, first the problems arising from its asymmetric nature should be healed as soon as possible. Then its scope should be deepened and widened further.

In order to deepen the customs union the Turkish side needs to fully align all of its technical regulations and technical barriers to trade with those of the EU. The EU side should remove the visa requirement that constitutes a substantial obstacle for Turkish citizens doing business with the EU and solve the issue of transit road transport permits that restricts free movement of goods. Widening the customs union towards hitherto excluded sectors, like agriculture, services and public procurement, is equally important for strengthening economic relations and, therefore, for facilitating Turkey's accession. For this purpose Turkey needs to liberalize its highly protective agricultural trade with the EU and adopt the EU's CCT for agricultural products against third counties on the one hand and open up its service and public procurement markets to EU firms on the other hand.

The revision of the customs union, taking into account all these concerns, has become an urgent need. Accordingly, both parties agreed to revise the customs union on 12 May 2015 and stated their support in the refugee deal on 18 March 2016 for ongoing preparatory studies in this respect. The European Commission that prepared the customs union impact report asked the Council for negotiation mandate on 21 December 2016. The negotiations for revision of the customs union are expected to launch within 2017 after the Council decides on the EU's common negotiation position and gives the Commission negotiation mandate.

Turkey's candidacy to the EU since 1999 has been a ground-breaking development in Turkey–EU relations since it triggered a process of intensive reform in Turkey with a view to fulfilling the conditions for opening accession negotiations. Turkey has come closer to the EU by intensifying its efforts at democratization and adopting EU norms and principles in areas such as fundamental rights and freedoms, minority rights and civil-military relations. Accession negotiations opened on 3 October 2005 could not be finalized to this day due to a number of political obstacles, most prominently the Cyprus issue. Turkey turned its attention mostly to internal political conflict and its quest to be a determining actor in regional politics, especially in the Middle East. However, the onset of the Arab uprisings and increasing instability in the region forced Turkey to seek to reinforce its ties to the EU. The EU, itself in a precarious position after the effects of the global crisis and problems in maintaining its integrity, could not offer Turkey membership in the near future. The refugee crisis was a wake-up call to both parties since it showed that Turkey was an indispensable partner for the EU even in the resolution of some of its most urgent problems. However, Turkey had to keep its European reform agenda always moving if it wanted to avail itself of such opportunities as the one that arose over the refuge crisis. Especially its track record in democratization would prove to be vital in determining its status vis-à-vis the EU – that is as a potential member likely to join the Union in the future or as a forever partner that lost its prospect of accession.

The EU's impact on democratization processes should be seen as conditioning domestic change, particularly by helping those working for the establishment of democratic regimes in their countries. Conversely, unconvincing application of conditionality in terms of credibility, consistency and strength tends to give strong support to conservatives and resistant elements in society while reducing the incentives for political elites to strive to comply with the remaining political criteria. To implant a long-lasting and stable democratic regime, the active and voluntary participation and support of a wide range of groups and actors have to be obtained and maintained in the long run. An effective conditionality with a strong membership perspective will considerably contribute to the enduring consent and commitment of domestic actors. Taking stock of Turkey's 17-year candidacy process shows us that EU conditionality has been effective only to a limited extent on Turkey's democratic transformation process. The non-meritocratic and inconsistent nature of accession negotiations coupled with ambiguity about the end result of the negotiations has considerably restricted the impact of EU political conditionality in Turkey.

Without a consistent and credible membership perspective, the role and motivation of EU supporters in the country to get EU membership and political reforms back on track have decreased. The stalling of the accession process and the EU's fading attraction for Turkish society, combined with the further consolidation of the AKP's dominant party position and its declining interest in the EU, have led to seriously decreasing commitment to EU-led political reforms and a weakening of Turkish democracy. In the recent period, the extensive reforms Turkey carried out in order to fulfil the criteria for visa liberalization can be noted as an exemplary case of conditionality in action. Even there, the remaining five criteria, including the revision of the antiterror legislation, proved to be a stumbling block in the process. Considering the 15 July coup attempt and concomitant developments at the expense of Turkish democracy under the conditions of state of emergency, Turkey needs credible and strong EU conditionality more than ever before in order to mobilize the supporters of liberal democracy and to generate social pressure in the country in favour of democratic revitalization. Without a strong EU anchor,

Turkey will further deviate from its reformist direction, consolidating the recent tendency towards more authoritarian rule.

Even if Turkey moves forward in its democratization process and succeeds in reversing its retreat in terms of fundamental rights and freedoms, the Cyprus issue continues to mar progress in the relations. It is obvious that the Cyprus dispute has a high potential to hinder the course of the accession negotiations as currently experienced and delay Turkey's EU membership. The outcome of the negotiations is closely connected to that of the long-standing Cyprus dispute. Problems in Turkey–EU relations started with Greece's EU membership in 1981 before being aggravated by the accession of the Greek-controlled Republic of Cyprus, which made the EU an official party to the dispute. These developments have hindered Turkey's membership ambitions. Before Greek Cypriot membership, Turkey wholeheartedly supported the Annan Plan, which was considered as the most rational initiative so far and therefore strongly backed by the international community and the EU, and actively worked to make the Turkish Cypriot community approve the plan in the referendum. While 65 per cent of Turkish Cypriots accepted the plan, which was defended by the liberal and left political parties, intellectuals and civil society organizations, the Greek Cypriot community, which had already guaranteed its EU membership, rejected the plan. This meant that the best opportunity to reunify Cyprus was lost. This situation has particularly concerned Turkey as its own accession process was undermined, while Turkish Cypriots have continued to suffer economic and political isolation.

Turkish officials have been reiterating Turkey's commitment to reunification broadly in line with the Annan Plan. After a period of break due to the dispute over hydrocarbon energy reserves in the eastern Mediterranean, talks between the two sides of the island restarted in May 2015 and, therefore, a new chance for resolution emerged. Turkey's support this time is less manipulating and interfering in the sense that it seems content to let the Turkish Cypriots negotiate their own agreement, as Emine Çolak, the former Turkish Cypriot foreign minister, stated (Hürriyet Daily News 2015b). This distant approach by Turkey upon the preference of the newly elected Turkish Cypriot leader, who argues for the necessity of becoming self-sufficient in economic, political and administrative terms, is regarded as an important factor explaining the current constructive atmosphere. Additionally, Mustafa Akıncı immediately started after being elected to work for first resuming the talks and then concluding a settlement as soon as possible and concluding a settlement by the end of 2015, as he pledged during his campaign, and accordingly he tries to do his best in the negotiations. He frequently and strongly emphasizes the importance of economic interdependence as a tool for settlement by referring to the vitality of natural gas, water and electricity for mutual economic development. Nikos Anastasiades seems also more positive compared to past leaders. If the southern part of the island can maintain its political will, a political settlement seems closer than ever before. Compared to the 2004 referendum, Greek Cypriots experienced a severe economic crisis in 2013. This has made them more cooperative since they needed an opening which would help allay their economic problems. As suggested by the Turkish side, the economic crisis in Southern Cyprus and newly discovered offshore hydrocarbon reserves in the eastern Mediterranean can be turned into an opportunity for ending long-lasting division between the two communities.

Considering the favourable change in the atmosphere and prevailing conditions of the current situation the negotiation process seems this time to be more promising. However, both of the leaders who want peace and solution still need encouragement and strong support in order to overcome hurdles, allay concerns, gain confidence and finally bring the process to a successful conclusion. At this point, the EU's role will be the principal determinant factor. It is vital to help Anastasiades and Akıncı overcome traditional barriers to an agreement that prevented the parties from reaching a resolution many times in the past.

The EU's role is particularly critical in pushing the Greek Cypriot government to keep its positive stance and to take a more conciliatory stance, particularly over sticky issues – namely property, territory and guarantees. The EU could use the recently experienced economic crisis and the dispute over hydrocarbon energy reserves in the eastern Mediterranean as an opportunity for this purpose. The existing situation of disregarding the Turkish Cypriot community is unsustainable, for the future of both the island and the EU. Therefore, the EU should keep its promise to end the economic isolation of Northern Cyprus while discouraging the Greek Cypriot government from continuing to represent the island alone.

The Cyprus issue is not such a complicated and unsolvable issue so as to obstruct Turkey–EU relations. Rather, it has been EU's lack of leadership in resolving the issue, especially in the Annan Plan process, that has rendered this issue so complicated and hard to solve. The EU's acceptance of the southern part of the island as the sole representative of the whole island without ensuring prior reunification within the framework of a political settlement made the solution elusive. Today a solution seems possible, maybe more possible than ever before, and the EU has an important chance now to counterbalance its unfortunate policies in this respect.

It seems that the Cyprus issue provided a very convenient pretext to delay Turkey's accession negotiations and hence eventual membership to the Union. The difference in the EU's and Turkey's approaches to the Cyprus conundrum could be viewed as a manifestation of some deeper differences and incompatibilities in the relationship. These revolved around the concept of integration capacity and were linked to the difficulties the EU would have in accepting Turkey as a full-scale member of the Union. Turkey's potential impact on the EU's institutions and decision-making as a country of 80 million, its cultural traits and approaches to religion, the potential share it is likely to take from the EU budget and the security implications of accepting a country bordering the Middle East constituted an important consideration in evaluating the EU's capacity to integrate Turkey as a future member state. Although German chancellor Merkel approached Turkey to curb the flow of refugees towards the EU, she made her view about Turkey's membership clear: a privileged or strategic partnership rather than membership. This still constitutes the dominant viewpoint in the EU right now considering current course of the relations in the shadow of rising support for far right parties and growing anti-enlargement tendencies in the EU on the one hand and increasingly more authoritarian and less democratic regime in Turkey on the other hand.

Turkey's shortcomings in the area of democracy, rule of law and fundamental rights further intensify any objections to Turkey's membership based on assessments about the EU's integration capacity. For Turkey to be a member of the EU, its potential contributions to the EU should prevail over the burdens and risks its membership would entail for the EU. However, it should also be considered that integration capacity may not always be an assessment based on rational calculations. Prejudices, images, stereotypes and misconceptions always play a role in the formation of a policy towards a country by shaping the predispositions of decision makers as well as influencing public opinion. Thus considerations about the integration capacity of the EU regarding Turkey will be affected by the EU citizens' ideas and images regarding Turkey as well as concrete facts and developments in the country.

The EU's approach towards Turkey is also affected by the need it feels to engage the country in the resolution of European challenges. Recently, the twin issues of migration and mobility have occupied a central position in Turkey and EU relations. Turkey's quest for visa-free travel to the Schengen Area has been met by the EU's demand for signing the Readmission Agreement. Following eight years of negotiations, the Readmission Agreement was signed on 16 December 2013, making it possible upon its implementation for the EU to return illegal migrants to Turkey if they have passed through Turkish territory on their way to EU countries. At the same time, the 'Roadmap towards a Visa-Free Regime for Turkey' was also adopted, including the conditions Turkey had to fulfil in order for its citizens to qualify for visa-free access to the Schengen Area. The recent refugee deal between Turkey and the EU also impacted on the visa liberalization process by bringing forward the target date first to October 2016 and then to June 2016. The prospect of visa-free travel to the EU exerts a symbolic significance for Turkey–EU relations since it may be evaluated as a sign of acceptance to the European space for Turkish citizens. It remains to be seen whether Turkey will continue with the fulfilment of the criteria outlined in the roadmap and the Second Progress Report prepared by the Commission, and visas will in fact be abolished in June or October of this year.

Despite the pledge to re-energize the relations at the Turkey–EU summit on 29 November 2016, negotiations have not yet gained a renewed momentum. However, the refugee deal reached between Turkey and the EU ignited a process of strengthened cooperation with a view to stemming the flow of refugees towards the EU via Turkey. Turkey is asked to reinforce its efforts to integrate the Syrian refugees on Turkish soil, to fight against migrant smuggling networks, to increase the capacity to control its borders and to engage in intensive cooperation with EU agencies, such as Frontex and Eurojust.

Unable to find support among the member states for taking in more refugees, German chancellor Angela Merkel increasingly turned to Turkey as the only possible solution of dealing with the continuing influx of refugees. The Turkish president and prime minister were concerned with engaging in a fairer burden-sharing with the EU with regard to managing the refugee flow, taking the opportunity to force the EU to a deal on the visa issue with a target date and to make sure that this new agenda in Turkey–EU relations will also have a positive side effect on the accession process. Faced with multiple problems both on the home front and abroad, such as the deterioration of the conflict in the south-east and the foreign policy shortcomings regarding the Syrian War, the Turkish government took advantage of the EU's urgent need to engage Turkey, to reignite the relationship and to also impress the Turkish public with the government's 'success' on the European stage.

The Turkey–EU refugee deal showed the EU leaders in a bad light and attracted major criticism from the media and political groups, such as the ALDE, since they had to leave aside criticisms about Turkey's worsening record on political rights, such as media freedom, rule of law and freedom of expression. The EU was accused of engaging with a country which was criticized for becoming increasingly authoritarian. Commissioners, such as the first vice-president, Franz Timmermans, and the commissioner for enlargement negotiations and neighbourhood policy, Johannes Hahn, and EU leaders, such as Angela Merkel, visited Turkey more frequently than ever before to broker a deal and trigger more cooperation from Turkish officials.

When viewed from the perspective of the EU's focus on promoting democracy and human rights, this could be deemed as the end of the EU's famous 'conditionality' policy towards candidate and third countries. One very important aspect of this policy, the progress reports that the Commission published each year, was postponed until after the 1 November elections in Turkey. Although not officially admitted, it was most probably a move by the EU not to put pressure on the AKP government just before the elections by making public a generally critical report and gaining some leverage to broker a deal to stem the flow of refugees from Syria. The EU, stuck between its principles and interests vis-à-vis Turkey, gave in to the urgency of the refugee situation and approached Turkey despite its deficiencies in the democracy and human rights situation. President of the European Council Donald Tusk and president of the European Parliament Martin Schulz underlined that fulfilling the political criteria was necessary for Turkey to move forward in the accession track, but still such statements had limited ability to ease some vocal criticisms since actions speak louder than words.

The EU–Turkey summit on 7 March 2016 came as a surprise to most EU leaders and onlookers since Prime Minister Davutoğlu came to the table with new demands, such as bringing forward the target date for visa-free travel to June 2016 and requesting an additional €3 billion of funds from the EU until 2018. Davutoğlu also proposed that Turkey should take back all migrants travelling to the Aegean islands from Turkish shores while the EU is to accept one Syrian refugee for every Syrian sent back to Turkey on the Aegean route. Despite the fact that several NGOs criticized the deal on the grounds of infringing on refugee rights, the deal was adopted at the Turkey–EU summit on 18 March. Since then, the deal succeeded in effectively reducing the number of migrants using the eastern Mediterranean route from Turkey's Aegean shore to the Greek islands. Visa-free travel for Turkish citizens could not be attained until the target date of June 2016. It is still an issue in the relations, and we will see whether the EU will lift the visa requirement in exchange for Turkey's continued cooperation in fending off unwanted migration.

In the aftermath of the 15 July coup attempt and the ensuing estrangement between Turkey and the EU, even termination of Turkey's accession negotiations is in the cards. Turkey's swift return to a normal democratic system after the ending of the state of emergency and carrying out of reforms with a view to rectifying respect for rule of law, human rights and fundamental freedoms are definitely needed for the revitalization of the relations. In its current state, Turkey's membership in the EU is considered likely neither in Turkey nor in the EU. In a way, Turkey has fallen out of 'Europe', in terms of adhering to its ideals, internalizing its values and accepting its moral superiority. While several EU officials and member state leaders criticized Turkey for its regression in human rights and freedoms, President Erdoğan and other leading governmental figures did not miss any opportunity to lay bare the hypocrisy of the Union. One recent example was the British EU membership referendum. Though Britain has been one of the few supporters of Turkey's EU membership in the EU, the issue was raised by the 'Leave' camp during the referendum campaign, and in order to placate anxiety about Turkey's possible membership, Prime Minister Cameron said that he did not expect Turkey to become a member of the EU until 3000. Erdoğan made reference to this dilemma and directly targeted Cameron in a speech he made following the Brexit vote: 'Cameron, you did not say that when we came together . . . That was what you used to say: "We are always beside you; We are making every effort for Turkey's accession to the EU". What happened now?' (BBC 2016). Hence, antagonistic positions based on unfulfilled expectations and a milieu of distrust and misunderstanding continue to mar progress in the relations. For there to be a realistic chance of Turkey's accession to the EU, Turkey should set its democracy and human rights record straight while the EU should be able to revitalize its integration by resolving the current difficulties it has been facing, such as the Brexit issue, migration and economic stagnation, and adopt a constructive approach to Turkey. The result of the referendum to be held on April 16 regarding the transition to an executive presidential regime will also have a determining effect on Turkey's EU perspective.

Finally, the determining question in Turkey–EU relations at the moment is the following: will such dynamic processes as the visa liberalization dialogue and the modernization of the customs union bring Turkey closer to the goal of final integration – that is membership – or will these processes pave the way to a special partnership between the parties, which is short of full accession? The answer to this question lies in developments in both Turkey and the EU. If Turkey progresses towards fulfilling the conditions of a liberal democracy with protection of fundamental rights and freedoms, respect for separation of powers and rule of law, it will be able to realistically continue its bid for membership and argue in favour of its European vocation. If Turkey becomes further embroiled in a regime crisis with increasing authoritarian tendencies and limitation of rights and freedoms, then hopes for membership in the EU will become even dimmer. On the part of the EU, an EU that has resolved its internal problems over critical issues, such as the Economic and Monetary Union, Schengen Area, internal market and growth strategies, as well as disparities and lack of solidarity among the member states, will be in a better position to welcome a country such as Turkey.

References

Açıkmeşe, S. A. 2010. Cycles for Europeanisation in Turkey: The Domestic Impact of EU Political Conditionality. *UNISCI Discussion Papers*, 23 May. [Online]. Available at: www.ucm.es/BUCM/tevists/cps/16962206/articulos/UNIS1010230129A.PDF [accessed: 5August 2011].

Akgül, M. and Kırlıdoğ, M. 2015. Internet Censorship in Turkey. *Internet Policy Review: Journal on Internet Regulation*, 4(2), 3 June. [Online]. Available at: http://policyreview.info/articles/analysis/internet-censorship-turkey [accessed: 5 November 2015].

Akgün, M. 2013. Kıbrıs'ta çözümün tam zamanı (It Is Time for Solution in Cyprus). *Star*, 30 March. [Online]. Available at: http://m.stargazete.com.tr/mobilyazar.asp?Newsid=740631 [accessed: 2 June 2013].

Akman, M. S. 2013. Dynamics of the European Union's Trade Strategy and Its Imperatives on Turkish Trade Policy, in *Turkey's Accession to the European Union: Political and Economic Challenges*, edited by B. Akçay and B. Yılmaz. Boulder: Lexington, 127–60.

Akman, M. S. 2012. Türkiye-Avrupa Birliği Gümrük Birliği İlişkisi ve Ortak Dış Ticaret Politikası (Turkey–EU Customs Union Relationship and Common Commercial Policy), in *Avrupa Birliği: Tarihçe, Teoriler, Kurumlar ve Politikalar (European Union: History, Theories, Institutions and Policies)*, edited by B. Akçay and İ. Göçmen. Ankara: Seçkin, 217–42.

Akman, M. S. 2010. The European Union's Trade Strategy and Its Reflections on Turkey: An Evaluation from the Perspective of Free Trade Agreements. *Sosyal Bilimler Enstitüsü Dergisi*, Dokuz Eylül Üniversitesi, 12(2), 17–45. [Online]. Available at: www.sbe.deu.edu.tr/dergi/cilt12.%20say%C4%B12/akman.pdf [accessed: 2 August 2013].

AKP Party Programme. 2015. [Online]. Available at: https://www.akparti.org.tr/english/akparti/parti-programme#bolum [accessed: 1 November 2015].

Aksu, F. 2004. Ege ve Kıbrıs Sorunlarının Çözümünde Avrupa Birliği'nin Tutumu (The EU's Approach in the Resolution of the Aegean and Cyprus Questions). *Stratejik Araştırmalar Dergisi*, (3), February, 103–32.

Aljazeera. 2012. 22 June. [Online]. Available at: www.aljazeera.com/news/europe/2012/06/2012622811474159.html [accessed: 8 May 2015].

Amnesty International. 2016a. *Turkey: Release Detained Academics and Uphold Freedom of Expression*, 21 April. [Online]. Available at: https://www.amnesty.org/en/latest/news/2016/04/turkey-academics/ [accessed: 19 May 2013].

Amnesty International. 2016b. *Turkey: Illegal Mass Returns of Syrian Refugees Expose Fatal Flaws in EU–Turkey Deal*, Press Release, 1 April. [Online]. Available at: https://www.amnesty.org/en/press-releases/2016/04/turkey-illegal-mass-returns-of-syrian-refugees-expose-fatal [accessed: 1 April 2016].

Amnesty International. 2013. *Gezi Park Protests*, October, EUR 44/022/2013. [Online]. Available at: https://www.amnestyusa.org/sites/default/files/eur440222013en.pdf [accessed: 5 November 2015].

Anadolu News Agency. 2015. *European Commission Calls 1915 Events 'Tragedy'*, 16 April. [Online]. Available at: www.aa.com.tr/en/politics/494923-european-commission-calls-1915-events-tragedy [accessed: 28 July 2015].

Arıkan, H. 2006. *Turkey and the EU: An Awkward Candidate for EU Membership?* Aldershot: Ashgate.

Arıkan, H. 2003. *Turkey and the EU: An Awkward Candidate for EU Membership*? Aldershot: Ashgate.

Atacan, F. 2006. Explaining Religious Politics at the Crossroads: AKP-SP, in *Religion and Politics in Turkey*, edited by A. Çarkoğlu and B. Rubin. Oxon: Routledge, 45–58.

Avcı, G. 2011. The Justice and Development Party and the EU: Political Pragmatism in a Changing Environment. *South European Society and Politics*, 16(3), September, 409–21.

Ayad, C., Ayad, C., Jego, M. and Semo, M. 2016. Recep Tayyip Erdoğan: "Western Leaders Preferred to Leave Turkish People to Themselves". *Le Monde*, 8 August. [Online]. Available at: www.lemonde.fr/europe/article/2016/08/08/recep-tayyip-erdogan-western-leaders-prefered-to-leave-turkish-people-to-themselves_4979866_3214.html [accessed: 10 August 2016].

Ayasun, A. 2016. Erdoğan Renews Support for Death Penalty Despite Western Disapproval. *Turkey Times*, 14 October. [Online]. Available at: www.turkeytms.com/2016/10/14/erdogan-renews-support-for-death-penalty-despite-western-disapproval/ [accessed: 4 November 2016].

Aydın-Düzgit, S. and Keyman, E. F. 2012. EU–Turkey Relations and the Stagnation of Turkish Democracy. *Istanbul Policy Center (IPC)*, Global Turkey in Europe Series, Working Paper 2. [Online]. Available at: http://ipc.sabanciuniv.edu/wp-content/uploads/2012/12/GTE_WP_021.pdf [accessed: 18 June 2013].

Aydın-Düzgit, S. and Keyman, E. F. 2004. European Integration and the Transformation of Turkish Democracy. *Centre for European Policy Studies*, EU–Turkey Working Papers, 2 August. [Online]. Available at: http://file.setav.org/Files/Pdf/european-integration-and-the-transformation-of-turkish-democracy-ceps-2004.pdf [accessed: 8 August 2013].

Babacan, N. 2016. Turkey Faces Division 'If No Shift to Presidency', *Hürriyet Daily News*, 1 November. [Online]. Available at: www.hurriyetdailynews.com/turkey-faces-division-if-no-shift-to-presidency.aspx?PageID=238&NID=105589&NewsCatID=338 [accessed: 04 November 2016].

Bağcı, H. 2000. Helmut Schmidt's 'Realist' View of Turkey. *Hürriyet Daily News*, 19 October. [Online]. Available at: www.hurriyetdailynews.com/helmut-schmidts-realist-view-of-turkey.aspx?pageID=438&n=helmut-schmidts-realist-view-of-turkey-2000-10-19 [accessed: 1 November 2015].

Bahceli, T. 2003. Cycles of Tension and Rapprochement: Prospects for Turkey's Relations with Greece, in *Turkey's Foreign Policy in the 21st Century: A Changing Role in World Politics*, edited by T. Y. Ismael and M. Aydın. Aldershot and Burlington: Ashgate, 161–79.

Barysch, K. 2007. What European Think about Turkey and Why? *Centre for European Reform Essays*, September. [Online]. Available at: www.cer.org.uk/sites/default/files/publications/attachments/pdf/2011/essay_turkey_barysch_25sept07-1392.pdf [accessed: 30 October 2015].

Başaran, R. 2016. Kemal Kılıçdaroğlu: Türkiye'yi tampon il yaptılar (They Have Made Turkey into a Buffer Zone). *Hürriyet*, 10 March. [Online]. Available at: www.hurriyet.com.tr/kemal-kilicdaroglu-turkiyeyi-tampon-il-yaptilar-40066741 [accessed: 28 April 2016].

Baylies, C. 1995. Political Conditionality and Democratisation. *Review of African Political Economy*, 22(65), 321–37.

BBC News. 2016. *Hungary PM Claims EU Migrant Quota Referendum Victory*, 3 October. [Online]. Available at: www.bbc.com/news/world-europe-37528325 [accessed: 25 October 2016].

BBC News. 2002. *Turkey Entry 'Would Destroy EU'*, 8 November. [Online]. Available at: http://news.bbc.co.uk/2/hi/europe/2420697.stm [accessed: 1 November 2015].

BBC News Europe. 2010. *France Sends Roma Gypsies Back to Romania*, 20 August. [Online]. Available at: www.bbc.co.uk/news/world-europe-11020429 [accessed: 23 July 2015].

BBC Turkish. 2016. *Erdoğan: AB müzakerelerini referanduma götürebiliriz (Erdoğan: We Can Take EU Negotiations to a Referendum)*, 23 June. [Online]. Available at: www.bbc.com/turkce/haberler/2016/06/160623_erdogan_ab_muzakere_referandum [accessed: 9 August 2016].

Bianet. 2014. *BIA Media Monitoring Report 2014*. [Online]. Available at: http://bianet.org/english/freedom-of-expression/162786-media-s-3-years-a-summary-with-graphics [accessed: 23 August 2015].

Bianet. 2011. *BIA Media Monitoring Report 2011*. [Online]. Available at: http://bianet.org/english/freedom-of-expression/136599-bia-media-monitoring-report-2011-full-text [accessed: 23 August 2015].

Birand, M. A. 1996. *Türkiye'nin Gümrük Birliği Macerası (Turkey's Customs Union Adventure)*. Istanbul: Milliyet.

Birand, M. A. 1990. *Türkiye'nin Ortak Pazar Macerası: 1959–1990 (Turkey's Common Market Adventure)*. Istanbul: Milliyet.

Birand, M. A. 1978. Turkey and the European Community. *The World Today*.

Bölinger, M. 2015. Merkel's Disputed Visit to Turkey Is a Political Minefield. *Deutsche Welle*, 15 October. [Online]. Available at: www.dw.com/en/merkels-disputed-visit-to-turkey-is-a-political-minefield/a-18784725 [accessed: 10 August 2016].

Bourguignon, R. 1990. A History of the Association Agreement between Turkey and the European Community, in *Turkey and European Community*, edited by A. Evin and G. R. Dento. Opladen: Springer, 51–64.

Brewin, C. 2000. *The European Union and Cyprus*. Huntingdon and Cambridgeshire: Eothen.

Can, H. and Özen, Ç. 2005. *Türkiye-Avrupa Topluluğu Ortaklık Hukuku (Turkey–EUropean Community Association Law)*. Ankara: Gazi Kitabevi.

Carothers, T. 1997. Democracy Assistance: The Question of Strategy. *Democratisation*, 4(3), 109–32.

Castles, S., Haas, H. and Miller, M. J. 2013. *The Age of Migration: International Population Movements in the Modern World*. 5th ed. Basingstoke: Palgrave Macmillan.

Çayhan, E. 1997. *Dünden Bugüne Türkiye-Avrupa Birliği İlişkileri ve Siyasal Partilerin Konuya Bakışı (Turkey–EU Relations and the Positions of the Political Parties on the Subject)*. Istanbul: Boyut.

Ceran, A. 2016. Data Protection Agenda of Brussels and Ankara: Same Goal/Different Motives. *Economic Development Foundation (İKV), Monthly*, Issue: 15 January. [Online]. Available at: www.ikv.org.tr/images/files/IKV-newsleter-January(1).pdf [accessed: 3 April 2016].

Chadwick, V. 2016. Austrian Chancellor: Turkey's EU Accession Talks a 'Diplomatic Fiction'. *Politico*, 4 August. [Online]. Available at: www.politico.eu/article/austria-Turkey–EU-talks-news-fiction-kern-christian-kern-europe-membership-erdogan-migration/ [accessed: 8 August 2016].

Clinton, W. J. 1999. *Public Papers of the Presidents of the United States*. [Online]. Available at: https://books.google.com.tr/books?id=hCbhAwAAQBAJ&pg=PA2091&lpg=PA2091&dq=clinton+helsinki+summit+turkey+EU&source=bl&ots=bOHYfg6bTV&sig=5X6vClRZEcNLZmTmb9G2elu64nM&hl=tr&sa=X&ved=0CEIQ6AEwBGoVChMItY6H69zsyAIVBkYPCh15zwz0#v=onepage&q=clinton%20helsinki%20summit%20turkey%20EU&f=false [accessed: 1 November 2015].

CNN. 2012. *French Senate Passes Armenian Genocide Bill*, 24 January. [Online]. Available at: http://edition.cnn.com/2012/01/23/world/europe/france-armenia-genocide/ [accessed: 28 July 2015].

Council of Europe. 1957. *European Agreement on Regulations governing the Movement of Persons between Member States of the Council of Europe*, European Treaty Series, No. 25, Paris, 13 December. [Online]. Available at: https://rm.coe.int/CoERMPublicCommonSearchServices/DisplayDCTMContent?documentId=0900001680064588 [accessed: 15 March 2015].

Council of the European Union. 2016. *EU–Turkey Statement*, Press Release, 18 March, 144/16, Brussels. [Online]. Available at: www.consilium.europa.eu/en/press/press-releases/2016/03/18-EU–Turkey-statement/ [accessed: 3 April 2016].

Council of the European Union. 2013. *Statement by the Spokesperson of High Representative Catherine Ashton on Violence in Turkey*, A 295/13, 2 June, Brussels. [Online]. Available at: www.consilium.europa.eu/uedocs/cms_Data/docs/pressdata/EN/foraff/137372.pdf [accessed: 28 July 2015].

Council of the European Union. 2006. Press Release, 2770th Council Meeting General Affairs, 11 December, 16289/06 (Press 352), Brussels. [Online]. Available at: www.consilium.europa.eu/ueDocs/cms_Data/docs/pressData/en/gena/92122.pdf [accessed: 18 September 2013].

Council of the European Union. 2005. Enlargement: Turkey Declaration by the European Community and Its Member States, 21 September, No:12541/05 (Presse 243). [Online]. Available at: europa.eu/rapid/press-release_PRES-05-243_en.pdf [accessed: 06 November 2016].

Craig, P. and de Burca, G. 2015. *EU Law: Texts, Cases and Materials*. Sixth Edition. Oxford: Oxford University Press.

Cremona, M. 2009. The European Union and Regional Trade Agreements, in *European Yearbook of International Economic Law 2010*, edited by C. Herrmann and J. P. Terhechte. Heidelberg: Springer, 245–68.

Cyprus Mail. 2014. *Joint Declaration: Final Version as Agreed between the Two Leaders*, 11 February. [Online]. Available at: http://cyprus-mail.com/2014/02/11/joint-declaration-final-version-as-agreed-between-the-two-leaders/ [accessed: 23 August 2015].

Dagdeverenis, D. 2014. EU Public Opinion and Turkey's EU Membership. *Bridging Europe*, EU–Turkey Dialogue Initiative Working Paper, No. 2. [Online]. Available at: www.bridgingeurope.net/uploads/8/1/7/1/8171506/working_paper_on_eu_public_opinion_on_turkey_dagdeverenis_august.pdf [accessed: 17 July 2015].

Dahlman, C. 2004. Turkey's Accession to the EU: The Geopolitics of Enlargement. *Eurasian Geography and Economics*, 45(8), 553–74.

Davutoğlu, A. 2008. Turkey's Foreign Policy Vision: An Assessment of 2007. *Insight Turkey*, 10(1), 77–96.

Delanty, G. 1995. *Inventing Europe: Idea, Identity, Reality*. Hampshire: Palgrave Macmillan.

Demirel, F. 2013. The Kurdish Problem and the Peace Process in Turkey. *Muftah*, 4 November. [Online]. Available at: http://muftah.org/the-kurdish-problem-the-peace-process-in-turkey/#.VhqoDMdfFyi [accessed: 22 April 2015].

Derviş, K., Gros, D., Öztrak, F., Işık, Y. and Bayar, F. 2004. Turkey and the European Budget: Prospects and Issues, *Center for European Policy Studies*, EU–Turkey Working Paper, No: 6, August. [Online]. Available at: http://aei.pitt.edu/6760/1/1148_06.pdf [accessed: 30 October 2015].

Deutsche Welle. 2004. *Germany Supports Turkey's EU Membership Bid*, 24 February. [Online]. Available at: www.dw.com/en/germany-supports-turkeys-eu-membership-bid/a-1121703 [accessed: 1 November 2015].

Diez, T. 2004. Europe's others and the Return of Geopolitics. *Cambridge Review of International Affairs*, 17(2), 319–35.

DPT. 2001. *Turkey–EUropean Union Association Council Decisions 1964–2000*, Vol. 2, Publication No. DPT: 2596, State Planning Organisation, Ankara. [Online]. Available at: www.ab.gov.tr/files/_files/okk_eng.pdf [accessed: 22 November 2015].

Dünya. 2011. *President Gul Received a King's Welcome in the UK*, 23 November. [Online]. Available at: www.dunya.com/mobi/president-gul-received-a-kings-welcome-in-uk-138467h.htm [accessed: 24 July 2015].

Economic Development Foundation (İKV). 2014. *The Visa Requirements for Turkish Citizens Are against the Spirit Not Only of Turkey's EU Integration But Also of European Integration.* 28 May. [Online]. Available at: http://oldweb.ikv.org.tr/icerik_en.asp?konu=haberler&id=695&baslik=%93THE%20VISA%20REQUIREMENTS%20FOR%20TURKISH%20CITIZENS%20ARE%20AGAINST%20THE%20SPIRIT%20NOT%20ONLY%20OF%20TURKEY%92S%20EU%20INTEGRATION%20BUT%20ALSO%20OF%20THE%20EUROPEAN%20INTEGRATION%94 [accessed: 10 January 2015].

Economist. 1997. Turkey and Europe: Just Not Our Sort. *The Economist*, 15 March.

Egemen Bağış Website. 2011. *Yahudi Soykırımı Auschwitz'de ele alındı (Jewish Genocide Is Tackled in Auschwitz)*, 1 February. [Online]. Available at: http://egemenbagis.com/tr/1822 [accessed: 24 July 2015].

Elsig, M. 2009. *European Union Trade Policy after Enlargement: Does the Expanded Trade Power Have New Clothes?* Swiss National Centre of Competence in Research, Working Paper No 2009/22 March.

Elsig, M. 2007. The EU's Choice of Regulatory Venues for Trade Negotiations: A Tale of Agency Power? *Journal of Common Market Studies*, 45(4), 927–48.

Eraktan, G. 2013. Turkish Agriculture in Case of EU Membership or Nonmember Status, in *Turkey's Accession to the European Union: Political and Economic Challenges*, edited by B. Akçay and B. Yılmaz. Lanham: Lexington Books, 181–210.

Eralp, A. 2004. Turkey and the European Union, in *The Future of Turkish Foreign Policy*, edited by L. G. Martin and D. Keridis. Cambridge: MIT Press, 63–82.

Erdenir, B. 2012. Vize (Visa), in *Avrupa Birliği: Tarihçe, Teoriler, Kurumlar ve Politikalar (European Union: History, Theories, Institutions and Policies)*, edited by B. Akçay and İ. Göçmen. Ankara: Seçkin, 471–95.

Ergin, S. 1998. Yılmaz-Kohl İlişkisi Nerede Koptu? (Where Did the Yılmaz-Kohl Relationship Break Off? *Hürriyet*, 12 March. [Online]. Available at: http://hurarsiv.hurriyet.com.tr/goster/haber.aspx?id=-9589 [accessed: 26 January 2014].

Ethier, D. 2003. Is Democracy Promotion Effective? Comparing Conditionality and Incentives. *Democratisation*, 10(1), 99–120.

Euractiv. 2009. Privileged Partnership Offers Turkey Neither Privilege Nor Partnership, 9 July. [Online]. Available at: https://www.euractiv.com/section/enlargement/opinion/privileged-partnership-offers-turkey-neither-privilege-nor-partnership/ [accessed: 29.10.2016].

EuroBarometer 82. 2014. *Public Opinion in the European Union*, Fall. [Online]. Available at: http://ec.europa.eu/public_opinion/archives/eb/eb82/eb82_first_en.pdf [accessed: 9 June 2014].

EuroBarometer 71. 2009. *Public Opinion in the European Union*, September. [Online]. Available at: http://ec.europa.eu/public_opinion/archives/eb/eb71/eb71_std_part1.pdf [accessed: 9 June 2014].

EuroBarometer 61. 2004. *Public Opinion in the EU15*, Spring. [Online]. Available at: http://ec.europa.eu/public_opinion/archives/eb/eb61/eb61_en.htm [accessed: 9 June 2014].

Euronews. 2010. *Interview with Turkey's European Affairs Minister Egemen Bağış*, 13 September. [Online]. Available at: www.euronews.com/2010/09/13/interview-with-turkey-s-european-affairs-minister-egemen-bagis/ [accessed: 24 July 2015].

European Commission. 2016. *Turkey 2016 Progress Report*, 9 November, Brussels. [Online]. Available at: http://www.ab.gov.tr/files/5%20Ekim/20161109_report_turkey.pdf [accessed: 25 November 2016].

European Commission. 2016a. *Staff Working Document Accompanying the Document Second Report on Progress by Turkey in Fulfilling the Requirements of Its Visa Liberalisation Roadmap*, {COM(2016) 140 final}, 4 March, Brussels. [Online]. Available at: http://ec.europa.eu/dgs/home-affairs/e-library/documents/policies/international-affairs/general/docs/turkey_second_progress_report_commission_staff_working_en.pdf [accessed: 10 August 2016].

European Commission. 2016b. *Report from the Commission to the European Parliament and the Council: Third Report on Progress by Turkey in Fulfilling the Requirements of Its Visa Liberalisation Roadmap*, {COM(2016) 278 final}, 4 May, Brussels. [Online]. Available at: http://ec.europa.eu/dgs/home-affairs/what-we-do/policies/european-agenda-migration/proposal-implementation-package/docs/20160504/third_progress_report_on_turkey_visa_liberalisation_roadmap_en.pdf [accessed: 4 August 2016].

European Commission. 2016c. *Temporary Reintroduction of Border Control*, Directorate-General Migration and Home Affairs. [Online]. Available at: http://ec.europa.eu/dgs/home-affairs/what-we-do/policies/borders-and-visas/schengen/reintroduction-border-control/index_en.htm [accessed: 10 August 2016].

European Commission. 2016d. *European Solidarity: A Refugee Relocation System*. [Online]. Available at: http://ec.europa.eu/dgs/home-affairs/what-we-do/policies/european-agenda-migration/backgroundinformation/docs/2_eu_solidarity_a_refugee_relocation_system_en.pdf [accessed: 31 August 2016].

European Commission. 2016e. Managing the Refugee Crisis: Commission Reports on Implementation of EU–Turkey Joint Action Plan, 10 February Brussels. [Online]. Available at: http://europa.eu/rapid/press-release_IP-16-268_en.htm [accessed: 4 November 2016].

European Commission. 2016f. *Communication from the Commission to the EP, the European Council and the Council: Second Report on the Progress Made in the Implementation of the EU–Turkey Statement*, {COM(2016) 349 final}, 15 June, Brussels. [Online]. Available at: http://ec.europa.eu/dgs/home-affairs/what-we-do/policies/european-agenda-migration/proposal-implementation-package/docs/20160615/2nd_commission_report_on_progress_made_in_the_implementation_of_the_EU–Turkey_agreement_en.pdf [accessed: 10 August 2016].

European Commission. 2015a. *Turkey 2015 Progress Report*, SWD (2015) 216, Brussels. [Online]. Available at: www.ab.gov.tr/files/000files/2015/11/2015_turkiye_raporu.pdf [accessed: 25 November 2015].

European Commission. 2015b. Draft Action Plan: Stepping Up EU–Turkey Cooperation on Support of Refugees and Migration Management in View of the Situation in Syria and Iraq, Brussels, 6 October. [Online]. Available at: http://europa.eu/rapid/press-release_MEMO-15-5777_en.htm [accessed: 29 October 2015].

European Commission. 2015c. *EU–Turkey Joint Action Plan*, Fact Sheet, MEMO/15/5860, Brussels, 15 October. [Online]. Available at: http://europa.eu/rapid/press-release_MEMO-15-5860_en.htm [accessed: 16 January 2016].

European Commission. 2015d. *EU and Turkey Announce Modernisation of Customs Union*, 12 May, Brussels. [Online]. Available at: http://trade.ec.europa.eu/doclib/press/index.cfm?id=1307 [accessed: 29 October 2016].

European Commission. 2014a. *Turkey 2014 Progress Report*, COM(2014)700, Brussels. [Online]. Available at: http://ec.europa.eu/enlargement/pdf/key_documents/2014/20141008-turkey-progress-report_en.pdf [accessed: 21 July 2014].

European Commission. 2014b. *Commission Implementing Decision of 18 February 2014 Setting Out the List of Regions Eligible for Funding from the European Regional Development Fund and the European Social Fund and of Member States Eligible for Funding from the Cohesion Fund for the Period 2014–2020 (notified under document C(2014) 974)*, 2014/99/EU, OJ L 50, 20 February. [Online]. Available at: http://eur-lex.europa.eu/legal-content/EN/TXT/?uri=CELEX:32014D0099 [accessed: 16 January 2016].

European Commission. 2014c. *Report from the Commission to the European Parliament and the Council on Progress by Turkey in Fulfilling the Requirements of Its Visa Liberalisation Roadmap*, COM(2014) 646 final, 20 October, Brussels. [Online]. Available at: http://eur-lex.europa.eu/legal-content/EN/TXT/PDF/?uri=CELEX:52014DC0646&from=EN [accessed: 10 August 2016].

European Commission. 2013a. *Crucial Moment in EU–Turkey Relations*. Stefan Füle's Website, 12 June. [Online]. Available at: http://ec.europa.eu/archives/commission_2010-2014/fule/headlines/news/2013/06/20130612_en.htm [accessed: 28 July 2015].

European Commission. 2013b. *Roadmap towards a Visa-free Regime with Turkey*, 16 December. [Online]. Available at: http://ec.europa.eu/dgs/home-affairs/what-is-new/news/news/docs/20131216-roadmap_towards_the_visa-free_regime_with_turkey_en.pdf [accessed: 8 November 2015].

European Commission. 2012a. *Turkey 2012 Progress Report*, COM(2012)600, Brussels. [Online]. Available at: http://madde14.org/english/images/c/cd/2012ecpr.pdf [accessed: 21 July 2014].

European Commission. 2012b. Press Release, *Positive EU–Turkey Agenda Launched in Ankara*, 17 May, Memo/12/359, http://europa.eu/rapid/press-release_MEMO-12-359_en.htm [accessed: 29 October 2016].

European Commission. 2006a. *Enlargement Strategy and Main Challenges 2006–2007*, COM(2006) 649, Brussels, 8 November. [Online]. Available at: http://ec.europa.eu/enlargement/pdf/key_documents/2006/nov/com_649_strategy_paper_en.pdf [accessed: 4 November 2016].

European Commission. 2006b. *Special Report on the EU's Capacity to Integrate New Members*, Annex I to 2006–7 Enlargement Strategy, 8 November, COM(2006) 649 final, Brussels.

European Commission. 2005a. *Declaration of the President of the European Commission José Manuel Barroso on the opening of accession negotiations with Turkey*. [Online]. Available at: http://europa.eu/rapid/press-release_IP-05-1219_en.htm [accessed: 26 January 2017].

European Commission. 2005b. *Negotiating Framework for Turkey*, Luxembourg, 3 October. [Online]. Available at: http://ec.europa.eu/enlargement/pdf/turkey/st20002_05_tr_framedoc_en.pdf [accessed: 18 October 2005].

European Commission. 2004a. *2004 Regular Report on Turkey's Progress Towards Accession*, COM(2004)656, Brussels. [Online]. Available at: www.ab.gov.tr/files/AB_Iliskileri/Tur_En_Realitons/Progress/Turkey_Progress_Report_2004.pdf [accessed: 24 December 2008].

European Commission. 2004b. *Issues Arising from Turkey's Membership Perspective*. Commission Staff Working Document, COM (2004) 656 final, 6 October, Brussels. [Online]. Available at: http://ec.europa.eu/enlargement/archives/pdf/key_documents/2004/issues_paper_en.pdf [accessed: 3 August 2015].

European Commission. 2004c. *Communication from the Commission to the Council and the European Parliament: Recommendation of the European Commission on Turkey's Progress towards Accession*, COM(2004) 656 final, 6 October, Brussels. [Online]. Available at: http://eur-lex.europa.eu/LexUriServ/LexUriServ.do?uri=COM:2004:0656:FIN:EN:PDF [accessed: 29 January 2014].

European Commission. 1998. *Regular Report from the Commission on Turkey's Progress towards Accession*. [Online]. Available at: http://ec.europa.eu/enlargement/archives/pdf/key_documents/1998/turkey_en.pdf [accessed: 26 January 2014].

European Commission. 1993. *Commission Opinion on the Application by the Republic of Cyprus for Membership*, Paragraph 47. Brussels, June 30, Doc. COM(93) 313 fin.

European Commission. 1990. *Communication to the Council on Relations with Turkey*, SEC (90) 1017 final. Brussels.

European Commission. 1989. *Commission's Opinion on Turkey Request for Accession to the Community*, SEC (89) 2290 final/2, 20 December, Brussels. [Online]. Available at: http://aei.pitt.edu/4475/1/4475.pdf [accessed: 22 May 2013].

European Commission. 1976. *Commission Opinion on Greek Application for Membership of the European Communities*, Bulletin of the European Communities, February 1976, n° Supplement 2/1976. 29 January, Luxembourg: Office for Official Publications of the European Communities. [Online]. Available at: www.cvce.eu/content/publication/1999/1/1/add5c5dd-118f-412d-bf8a-277a9fc1f239/publishable_en.pdf [accessed: 7 June 2013].

European Council. 2015. *EU–Turkey Statement*, 29 November. [Online]. Available at: www.consilium.europa.eu/en/press/press-releases/2015/11/29-EU–Turkey-meeting-statement/ [accessed: 29 November 2015].

European Council. 2004. *Presidency Conclusions*, Brussels, 16–17 December. [Online]. Available at: www.consilium.europa.eu/ueDocs/cms_Data/docs/pressData/en/ec/83201.pdf [accessed: 14 April 2016].

European Council. 2002. *Presidency Conclusions*, Copenhagen, 12–13 December. [Online]. Available at: http://ue.eu.int/ueDocs/cms_Data/docs/pressData/en/ec/73842.pdf [accessed: 3 March 2004].

European Council. 1999. *Presidency Conclusions*, Helsinki, 10–11 December. [Online]. Available at: www.consilium.europa.eu/ueDocs/cms_Data/docs/pressData/en/ec/ACFA4C.htm [accessed: 23 January 2000].

European Council. 1997. *Presidency Conclusions*, Luxembourg, 12–13 December. [Online]. Available at: www.consilium.europa.eu/ueDocs/cms_Data/docs/pressData/en/ec/032a0008.htm [accessed: 18 August 1998].

European Council. 1994. *Presidency Conclusions*, Essen, 9–10 December. [Online]. Available at: www.ab.gov.tr/files/ardb/evt/1_avrupa_birligi/1_4_zirveler_1985_sonrasi/1994_12_essen_zirvesi_baskanlik_sonuc_bildirgesi_en.pdf [accessed: 8 June 2013].

European Council. 1993. *Presidency Conclusions*, Copenhagen, 21–22 June. [Online]. Available at: www.consilium.europa.eu/ueDocs/cms_Data/docs/pressData/en/ec/72921.pdf [accessed: 5 June 2014].

European External Action Service. 2016. *Statement by Federica Mogherini and Johannes Hahn on the Detention of Several HDP Members, Including the Party's Co-Chairs*, 4 November. [Online]. Available at: https://eeas.europa.eu/headquarters/headquarters-homepage/14039/statement-by-federica-mogherini-and-johannes-hahn-on-the-detention-of-several-hdp-members-including-the-partys-co-chairs_en [accessed: 05 November 2016].

European Parliament. 2016. *Visa Liberalisation for Turkey: EU Criteria Must Be Met, say MEPs*, Press release, 10 May. [Online]. Available at: www.europarl.europa.eu/news/en/news-room/20160509IPR26368/Visa-liberalisation-for-Turkey–EU-criteria-must-be-met-say-MEPs [accessed: 4 August 2016].

European Parliament. 2015. *Irregular Immigration in the EU: Facts and Figures*, April. [Online]. Available at: www.europarl.europa.eu/RegData/etudes/BRIE/2015/554202/EPRS_BRI(2015)554202_EN.pdf [accessed: 8 November 2015].

European Parliament. 2013. *European Parliament Resolution on the Situation in Turkey*, (2013/2664(RSP)), 11 June. [Online]. Available at: www.europarl.europa.eu/sides/getDoc.do?type=MOTION&reference=B7-2013-0309&language=EN [accessed: 28 July 2015].

European Stability Initiative. 2015. *New Facts and Figures on Western Balkan Asylum Seekers*, 6 April. [Online]. Available at: www.esiweb.org/pdf/New%20facts%20and%20figures%20on%20WB%20asylum%20claims%206%20April%202015.pdf [accessed: 8 November 2015].

European Stability Initiative. 2011. *Visa Free Travel and Asylum*. 30 June. [Online]. Available at: www.esiweb.org/index.php?lang=en&id=532 [accessed: 8 November 2015].

Eurostat. 2015a. *GDP Per Capita in PPS*, 1 June. [Online]. Available at: http://ec.europa.eu/eurostat/tgm/table.do?tab=table&init=1&language=en&pcode=tec00114&plugin=1 [accessed: 5 November 2015].

Eurostat. 2015b. *Asylum Quarterly Report*, 16 September. [Online]. Available at: http://ec.europa.eu/eurostat/statistics-explained/index.php/Asylum_quarterly_report [accessed: 8 November 2015].

EU–Turkey Association's Annual Report. 1994. *Minutes of the 35th Meeting of the EC-Turkey Association Council*. EC-TR 126/94 (FIN), Office for Official Publications for European Communities, Luxembourg.

Federal Ministry for Europe, Integration and Foreign Affairs. 2004. *Foreign Minister Ursula Plassnik Ahead of EU Summit*, 13 December. [Online]. Available at: www.bmeia.gv.at/en/foreign-ministry/news/press-releases/2004/foreign-minister-plassnik-ahead-of-eu-summit.html [accessed: 29 January 2014].

Felbermayr, G. J. and Larch, M. 2013. The Transatlantic Trade and Investment Partnership (TTIP): Potentials, Problems and Perspectives. *CESifo Forum*, 14(2), June, 49–60. [Online]. Available at: www.cesifo-group.de/portal/page/portal/DocBase_Content/ZS/ZS-CESifo_Forum/zs-for-2013/zs-for-2013-2/forum2-13-special3.pdf [accessed: 14 June 2015].

Fihel, A., Janicka, A., Kaczmarczyk, P. and Nestorowicz, J. 2015. *Free Movement of Workers and Transitional Arrangements: Lessons from the 2004 and 2007 Enlargements*. Warsaw: Centre of Migration Research University of Warsaw.

Financial Times. 2016. *Britain Should Vote to Stay in the EU*, 5 June. [Online]. Available at: www.ft.com/cms/s/2/3748166e-3151-11e6-ad39-3fee5ffe5b5b.html#axzz4GqD8LAnq [accessed: 10 August 2016].

Flam, H. 2005. Economic Effects of Turkey's Membership on the European Union, in *Turkey: Economic Reform and Accession to the European Union*, edited by B. M. Hoekman and S. Togan. Washington: World Bank, 341–52.

France 24. 2013. *Roma Deportations Split French Government*, 27 September. [Online]. Available at: www.france24.com/en/20130927-france-division-socialist-party-roma-gypsies-people-valls-duflot-immigration-elections [accessed: 8 November 2015].

Freedom House. 2017. *Freedom in the World, Turkey*. [Online]. Available at: https:// freedom house.org/report/freedom-world/2017/turkey [accessed: 28 February 2017].

Freedom House. 2016. *Freedom of the Press, Turkey*. [Online]. Available at: https:// freedom house.org/report/ freedom-press/2016/turkey [accessed: 23 January 2016].

Freedom House. 2015a. *Freedom of the Press, Turkey*. [Online]. Available at: www. freedomhouse.org/report/freedom-press/2015/turkey [accessed: 23 August 2015].

Freedom House. 2015b. *Freedom in the World, Turkey*. [Online]. Available at: www. freedomhouse.org/report/freedom-world/2015/turkey [accessed: 23 August 2015].

Freedom House. 2011. *Freedom of the Press, Turkey*. [Online]. Available at: www.freedom house.org/report/freedom-press/2011/turkey [accessed: 23 August 2015].

Frontex. 2016a. *Eastern Mediterranean Route*. [Online]. Available at: http://frontex.europa. eu/trends-and-routes/eastern-mediterranean-route/ [accessed: 04 November 2016].

Frontex. 2016b. *Western Balkan Route*. [Online]. Available at: http://frontex.europa.eu/ trends-and-routes/western-balkan-route/ [accessed: 04 November 2016].

Frontex. 2015. *710,000 Migrants Entered EU in First Nine Months of 2015*, 13 October. [Online]. Available at: http://frontex.europa.eu/news/710-000-migrants-entered-eu-in-first-nine-months-of-2015-NUiBkk [accessed: 8 November 2015].

Füle, S. "EU–Turkey Bound Together", Conference of Ministry for EU Affairs "Rethinking Global Challenges: Constructing a Common Future for Turkey and the EU". Istanbul, Turkey, 07.06.2013. [Online] Available at: http://europa.eu/rapid/press-release_ SPEECH-13- 517_en.htm [accessed: 26 January 2017].

Giauque, J. G. 2002. *Grand Designs and Visions of Unity: The Atlantic Powers and the Reorganization of Western Europe*. Chapel Hill: The University of North Carolina Press.

Gill, G. 2000. *The Dynamics of Democratisation: Elites, Civil Society and the Transition Process*. New York: The St. Martin Press.

Gow, D. and MacAskill, E. 2004. Turkish Accession Could Spell End of EU, Says Commissioner. *The Guardian*, 8 September. [Online]. Available at: www.theguardian.com/ world/2004/sep/08/turkey.eu [accessed: 26 August 2015].

Grigoriadis, I. N. 2003. *The Changing Role of the EU Factor in Greek-Turkish Relations*, London School of Economics and Political Science Hellenic Observatory 1st PhD Symposium on Modern Greece. London, 21 June. [Online]. Available at: www.lse.ac.uk/ europeanInstitute/research/hellenicObservatory/pdf/1st_Symposium/GrigoriadisIoan nis.pdf [accessed: 1 November 2015].

Groenendijk, K. and Guild, E. 2011. *Visa Policy of Member States and the EU towards Turkish Nationals after Soysal*. Economic Development Foundation (İKV), Publication No: 249, 2nd ed. September.

Grugel, J. 2005. Democratisation and the Realm of Politics in International Political Economy, in *Globalising International Political Economy*, edited by N. Phillips. New York: Palgrave Macmillan, 193–220.

Grugel, J. 1999. *Democracy without Borders*. London: Routledge.

The Guardian. 2016a. *Turkish Journalists Released from Jail after Court Rules Press Freedom Violated*, 26 February. [Online]. Available at: https://www.theguardian.com/ world/2016/feb/26/turkish-journalists-released-jail-court-rules-press-freedom-violated-dundar [accessed: 23 April 2016].

The Guardian. 2016b. *Turkey Rounds Up Academics Who Signed Petition Denouncing Attacks on Kurds*, 15 January. [Online]. Available at: https://www.theguardian.com/world/2016/jan/15/turkey-rounds-up-academics-who-signed-petition-denouncing-attacks-on-kurds [accessed: 8 February 2016].

Gülmez, S. B. 2008. The EU Policy of the Republican People's Party: An Inquiry on the Opposition Party and Euro-Skepticism in Turkey. *Turkish Studies*, 9(3), 423–36.

Gümüşçü, Ş. and Keyman, E. F. 2014. Ruling vs. Governing: Pluralism and Democracy in Turkey, Egypt and Tunisia. *The German Marshall Fund of the United States (GMF)*, On Turkey, Analysis, 15 April. [Online]. Available at: http://ipc.sabanciuniv.edu/wp-content/uploads/2014/04/1397580368Gumuscu_Keyman_RulingGoverning_Apr14.pdf [accessed: 24 April 2015].

Gümüşçü, Ş. and Keyman, E. F. 2013. Islamism, Electoral Hegemony, and Democracy: Lessons from Turkey, Egypt and Tunisia. *The German Marshall Fund of the United States (GMF)*, On Turkey, Analysis, 16 December. [Online]. Available at: http://ipc.sabanciuniv.edu/en/wp-content/uploads/2013/12/1387214390Gumuscu_Keyman_IslamismElectoralHegemonyDemocracy_Dec13.pdf [accessed: 24 April 2015].

Güneş, D., Mavuş, M. and Oduncu, A. 2013. AB-ABD Serbest Ticaret Anlaşması ve Türkiye Üzerine Etkileri (EU-US Free Trade Agreement and Its Impacts on Turkey). *Ekonomi Notları*, Türkiye Cumhuriyet Merkez Bankası, 2013–30, 26 November. [Online]. Available at: www.tcmb.gov.tr/wps/wcm/connect/e23c8575-44bd-4eab-ab52-c14286482258/EN1330.pdf?MOD=AJPERES [accessed: 29 June 2014].

Guttenberg, Karl-Theodor zu. 2005. We Need an Option Short of Full Membership. *European Affairs*, 6(4), updated 11 November 2009, www.europeaninstitute.org/index.php/37-european-affairs/fall-2005/177-we-need-an-option-short-of-full-membership [accessed: 29 October 2016].

Habermas, J. and Derrida, J. 2003. February 15, or What Binds Europeans Together: A Plea for a Common Foreign Policy Beginning in the Core of Europe. *Constellations*, 10(3), 291–7.

Habertürk. 2016. AB Bakanı Ömer Çelik: Tablo Değişmezse Anlaşmayı Feshederiz (EU Minister Ömer Çelik: We Will Abolish the Agreement If the Picture Does Not Change), 4 November. [Online]. Available at: www.haberturk.com/dunya/haber/1319343-ab-bakani-omer-celik-tablo-degismezse-anlasmayi-feshederiz [accessed: 06 November 2016].

Habertürk. 2014. *Anayasa Mahkemesi'nden Flaş İlker Başbuğ kararı! (Ruling of the Constitutional Court about İlker Başbuğ)*, 6 March. [Online]. Available at: www.haberturk.com/gundem/haber/927324-anayasa-mahkemesinden-flas-ilker-basbug-karari [accessed: 17 April 2015].

Hale, W. 2002. *Turkish Foreign Policy 1774–2000*. London: Frank Cass.

Hale, W. and Özbudun, E. 2010. *Islamism, Democracy and Liberalism in Turkey: The Case of the AKP*. Oxon: Routledge.

Hallstein, W. 1963. *Address by Professor Dr. Walter Hallstein, President of the Commission of the European Economic Community, on the Occasion of the Signature of the Association Agreement with Turkey*, Archive of European Integration, 12 September, Ankara. [EU Speech]. [Online]. Available at: http://aei.pitt.edu/14311/ [accessed: 3 March 2016].

Human Rights Watch. 2015. *World Report 2015: Turkey, Events of 2014*. [Online]. Available at: https://www.hrw.org/world-report/2015/country-chapters/turkey [accessed: 5 November 2015].

Huntington, Samuel P. 1991. *Third Wave: Democratisation in the Late Twentieth Century*. Norman: University of Oklahoma Press.

Hürriyet. 2006. *Maraş Kıbrıs'ta İpleri Kopardı (Maraş- Varosha Broke Ties in Cyprus)*, 28 November. [Online]. Available at: www.hurriyet.com.tr/maras-kibris-ta-ipleri-kopardi-5514979?nomobile=true [accessed: 04 November 2016].

Hürriyet. 2004. *CHP'den AB'nin Tuzakları Raporu (The Report by the CHP on the EU's Pitfalls)*, 24 November. [Online]. Available at: http://webarsiv.hurriyet.com.tr/2004/11/24/558437.asp [accessed: 29 January 2014].

Hürriyet. 2000. *AB ile gizli mektup trafiği (Confidential Letter Traffic with the EU)*, 20 March. [Online]. Available at: http://hurarsiv.hurriyet.com.tr/goster/haber.aspx?id=-141273 [accessed: 24 January 2014].

Hürriyet. 1999. *Tarihi mektuplar (Historical Letters)*, 5 June. [Online]. Available at: http://arama.hurriyet.com.tr/arsivnews.aspx?id=-83722 [accessed: 26 January 2014].

Hürriyet Daily News. 2015a. *Ankara to Return EP Report on Turkey: Turkish EU Minister*, 10 June. [Online]. Available at: www.hurriyetdailynews.com/ankara-to-return-ep-report-on-turkey-turkish-eu-minister-.aspx?pageID=238&nID=83782&NewsCatID=510 [accessed: 28 July 2015].

Hürriyet Daily News. 2015b. *Turkey Not Manipulating Cyprus Peace Talks*, 3 August. [Online]. Available at: www.hurriyetdailynews.com/turkey-not-manipulating-cyprus-peace-talks.aspx?pageID=238&nID=86304&NewsCatID=510 [accessed: 9 September 2015].

Hürriyet Daily News. 2013. *Turkish PM Erdoğan and EU Commissioner Füle in Crossfire over Gezi Park Protests*, 7 June. [Online]. Available at: www.hurriyetdailynews.com/turkish-pm-erdogan-and-eu-commissioner-fule-in-crossfire-over-gezi-park-protests.aspx?pageID=238&nid=48441 [accessed: 28 July 2015].

Hürriyet Daily News. 2001. *Ex-Chancellor Schmidt against Turkey EU Membership*, 8 June. [Online]. Available at: www.hurriyetdailynews.com/ex-chancellor-schmidt-against-Turkey–EU-membership.aspx?pageID=438&n=ex-chancellor-schmidt-against-Turkey–EU-membership-2001-06-08 [accessed: 1 November 2015].

Hürriyet Daily News. 1998. *. . . And They Closed Refah*, 17 January. [Online]. Available at: www.hurriyetdailynews.com/-and-they-closed-refah.aspx?pageID=438&n= . . . -and-they-closed-refah-1998-01-17 [accessed: 5 November 2015].

Hürriyet Daily News. 1997. *From the Papers*, 20 December. [Online]. Available at: www.hurriyetdailynews.com/from-the-papers.aspx?pageID=438&n=from-the-papers-1997-12-20 [accessed: 1 November 2015].

Huysmans, J. 2000.The European Union and Securitization of Migration. *Journal of Common Market Studies*, 38(5), 751–77.

İnal, N. N. and Yeğenoğlu, D. 2005. German and French Leaders' Views on Turkey's EU Membership. *The Washington Institute*, POLICYWATCH No: 1007, 27 June. [Online]. Available at: www.washingtoninstitute.org/policy-analysis/view/german-and-french-leaders-views-on-turkeys-eu-membership [accessed: 5 November 2015].

Independent Commission on Turkey. 2014. *Turkey in Europe: The Imperative for Change*, The Third Report, March. [Online]. Available at: www.independentcommissionon turkey.org/pdfs/2014_english.pdf [accessed: 16 January 2016].

Independent Commission on Turkey. 2004. *Turkey in Europe: More than a Promise?* September. [Online]. Available at: www.independentcommissiononturkey.org/pdfs/2004_english.pdf [accessed: 16 January 2016].

InfoCuria. 2013. *Leyla Ecem Demirkan v Bundesrepublik Deutschland*. Case-law of the Court of Justice. Judgment of the Court (Grand Chamber) of 24 September 2013, Case C-221/11. [Online]. Available at: http://curia.europa.eu/juris/document/document.jsf?text=&docid=142081&pageIndex=0&doclang=EN&mode=lst&dir=&occ=first&part=1&cid=53399 [accessed: 8 November 2015].

InfoCuria. 2009. *Mehmet Soysal and Ibrahim Savatli v Bundesrepublik Deutschland.* Case-law of the Court of Justice. Judgment of the Court (First Chamber) of 19 February 2009, Case C-228/06. [Online]. Available at: http://curia.europa.eu/juris/document/document.jsf;jsessionid=9ea7d2dc30ddae939a167eb8473da553d6982619223f.e34KaxiLc3qMb40Rch0SaxuRc3b0?text=&docid=74024&pageIndex=0&doclang=EN&mode=lst&dir=&occ=first&part=1&cid=35966 [accessed: 8 November 2015].

InfoCuria. 1990. *S. Z. Sevince v Staatssecretaris van Justitie.* Case-law of the Court of Justice. Judgment of the Court of 20 September 1990, Case C-192/89. [Online]. Available at: http://curia.europa.eu/juris/liste.jsf?language=en&num=C-192/89 [accessed: 24 January 2015].

InfoCuria. 1987. *Meryem Demirel v Stadt Schwabish Gmünd.* Case-law of the Court of Justice. Judgment of the Court of 30 September 1987, Case 12/86. [Online]. Available at: http://curia.europa.eu/juris/liste.jsf?language=en&num=C-12/86 [accessed: 24 January 2015].

InfoCuria. 1983. *Societa Italiana per l'Oleodotto Transalpino (SIOT) v Ministero dele finanze. . . .* Case-law of the Court of Justice. Judgment of the Court of 16 March 1983, Case 266/81. [Online]. Available at: http://curia.europa.eu/juris/liste.jsf?language=en&num=C-266/81 [accessed: 17 October 2015].

InfoCuria. 1973. *Riseria Luigi Geddo v. Ente Nazionale Risi.* Case-law of the Court of Justice. Judgment of the Court of 12 July 1973, Case 2–73. [Online]. Available at: http://curia.europa.eu/juris/liste.jsf?language=en&jur=C,T,F&num=2-73&td=ALL [accessed: 17 October 2015].

International Crisis Group. 2016. The Human Cost of the PKK Conflict in Turkey: The Case of Sur. *Europe Briefing*, No. 80, 17 March. [Online]. Available at: www.crisisgroup.org/en/regions/europe/turkey-cyprus/turkey/b080-the-human-cost-of-the-pkk-conflict-in-turkey-the-case-of-sur.aspx [accessed: 11 April 2016].

International Crisis Group. 2009. Cyprus: Reunification or Partition. *Europe Report*, No. 201, 30 September. [Online]. Available at: www.crisisgroup.org/~/media/Files/europe/201_cyprus___reunification_or_partition.pdf [accessed: 28 June 2013].

Juncos, A. E. and Perez-Solorzano Borragan, N. 2013. Enlargement, in *European Union Politics*, edited by M. Cini and N. Perez-Solorzano Borragan. Oxford: Oxford University Press, 226–39.

Kabaalioğlu, H. 2012. Turkey's Relations with the European Union: Customs Union and Accession Negotiations, in *Turkey and the European Union: Different Dimensions*, edited by P. C. Müller-Graff and H. Kabaalioğlu. Baden-Baden: Nomos, 11–23.

Kabaalioğlu, H. 1998. The Customs Union: A Final Step before Turkey's Accession to the European Union. *Marmara Journal of European Studies*, 6(1), 113–40.

Kaliber, A. 2012. Turkey's Cyprus Policy: A Case of Contextual Europeanisation, in *Turkey and the European Union: Processes of Europeanisation*, edited by Ç. Nas and Y. Özer. Burlington: Ashgate, 225–41.

Kambas, M. 2015. Cyprus Says Cannot Lift Veto on Turkey's EU Talks. *Reuters*, 19 October. [Online]. Available at: www.reuters.com/article/2015/10/19/us-cyprus-Turkey–EU-idUSKCN0SD0TH20151019#9R15bYQbyPE2xMQl.97 [accessed: 5 November 2015].

Karakaş, C. 2013, EU–Turkey: Integration without Full Membership or Membership without Full Integration? A Conceptual Framework for Accession Alternatives. *Journal of Common Market Studies*, 51(6), 1057–73.

Karakeçili, F. 2011. *15'inci Yılında Türkiye-AB Gümrük Birliği ve Yaşanan Temel Sorunlar (15th Anniversary of Turkey- EU Customs Union and Basic Problems).* Economic

Development Foundation (İKV), Değerlendirme Notu 31 (Evaluation Note 31), February. [Online]. Available at: http://ikv.org.tr/images/upload/data/files/31-15inci_ylinda_turkiye-ab_gumruk_birligi_yasanan_temel_sorunlar__subat_2011___2_.pdf [accessed: 12 June 2012].

Kaya, G. 2014. Free Movement of Turkish Citizens after the Soysal Judgment, in *Turkey and the European Union: Facing New Challenges and Opportunities*, edited by F. Cengiz and L. Hoffmann. London: Routledge, 121–37.

Kaygusuz, Ö. 2010. Türkiye-AB İlişkilerinin "Möbius" Şeridi: AKP Reformculuğu ve AB Çokkültürlülüğü (Möbius Strip of Turkey–EU Relations: AKP Reformism and EU Multiculturalism), in *AKP Kitabı: Bir Dönüşümün Bilançosu (The AKP Book: Balance Sheet of a Transformation)*, edited by İ. Uzgel and B. Duru, 2nd ed. Ankara: Phoenix, 410–38.

Keyman, E. F. and Öniş, Z. 2004. Helsinki, Copenhagen and Beyond: Challenges to the New Europe and the Turkish State, in *Turkey and European Integration: Accession Prospects and Issues*, edited by M. Uğur and N. Canefe. London: Routledge, 173–93.

Kilit, G. 2014. Türkiye'de Tarım Büyürken Sorunlar Azalıyor mu? AB Ortak Tarım Politikasına Uyum Sürecinin Etkileri (Do Problems Decrease in Turkey While Agriculture Grows? Impacts of the Harmonisation with the EU Common Agricultural Policy. *İKV Değerlendirme Notu (İKV Evaluation Note)*, No: 89, August. [Online]. Available at: http://ikv.org.tr/images/files/Degerlendirme%20%20notu%2089.pdf [accessed: 04 November 2016].

Kirişçi, K. 2014. *Syrian Refugees and Turkey's Challenges: Going beyond Hospitality*. Brookings. [Online]. Available at: https://www.brookings.edu/wp-content/uploads/2016/06/Syrian-Refugees-and-Turkeys-Challenges-May-14-2014.pdf [accessed: 10 August 2016].

Kirişçi, K. 2013. The Rise and Fall of Turkey as a Model for the Arab World. *Brookings*, 15 August. [Online]. Available at: www.brookings.edu/research/opinions/2013/08/15-rise-and-fall-turkey-model-middle-east [accessed: 5 November 2015].

Kirişçi, K. 2007. *The Limits of Conditionality and Europeanisation: Turkey's Dilemmas in Adopting the EU Acquis on Asylum*. Draft paper prepared for the panel on Immigration, asylum and supranational governance: Implications of Europeanisation at the EUSA Tenth Biennial International Conference, Montreal, 17–19 May 2007. [Online]. Available at: http://aei.pitt.edu/7936/01/kirisci-k-08g.pdf [accessed: June 2009].

Kirişçi, K. 2003. The Question of Asylum and Illegal Migration in European Union-Turk ish Relations, in *Turkey and the European Union: Domestic Politics, Economic Integration and International Dynamics*, edited by A. Çarkoğlu and B. Rubin. London: Frank Cass, 79–106.

Kirişçi, K. 2002. *12–13 December 2002 Copenhagen Summit of the European Council and Turkey*, Turkish Industrialists' and Businessmen's Association (TÜSİAD), Washington Office, 15 December. [Online]. Available at: www.tusiad.us/Content/uploaded/KIRISCICOPENHAGENTUSIADWDC.PDF [accessed: 9 May 2011].

Köse, M., Bayün, S., Akduman, M. and Barutçu, U. 2014. Limanların Rum Bandıralı Gemilere Açılması (Opening of Ports to Greek Cypriot Flag Ships). *Hukuk Gündemi (Law Agenda)*, No: 1. Ankara Bar Association. [Online]. Available at: www.ankarabarosu.org.tr/siteler/ankarabarosu/hgdmakale/2014-1/10.pdf [accessed: 21 July 2015].

Kramer, H. 1996. Turkey and the European Union: A Multi-Dimensional Relationship with Hazy Perspectives, in *Turkey between East and West: New Challenges for a Rising Regional Power*, edited by V. Mastny and R. C. Nation. Boulder: Westview Press, 203–32.

Kroet, C. 2016. Erdoğan Calls on EU to Deliver Cash, Visa-Free Travel. *Politico*, 26 July. www.politico.eu/article/recep-tayyip-erdogan-calls-on-eu-to-deliver-cash-visa-free-travel-migration-deal-turkey/ [accessed: 26 September 2016].

Kubicek, P. 2013. Moving Goalposts: Democratisation and EU Membership for Turkey. *Centre for Policy and Research on Turkey (Research Turkey)*, 4 November, 2(9), 1–8. [Online]. Available at: http://researchturkey.org/moving-goalposts-democratization-and-eu-membership-for-turkey/ [accessed: 21 April 2015].

Kubicek, P. 2003. International Norms, the European Union and Democratisation: Tentative Theory and Evidence, in *The European Union and Democratisation*, edited by P. Kubicek. London: Routledge, 1–29.

Küçükcan, T. 2008. Turkish Migrants, Social Capital, and Culturalist Discourse in Turkey–EU Relations, in *Religion, Politics and Turkey's EU Accession*, edited by D. Jung and C. Raudvere. New York: Palgrave Macmillan, 199–221.

Kylstad, I. 2010. Turkey and the EU: A 'New' European Identity in the Making? *LSE 'Europe in Question' Discussion Paper Series*, No: 27/2010. [Online]. Available at: www.lse.ac.uk/europeanInstitute/LEQS/LEQSPaper27.pdf [accessed: 1 November 2015].

LaGro, E. 2008. Why Is President Sarkozy Actually against Turkish Accession to the EU? Facts and Challenges. *Perceptions*, Spring–Summer, 57–77.

Lasok, D. 1991. The Ankara Agreement: Principles and Interpretation. *Marmara Journal of European Studies*, 1(1–2), 27–49.

Lepeska, D. 2015. The AKP's Golden Opportunity: Erdoğan's Victory and Turkey's Open Door Policy. *Foreign Affairs*, 2 November. [Online]. Available at: https://www.foreignaffairs.com/articles/turkey/2015-11-02/akps-golden-opportunity [accessed: 5 November 2015].

Letsch, C. 2014. A Year after the Protests, Gezi Park Nurtures the Seeds of a New Turkey. *The Guardian*, 29 May. [Online]. Available at: www.theguardian.com/world/2014/may/29/gezi-park-year-after-protests-seeds-new-turkey [accessed: 5 November 2015].

Linz, J. J. and Stepan, A. (1996). *Problems of Democratic Transition and Consolidation: Southern Europe, South America and Post-Communist Europe*. London and Baltimore: The John Hopkins University Press.

Mayer, M. M. 2008. *Germany's Preferences on the Ankara Agreement: Ministerial Actors between Cold War Security Concerns, Turkish European Ambitions and the Wirtschaftswunder*. Paper to the Fourth Pan-European Conference on EU Politics of the ECPR – Standing Group on the European Union, University of Latvia, Riga, 25–27 September. [Online]. Available at: www.jhubc. it/ecpr-riga/virtualpaperroom/121.pdf [accessed: 5 October 2012].

McLaren, L. M. 2007. Explaining Opposition to Turkish Membership of the EU. *European Union Politics*, 8(2), June, 251–78.

Mendelson, M. H. 1997. The Application of the Republic of Cyprus to Join the EU, in *The Status of the Two People in Cyprus*, 2nd ed., edited by N. M. Ertekün. Nicosia-TRNC: Okman, 137–179.

Milliyet. 1998. *Kohl'e Ağır Suçlama (Serious Accusation to Kohl)*, 7 March. [Online]. Available at: www.milliyet.com.tr/1998/03/07/dunya/dun00.html [accessed: 1 November 2015].

Ministry for EU Affairs. 2015. *Turkey's Programme for the Alignment with EU Acquis (2007–2013)*. [Online]. Available at: www.ab.gov.tr/index.php?p=6&l=2 [accessed: 1 November 2015].

Ministry of EU Affairs. 2005. *AB ile Müzakerelere Başlanmasının Yankıları (Repercussions of Launching Negotiations with the EU)*, 10 July. [Online]. Available at: www.abgs.gov.tr/index.php?p=37643&l=1 [accessed: 29 January 2014].

Ministry of Foreign Affairs of Turkey. 2015a. The Unofficial Translation of the Message of the Prime Minister of the Republic of Turkey, Recep Tayyip Erdoğan, on the Events of 1915, 23 April. [Online]. Available at: www.mfa.gov.tr/turkish-prime-minister-mr_-recep-tayyip-erdo%C4%9Fan-published-a-message-on-the-events-of-1915_-23-april-2014.en.mfa [accessed: 28 July 2015].

Ministry of Foreign Affairs of Turkey. 2015b. *Turkish Citizens Living Abroad.* [Online]. Available at: www.mfa.gov.tr/the-expatriate-turkish-citizens.en.mfa [accessed: 8 November 2015].

Ministry of Foreign Affairs of Turkey. 2013. *First Meeting of the EU–Turkey Visa Liberalisation Dialogue Agreed Minutes, Annex: Annotated Roadmap towards a Visa-Free Regime with Turkey (Rev. 1)*, 12 July. [Online]. Available at: www.mfa.gov.tr/data/agreed%20minutes%20ve%20annotated%20roadmap.pdf [accessed: 10 August 2016].

Ministry of Foreign Affairs of Turkey. 2011. *Relations with European Countries.* [Online] Available at: www.mfa.gov.tr/relations-with-european-countries.en.mfa [accessed: 26 January 2017].

Ministry of Foreign Affairs of Turkey. 2005. *Declaration by Turkey on Cyprus*, 29 July 2005. [Online]. Available at: www.mfa.gov.tr/declaration-by-turkey-on-cyprus_-29-july-2005.en.mfa [accessed: 5 November 2015].

Ministry of Foreign Affairs of Turkey. 2000. *The Statement of Prime Minister Ecevit Regarding the EU Accession Partnership Document and Cyprus November 11, 2000.* [Online]. Available at: www.mfa.gov.tr/the-statement-of-prime-minister-ecevit-regarding-the-eu-accession-partnership-document-and-cyprus_br_november-11_-2000.en.mfa [accessed: 25 January 2014].

Morelli, V. L. 2017. Cyprus: Reunification Proving Elusive. *Congressional Research Service*, CRS Report, 24 January. [Online]. Available at: www.fas.org/sgp/crs/row/R41136.pdf [accessed: 25 February 2017].

Möttöla, K. 1997. The OSCE: Institutional and Functional Developments in an Evolving European Security Order, in *The OSCE in the Maintenance of Peace and Security: Conflict Prevention, Crisis Management and Peaceful Settlement of Disputes*, edited by M. Bothe, N. Ronzitti and A. Rosas. The Hague: Kluwer Law International, 1–33.

Müftüler-Baç, M. 2004. Turkey's Accession to the European Union: Institutional and Security Challenges. *Perceptions*, 9, Autumn, 29–43.

Müftüler-Baç, M. 2001. *Türkiye ve AB: Soğuk Savaş Sonrası İlişkiler (Turkey and the EU: Post–Cold War Relations)*. Istanbul: Alfa.

Müftüler-Baç, M. and Keyman, E. F. 2015. Turkey's Unconsolidated Democracy: The Nexus between Democratisation and Majoritarianism in Turkey. *Istanbul Policy Center (IPC)*, Global Turkey in Europe, Policy Brief 19, January. [Online]. Available at: http://ipc.sabanciuniv.edu/en/wp-content/uploads/2015/01/GTE_PB_19.pdf [accessed: 27 May 2015].

N-tv. 2016. *Wie weiter mit der Türkei? "Verhandlungen ja, aber kein EU-Beitritt"*, 5 August. [Online]. Available at: www.n-tv.de/politik/Verhandlungen-ja-aber-kein-EU-Beitritt-article18351326.html [accessed: 8 August 2016].

Nachmani, N. 2002. What Says the Neighbour to the West? On Turkish-Greek relations, in *Turkey in World Politics: An Emerging Multiregional Power*, edited by B. Rubin and K. Kirişçi. Istanbul: Boğaziçi University Press, 93–121.

Nas, Ç. 2016a. EU's Deliberations on Its Future: Question of Enlargement and Turkey's Membership Perspective, *IKV Monthly*, No: 22, September. [Online]. Available at: http://ikv.org.tr/images/files/IKV%20MONTHLY-SEPTEMBER%20(No_22(1).pdf [accessed: 06 November 2016].

Nas, Ç. 2016b. Turkey–EU Refugee Deal and Visa Liberalisation: How to Secure Long-Term Cooperation, *IKV Brief*, No: 44. [Online]. Available at: http://ikv.org.tr/images/files/Turkey–EU%20Refugee%20Deal_%20IKV%20BRIEF.pdf [accessed: 04 November 2016].

Nielsen, N. 2016. Turkey Won't Reform Terrorism Law to Conform with EU Deal, *Euobserver*, 9 August, https://euobserver.com/foreign/134599 [accessed: 04 November 2016].

Oder, B. E. 2012. Turkish Constitutional Transformation and the EU: Europeanisation towards Constitutionalism?, in *Turkey and the European Union: Processes of Europeanisation*, edited by Ç. Nas and Y. Özer. Aldershot: Ashgate, 69–97.

Official Journal of the EU. 2014. *Agreement between the European Union and the Republic of Turkey on the Readmission of Person Residing without Authorization*, L134, 7 May, 3–27. [Online]. Available at: http://eur-lex.europa.eu/legal-content/EN/TXT/?uri=CELEX%3A22014A0507(01) [accessed: 04 November 2016].

Official Journal of the EC. 2001a. *Council Decision of 8 March 2001 on the Principles, Priorities, Intermediate Objectives and Conditions contained in the Accession Partnership with the Republic of Turkey*, (2001/235/EC), L85/13. [Online]. Available at: www.ab.gov.tr/files/AB_Iliskileri/Tur_En_Realitons/Apd/Turkey_APD_2001.pdf [accessed: 1 November 2015].

Official Journal of the EC. 2001b. *Council Regulation (EC) No 539/2001 of 15 March 2001 Listing the Third Countries Whose Nationals Must Be in Possession of Visas When Crossing the External Borders and Those Whose Nationals Are Exempt from That Requirement*. L81/1–7, 21 March. [Online]. Available at: http://eurlex.europa.eu/LexUriServ/LexUriServ.do?uri=OJ:L:2001:081:0001:0007:EN:PDF [accessed: 8 November 2015].

Official Journal of the EC. 1997. *Decision No 2/97 of the EC-Turkey Association Council of 4th June 1997 Establishing the List of Community Instruments Relating to the Removal of Technical Barriers to Trade and the Conditions and Arrangements Governing Their Implementation by Turkey*. (97/438/EC). L 191, 21 June. [Online]. Available at: http://eur-lex.europa.eu/legal-content/EN/TXT/?uri=CELEX%3A21997D0721(01) [accessed: 11 October 2015].

Official Journal of the EC. 1996. *Decision No 1/95 of the EC-Turkey Association Council of 22 December 1995 on Implementing the Final Phase of the Customs Union*. (96/142/EC), L 035, 13 February. [Online]. Available at: http://eur-lex.europa.eu/LexUriServ/LexUriServ.do?uri=CELEX:21996D0213(01):EN:HTML [accessed: 21 April 2014].

Official Journal of the EC. 1987. *Resolution on a Political Solution to the Armenian Question*, Doc. A2–33/87, No C 190/119, 18 June. [Online]. Available at: www.europarl.europa.eu/intcoop/euro/pcc/aag/pcc_meeting/resolutions/1987_07_20.pdf [accessed: 28 July 2015].

Official Journal of the EC. 1977a. *Agreement Establishing an Association between the European Economic Community and Turkey (signed at Ankara, 12 September 1963)*, L361/29, 31 December. [Online]. Available at: http://eur-lex.europa.eu/resource.html?uri=cellar:f8e2f9f4-75c8–4f62-ae3f-b86ca5842eee.0008.02/DOC_2&format=PDF [accessed: 22 September 2012].

Official Journal of the EC. 1977b. *Additional Protocol*, L 361/1, 31 December. [Online]. Available at: www.ab.gov.tr/files/AB_Iliskileri/tur_en_realitons/protocol_1977.pdf [accessed: 22 September 2012].

Official Journal of the EC. 1973. *Council Publication, in English and Danish, of the Texts of the Agreement Establishing an Association between the EEC and Turkey and the Additional Protocol*, 16(C113), 24 December, C113/28. [Online]. Available at: http://

ec.europa.eu/enlargement/pdf/turkey/association_agreement_1964_en.pdf [accessed: 8 November 2015].

Öniş, Z. 2009. Contesting for the 'Center': Domestic Politics, Identity Conflicts and the Controversy over EU Membership in Turkey. *İstanbul Bilgi University European Institute Working Papers*, No. 2, EU/2/2010, August. [Online]. Available at: http://eu.bilgi.edu.tr/media/files/2.pdf [accessed: 5 November 2015].

Öniş, Z. 2003. Domestic Politics, International Norms and Challenges to the State: Turkey–EU Relations in the Post-Helsinki Era. *Turkish Studies*, 4(1), 9–34. [Online]. Available at: http://homes.ieu.edu.tr/aburgin/IREU%20308%20Turkey–EU%20Relations/Önis%202003_Domestic%20politics%20international%20norms%20and%20challenges%20to%20the%20state_Turekey%20EU%20relations%20in%20the%20post%20Helsinki%20area.pdf [accessed: 9 May 2014].

Öniş, Z. and Yılmaz, Ş. 2009. Between Europeanization and Euro-Asianism: Foreign Policy Activism in Turkey during the AKP Era. *Turkish Studies*, Special Issue: *Turkey as a Trans-Regional Actor*, 10(1), 7–24.

Oskam, A., Longworth, N. and Molina Vilchez, I. 2005. Consequences for the EU-27 of Enlargement to Turkey, in *Turkey in the EU: Implications for Agriculture, Food and Structural Policy*, edited by A. M. Burrell and A. J. Oskam. Oxfordshire, Cambridge: CABI, 217–50.

Özler, Z. and Özsöz, M. 2010. *Visa Hotline Project: Final Report*. Istanbul: Economic Development Foundation Publications, No: 231.

Paçacı-Elitok, S. 2015. A Step Backward for Turkey: The Readmission Agreement and the Hope of Visa-free Europe. *IPC-Mercator Policy Brief*, December. [Online]. Available at: http://ipc.sabanciuniv.edu/wp-content/uploads/2015/12/A-Step-Backward-for-Turkey_The-Readmission-Agreement-and-the-Hope-of-Visa-Free-Europe.pdf [accessed: 20 April 2016].

Parker, G. 2016. Turkey Unlikely to Join EU 'until the Year 3000', says Cameron. *Financial Times*, 22 May. [Online]. Available at: www.ft.com/cms/s/0/de1efd42-2001-11e6-aa98-db1e01fabc0c.html#axzz4GqD8LAnq [accessed: 09 August 2016].

Paul, A. and Seyrek, D. M. 2015. Internet "Freedom" in Turkey. *EPC Commentary*, 2 March. [Online]. Available at: www.epc.eu/pub_details.php?cat_id=4&pub_id=5372 [accessed: 5 November 2015].

Pop, V. 2014. EU Parliament Approves Juncker Commission. *Euobserver*, 20 October. [Online]. Available at: https://euobserver.com/political/126182 [accessed: 23 July 2015].

Pop, V. 2010. Bulgaria and Romania Worried that Corruption May Delay Accession to Border-free Area. *Euobserver*, 20 July. [Online]. Available at: https://euobserver.com/justice/30511 [accessed: 5 November 2015].

Pridham, G. 2007. Change and Continuity in the European Union's Political Conditionality: Aims, Approach, and Priorities. *Democratisation*, 14(3), 446–71.

Pridham, G. 1999. The European Union, Democratic Conditionality and Transnational Party Linkages: The Case of Eastern Europe, in *Democracy without Borders, Transnationalisation and Conditionality in New Democracies*, edited by J. Grugel. London: Routledge, 59–75.

Redmond, J. 1994. *The Prospective European: The New Member of European Union*. New York: Harvester Wheatsheaf.

Rehn, O. 2008. *45 Years from the Signing of the Ankara Agreement: EU–Turkey Cooperation Continues*, Speech made at Conference on EU–Turkey Association Agreement,

Speech/08/581, 4 November. [Online]. Available at: http://europa.eu/rapid/press-release_SPEECH-08-581_en.htm [accessed: 19 September 2015].

Reporters without Borders. 2015. *World Press Freedom Index*. January. [Online]. Available at: http://index.rsf.org/#!/index-details/TUR [accessed: 23 August 2015].

Reporters without Borders. 2005. *World Press Freedom Index*. January. [Online]. Available at: http://en.rsf.org/press-freedom-index-2005,549.html [accessed: 23 August 2015].

Reuters. 2016. *Austrian Chancellor Suggests Ending EU Accession Talks with Turkey*, 3 August. [Online]. Available at: www.reuters.com/article/us-Turkey–EU-austria-idUSKCN10E2LX [accessed: 9 August 2016].

Rollo, J. 2006. Global Europe: Old Mercantilist Wine in New Bottles? *Aussenwirtschaft*, 61(4), 403–14.

Rumelili, B. 2012. Liminal Identities and Processes of Domestication and Subversion in International Relations. *Review of International Studies*, 38(2), 495–508.

Saatçioğlu, B. 2014. AKP's 'Europeanisation' in Civilianisation, Rule of Law and Fundamental Freedoms: The Primacy of Domestic Politics. *Journal of Balkan and Near Eastern Studies*, 16(1), 86–101.

Saatçioğlu, B. 2013. Turkey–EU Relations from the 1960s to 2012: A Critical Overview, in *Turkey's Accession to the European Union: Political and Economic Challenges*, edited by B. Akçay and B. Yılmaz. Lanham: Lexington, 3–23.

Saraçoğlu, T. 1991. Türkiye-Avrupa Topluluğu İlişkileri (Turkey–EUropean Community Relations). *Marmara Journal of European Studies*, 1(1–2), 49–55.

Sayarı, S. 2003. The United States and Turkey's Membership in the European Union. *The Turkish Yearbook of International Relations*, 34, 167–76.

Schimmelfennig, F. 2004. Strategic Calculation and International Socialisation: Membership Incentives, Party Constellations and Sustained Compliance in Central and Eastern Europe, Revised Draft submitted for *International Organisations* special issue on 'International Institutions and Socialisation in Europe'. [Online]. Available at: www.mzes.unimannheim.de/projekte/typo3/site/fileadmin/research%20groups/1/teamBreader/Schimmelfennig_Strategic%20calculation%20and%20international%20soc%26.pdf [accessed: July 2011].

Schimmelfennig, F., Engert, S. and Knobel, H. 2006. *International Socialisation in Europe: European Conditionality and Democratic Change*. Basingstoke: Palgrave.

Schimmelfennig, F., Engert, S. and Knobel, H. 2005. The Impact of EU Political Conditionality, in *The Europeanization of Central and Eastern Europe*, edited by F. Schimmelfening and U. Sedelmeier. Ithaca: Cornell University Press, 29–50.

Schimmelfennig, F., Engert, S. and Knobel, H. 2002. *The Conditions of Conditionality*. Paper to the Workshop 4: *Enlargement and European Governance*, ECPR Joint Session of Workshops, Turin, 22–7 March. [Online]. Available at: www.essex.ac.uk/ECPR/events/jointsessions/paperarchive/turin/ws4/Schimmelfennig.pdf [accessed: 16 June 2009].

Schimmelfennig, F. and Schwellnus, G. 2006. *Political Conditionality and Convergence: The EU's Impact on Democracy, Human Rights, and Minority Protection in Central and Eastern Countries*. Paper to the CEEISA Conference, Tartu, Estonia, 25–7 June. [Online]. Available at: www.eup.ethz.ch/people/schwellnus/papers/Schimmelfennig_Schwellnus.pdf [accessed: 17 May 2010].

Schimmelfennig, F. and Sedelmeier, U. 2005. Introduction: Conceptualising the Europeanisation of Central and Eastern Europe, in *The Europeanisation of Central and Eastern Europe*, edited by F. Schimmelfennig and U. Sedelmeier. Ithaca: Cornell University Press, 1–28.

Schimmelfennig, F. and Sedelmeier, U. 2004. Governance by Conditionality: EU Rule Transfer to the Candidate Countries of Central and Eastern Europe. *Journal of European Public Policy*, 11(4), 669–87.

Schmitter, Philippe C. 2001. The Influence of the International Context upon the Choice of National Institutions and Policies in Neo-Democracies, in *The International Dimensions of Democratisation: Europe and the Americas*, edited by L. Whitehead. Oxford: Oxford University Press, 26–54.

Secretariat General for EU Affairs. 2007. *Political Reforms in Turkey*. Ankara. [Online]. Available at: www.ab.gov.tr/files/pub/prt.pdf [accessed: 1 November 2015].

Seyrek, D. M. 2005. Annual Update: Turkey's Road to the EU. *Turkish Policy Quarterly*, 4(3), Fall, 111–118.

Şimşek, A. 2016. Erdoğan Slams EU's Lack of Solidarity amid Coup Attempt, *Anatolian Agency*, 13 August. [Online]. Available at: http://aa.com.tr/en/todays-headlines/erdogan-slams-eu-s-lack-of-solidarity-amid-coup-attempt/627737 [accessed: 4 November 2016].

Smale, A. and Eddy, M. 2016. German Parliament Recognizes Armenian Genocide Angering Turkey. *New York Times*, 2 June. www.nytimes.com/2016/06/03/world/europe/armenian-genocide-germany-turkey.html?_r=0 [accessed: 28 October 2016].

Smith, K. E. 2003. The Evolution and Application of EU Membership Conditionality, in *The Enlargement of the European Union*, edited by M. Cremona. Oxford: Oxford University Press, 105–40.

Soler i Lecha, E. 2014. Crises and Elections: What Are the Consequences for Turkey's EU Bid? *Istanbul Policy Center (IPC)*, Global Turkey in Europe, Policy Brief 13, March. [Online]. Available at: http://ipc.sabanciuniv.edu/wp-content/uploads/2014/03/GTE_PB_13.pdf [accessed: 23 April 2015].

Soler i Lecha, E. and Garcia, I. 2010. Spanish Perceptions, in *Turkey Watch: EU Member States Perceptions on Turkey's Accession to the EU*, edited by S. Akşit, O. Şenyuva and Ç. Üstün. Ankara: Center for European Studies, METU, 58–9.

Soysal, M. 2002. The Cyprus Problem and Turkey's Candidacy to EU Membership, in *The European Union Enlargement Process and Turkey*, edited by M. Dartan and Ç. Nas. Istanbul: Marmara University European Community Institute, 341–52.

Sözen, A. 2010. A Paradigm Shift in Turkish Foreign Policy: Transition and Challenges. *Turkish Studies*, 11(1), March, 103–23.

Sözen, A. 2005. A Model of Power-Sharing in Cyprus: From the 1959 London-Zurich Agreements to the Annan Plan, in *Greek-Turkish Relations in the Era of Détente*, edited by A. Çarkoğlu and B. Rubin. New York: Routledge, 61–77.

Spendzharova, A. B. 2003. Bringing Europe In? The Impact of EU Conditionality on Bulgarian and Romanian Politics. *Southeast European Politics*, 4(2–3), 141–56.

Stephanou, C. and Tsardanides, C. 1991. The EC Factor in the Greece-Turkey-Cyprus Triangle, in *The Greek-Turkish Conflict in the 1990s: Domestic and External Influences*, edited by D. Constas. London: Macmillan, 207–30.

Süvarierol, S. 2005. The Cyprus Obstacle on Turkey's Road to Membership in the European Union, in *Turkey and European Union: Domestic Politics, Economic Integration and International Dynamics*, edited by A. Çarkoğlu and B. Rubin. Portland: Frank Cass, 55–78.

Tamçelik, S. 2003. Kıbrıs ve Avrupa Birliği İlişkileri-II (Cyprus and EU Relations-II). *Sosyal Bilimler Dergisi (Journal of Social Sciences)*, 6, Manas University (Kirghizstan), 187–215. [Online]. Available at: http://journals.manas.kg/mjsr/oldarchives/Vol03_Issue06_2003/297.pdf [accessed: 22 May 2013].

TBMM. 2002. Statement by MP Mehmet Gül, Minutes of the TGNA, *TBMM Tutanak Dergisi*, Vol. 102, 2 August. [Online]. Available at: www.tbmm.gov.tr/tutanak/donem21/yil4/bas/b125m.htm [accessed: 26 January 2014].

Tezcan, E. 2013. Türkiye-Avrupa Birliği İlişkilerinin Ortaklık Boyutu: Hukuki Çerçeve (Association Dimension of Turkey–EUropean Union Relations: Legal Framework), in *Türkiye-Avrupa Birliği İlişkileri (Turkey–EUropean Union Relations)*, edited by B. Akçay and S. A. Açıkmeşe. Ankara: Turhan Kitabevi, 43–75.

Tocci, N. 2005. Europeanisation in Turkey: Trigger or Anchor for Reform. *South European Society and Politics*, 10(1), 73–83.

Tocci, N. and Bechev, D. 2012. Will Turkey Find Its Place in Post-Crisis Europe? *Global Turkey in Europe*, Istanbul Policy Center (IPC), Policy Brief 05, December. [Online]. Available at: http://ipc.sabanciuniv.edu/wp-content/uploads/2013/01/GTE_PB_05.pdf [accessed: 27 October 2014].

Today's Zaman. 2015. *ICT: Parties Close to Deal in Cyprus, Turkey's EU Accession to Be Revitalized*, 26 August. [Online]. Available at: www.todayszaman.com/anasayfa_ict-parties-close-to-deal-in-cyprus-turkeys-eu-accession-to-be-revitalized_397559.html [accessed: 8 October 2015].

Today's Zaman. 2013. *Davutoğlu Says Greek Cypriot Government Causing Disappointment*, 8 April. [Online]. Available at: www.todayszaman.com/news-312057-davutoglu-says-new-greek-cypriot-govt-causing-disappointment.html [accessed: 6 June 2013].

Togan, S. 2012. *The EU–Turkey Customs Union: A Model for Future Euro-Med Integration*. MEDPRO Technical Report No. 9/March. [Online]. Available at: www.medpro-foresight.eu/system/files/MEDPRO%20TR%20No%209%20WP5%20Togan.pdf [accessed: 24 April 2013].

Toksabay, E. and Carrell, P. 2016. Turkish, European Leaders Stand Their Ground in Impasse over Migrants Deal. *Reuters*, 12 May. [Online]. Available at: www.reuters.com/article/us-europe-migrants-turkey-minister-idUSKCN0Y30TA [accessed: 4 August 2016].

Tokyay, M. 2013. Cyprus Crisis: Opportunities and Challenges for Reunification. *SES Türkiye*, 17 April. [Online]. Available at: http://turkey.setimes.com/en_GB/articles/ses/articles/features/departments/world/2013/04/17/feature-01 [accessed: 7 June 2013].

Transatlantic Trends. 2014. *Country Profiles: Turkey 2014*. [Online]. Available at: http://trends.gmfus.org/transatlantic-trends/country-profiles-2014/country-profiles-turkey-2014/ [accessed: 3 September 2015].

Tsakaloyannis, P. 1980. The European Community and the Greek-Turkish Disputes. *Journal of Common Market Studies*, 19(1), 35–54.

Türkiye. 1999. *DSP Lideri: Mektubu Ciddiye Alıyorum*, 15 December. [Online]. Available at: www.turkiyegazetesi.com.tr/Genel/a34025.aspx [accessed: 25 January 2014].

Uğur, M. 1999. *The European Union and Turkey: An Anchor/Credibility Dilemma*. Aldershot: Ashgate.

UN Economic and Social Council. 2013. *An Analysis on the Impact of Road Transport Quotas (Submitted by the Government of the Republic of Turkey)*. [Online]. Available at: www.unece.org/fileadmin/DAM/trans/doc/2013/sc1/ECE-TRANS-SC1-2013-4e.pdf [accessed: 5 August 2014].

UNHCR. 2016. *Weekly Report*, 2 November. [Online]. Available at: http://data.unhcr.org/mediterranean/regional.php [accessed: 4 November 2016].

UNHCR. 2015. *Reservations and Declarations to the 1967 Protocol Relating to the Status of Refugees*. [Online]. Available at: www.unhcr.org/4dac37d79.html [accessed: 8 November 2015].

Üstün, Ç. 2010. *Turkey and European Security and Defense Policy: Compatibility and Security Cultures in a Globalised World*. London: I.B. Tauris.

Usul, A. R. 2011. *Democracy in Turkey: The Impact of EU Political Conditionality*. London: Routledge.

Vachudova, M. A. 2005. *Europe Undivided: Democracy, Leverage and Integration after Communism*. Oxford: Oxford University Press.

Whitehead, L. 2001.Three International Dimensions of Democratisation, in *The International Dimensions of Democratisation: Europe and the Americas*, edited by L. Whitehead. Oxford: Oxford University Press, 3–27.

World Bank. 2014. *Evaluation of the EU–Turkey Customs Union*. Report No. 85830-TR, 28 March. [Online]. Available at: www.worldbank.org/content/dam/Worldbank/document/eca/turkey/tr-eu-customs-union-eng.pdf [accessed: 17 May 2014].

Yavuz, M. H. 2004. İkicilik (Duality): Türk-Arap İlişkileri ve Filistin Sorunu 1947–1994 (Duality: Turkish-Arab Relations and the Palestinian Problem 1947–1994), in *Türk Dış Politikasının Analizi* (Analysis of Turkish Foreign Policy), edited by F. Sönmezoğlu. Instanbul: Der Publications, 235–252.

Yeşilada, B. 2013. *EU–Turkey Relations in the 21st Century*. Oxon: Routledge.

Yılmaz, K. 2015. TTIP and EU-Turkish Economic Relations: Deepening the Customs Union. *Istanbul Policy Centre (IPC)*, Global Turkey in Europe, Policy Brief 21, March. [Online]. Available at: www.iai.it/sites/default/files/gte_pb_21.pdf [accessed: 20 June 2015].

Yılmaz, K. 2011. The EU–Turkey Customs Union Fifteen Years Later: Better, Yet Not the Best Alternative. *South European Society and Politics*, 16(2), June, 235–49.

Yılmaz, M. 2010. 2010 Referandumu: Siyasi Partilerin Tutumları (2010 Referendum: Attitudes of Political Parties). *SETA Analiz (SETA Analysis)*, October. [Online]. Available at: http://file.setav.org/Files/Pdf/2010-referandumu-siyasi-partilerin-tutumlari.pdf [accessed: 25 September 2015].

Youngs, R. 2001. *The European Union and the Promotion of Democracy*. Oxford: Oxford University Press.

Zoeteweij-Turhan, M. H. 2015. Turkey on the Tightrope: From Readmission to Visa-Liberalisation Agreement? in *Rights of Third Country Nationals under EU Association Agreements: Degrees of Free Movement and Citizenship*, edited by D. Thym and M. H. Zoeteweij-Turhan. Leiden: Brill Nijhoff, 147–68.

Index

For Product Safety Concerns and Information please contact our EU
representative GPSR@taylorandfrancis.com
Taylor & Francis Verlag GmbH, Kaufingerstraße 24, 80331 München, Germany

www.ingramcontent.com/pod-product-compliance
Ingram Content Group UK Ltd.
Pitfield, Milton Keynes, MK11 3LW, UK
UKHW011011180926
475701UK00004B/677
9781032096865